The Austin Seven

THE MOTOR FOR THE MILLION
1922~1939

R.J.WYATT

DAVID & CHARLES
Newton Abbot   London   North Pomfret (VT)

Dedicated to the late Lord Austin of Longbridge

British Library Cataloguing in Publication Data

Wyatt, R. J.
    The Austin Seven. – 3rd ed.
    1. Austin 7 automobile – History
    I. Title
    629.2'222   TL215.A9

ISBN 0-7153-8394-9

First published by Macdonald & Co (Publishers) Ltd 1968
Second edition published by David & Charles (Publishers) Ltd 1972
Second impression of second edition 1976
Third impression of second edition 1978
Third edition 1982

Printed in Great Britain
by Redwood Burn Limited, Trowbridge
for David & Charles (Publishers) Limited
Brunel House   Newton Abbot   Devon

Contents

Author's Preface and Acknowledgments

This book was written following a conversation with Bill Boddy who, in 1965 suggested that the Austin Seven presented a subject of sufficient scope to warrant a volume of its own, as opposed to being included in my history of the Austin Motor Company from the firm's incorporation in 1905 until its founder's death during the last war.

I contacted my friend Bob Burgess, who had worked at "The Austin" – the name given to the Longbridge factory by those who live in and around the district bordering on the Lickey Hills – between 1916 and 1930, and who is one of those people fortunate enough to possess a photographic memory for events which took place many years before. I am indebted to him for the information which he provided and for his encouragement. My gratitude is also due to E. C. Gordon England, the late Cliff Lewis, J. F. Bramley, S. A. Haynes, Roland Harrison, Kevin Gover, Norman Milne, George Coldicutt and a host of other past and present Austin employees; my friend Peter Huntley for the excellent line drawings, and to Ron Beach, head of photography at Austin's, for taking the trouble to search through his old records to unearth most of the pictures of early Austin Sevens. The remainder are reproduced either by kind permission of the *Autocar*, or come from my own collection and from members of the Vintage Austin Register. The Temple Press were also kind enough to allow me to reproduce a number of articles and quotations from the *Motor* and the *Light Car and Cyclecar*.

The Austin Seven was invented and developed by Herbert Austin, an engineer born more than a century ago and trained in the Victorian era, as a reliable car for "the man in the street". He did not employ large teams of designers and stylists to make his basic ideas practical from the point of view of production, but worked out even the minor details himself and, more often than not, designed the machines to make the components as well. Not only could he accomplish any practical engineering job in the factory if called upon to do so, but he handled all the other functions involved in running one of the largest car production works in the country. He began at a period when the total output of the motor-car industry in the United Kingdom was in the region of 8,000 units a year, and still exercised control of his own concern as the trade progressed and finally became one of the country's major industries, with an annual production of more than 350,000 cars.

Perhaps he is best known for his finest achievement – the design and production of the first successful small car – and in this book I have endeavoured to trace the history of the model from its inception in 1922 and to describe its development throughout the 1920's and 1930's. Thousands of Austin Sevens still exist, many of them preserved by enthusiasts or in museums and, even today, some are still in regular use as a living memory of the soapbox on wheels, motorised pram – call it what you will, it will remain one of the most important cars in the history of motoring.

FOREWORD TO THE SECOND EDITION

A reprint of this book having been called for by its continuing popularity, the opportunity has been taken to correct a few minor errors in the original edition and to add one or two notes on information which subsequently became available.

A major addition, which it is hoped will enhance the value of the book to Austin Seven owners, is the inclusion, by courtesy of the British Leyland Motor Corporation, of a new appendix comprising facsimile extracts from Service Data Sheets which the Austin Motor Co Ltd in 1927 began issuing at regular intervals to their dealers and agents. These were bound into grey paper folders to provide some ten volumes until publication was discontinued in 1940. Complete sets are now very rare, and the extracts now included are the most important and relevant sections from a complete run. Prior to 1927, the information was available only from motoring journals, including the *Austin Magazine*, drivers' handbooks and the illustrated spare parts lists which were issued with each new car.

R. J. WYATT

FOREWORD TO THE THIRD EDITION

Perhaps the most important "discovery" in recent years was finding Stanley Edge, the clever draughtsman who shares with Lord Austin much of the credit for the Seven's original design. The important period of the car's inception can now be recorded for posterity and I am grateful to Stanley for all the information which he has provided.

R. J. WYATT

Introduction

"I look back upon the year 1922 as one that marks an important milestone in my life, for it was then that I introduced the now famous Seven which has made motoring possible for thousands who could not otherwise have enjoyed its advantages. The Seven has done more than anything previously accomplished to bring about the realisation of my ambition to motorise the masses. Of course, my little car was treated with a good deal of ridicule at first, but it cheers me up to notice that the appreciation which the Baby meets today is just as hearty as the erstwhile smiles were broad."

When Sir Herbert Austin made the above statement in 1929 it was already evident that the Austin Seven had changed the concept of motoring by providing a practical means of four-wheeled transport at a price low enough to enable a vast new section of the population to become car owners. Prior to its introduction in 1922 manufacturers had concentrated upon catering for those who were comparatively wealthy. The light car and cycle-car industries had made great efforts to find new markets for their products, and had failed to do so for many reasons.

The immediate post-war period was one of booming trade for the whole motor industry; no new cars, or motor cycles, had been built in Britain for several years, and there was sufficient money about to ensure a ready sale for anything upon two, three or four wheels. Sidecar combinations, cycle-cars and light cars were turned out by dozens of small firms anxious to supply the demand. Some of the small four-wheelers were quite good, but many were inferior articles and as a result the whole light car industry earned a bad name for itself and its products. As more of the well-known companies changed over their plants from munition work to car production, the smaller firms found themselves unable to compete. This was accompanied by the Slump of the early 'twenties. Austins were in serious financial trouble too and a Receiver was appointed to take control; the Company's future was in the balance, and yet this was the time that Sir Herbert chose to take the biggest gamble of his life – to produce a car for a new class of motorist.

His contention was that in view of the impoverished state of the people, particularly in Europe, economy must be the watchword. He saw that the need in future would be for a small car, and he did not miss the opportunity of providing the first practical answer to it.

As we all know now, he succeeded in his speculation. The fortunes of the Company in the 1920's improved as the demand for his revolutionary little car increased. The Seven remained in production until 1939, by which time nearly 300,000 had been sold – excluding those that were made under licence abroad.

Herbert Austin was born at Great Missenden, Buckinghamshire, in 1866. His father had been a farmer, as had his ancestors, so that it cannot be said that he inherited his aptitude for engineering.

Shortly after his birth the family moved to Wentworth in Yorkshire where his father became a farm bailiff to Earl Fitzwilliam. The young boy's early days were spent on the farm, and at Rotherham Grammar School, where his ability to make freehand drawings was encouraged. Later Austin said: "I was then – as I am now – best able to express myself by means of the pencil." Since his earliest days his greatest love had been for things mechanical and he soon developed a keen eye for geometrical drawing and an ability to convey sizes and proportions on paper.

When he left school his parents decided that he would be well suited to architecture. As his uncle was architect to Earl Fitzwilliam, Austin became an apprentice under him, but showed little interest in the profession, and before very long the Articles were cancelled.

His parents then thought that he should become an engineer and tried to get him apprenticed to the Great Northern Railway Company, but as there were no vacancies at the time for apprentices he was placed on their waiting list.

In 1884 his mother's brother, who was an engineer in Australia, visited the family, and after a brief holiday with the Austins the Great Northern Railway project was abandoned and young Austin returned to Melbourne with his uncle. Two days after their arrival in Australia he started work in his uncle's engineering shop in north Melbourne where the firm specialised in the manufacture of steel water pipes.

Two years later Austin moved to another Melbourne firm which imported and erected Crossley gas engines and printing presses, and in about 1888 he began working for the Longlands Foundry Company. It was there that he received what he later proudly described as "a thorough training as a mechanic". Whilst with Longlands Herbert Austin suggested improvements to some Wolseley sheep-shearing machinery for which his employers had acquired orders. These suggestions were adopted by Wolseley and they asked him to manage their Australian branch. Most sheep-shearing in Australia was, at that time, done by hand clippers and the problem of mechanising the process gave Austin his first opportunity to show his skill as an inventor. His ideas were so successful that he was prevailed upon by Wolseley to return to England in order to supervise the production of their sheep-shearing machines.

Within two years he was working on designs for his first motor car. By 1900 these ideas had developed sufficiently for him to have built a car and entered it in the 1,000 Miles Trial of that year. It won the Silver Medal and was awarded the first prize in its class. In 1901 the motor and machine-tool side of the firm was taken over by Vickers Sons and Maxim, and Herbert Austin was appointed General Manager of the new concern: the Wolseley Tool and Motor Car Company Limited.

He remained with them, producing his reliable horizontal-engined Wolseley cars until 1905 when he left to form his own Company. A friend provided additional capital and the newly formed concern took over a derelict factory at Longbridge in the village of Northfield, seven miles south of Birmingham. In 1906 the first Austin car was completed; a product typical of the period, and powered by Austin's first vertical cylindered engine. One hundred and forty-seven of these cars were manufactured in the first twelve months, and from this modest beginning the Company grew, until in 1914 – with an annual output of nearly a thousand cars – a point was reached at which more capital was necessary to expand. A Public Company was formed just six months before the outbreak of the First World War.

Almost at once nearly the whole resources of the factory were turned over to the production of shells and other war material, and during the next four years new buildings were erected all over the Longbridge site, thousands of new machines were installed, and by 1916, at the peak of activity, more than 22,000 workers were employed.

When the war ended in 1918 this vast plant became idle: its potential was enormous and Sir Herbert Austin – as he was then after being knighted for his wartime services as a producer of munitions – was faced with the problem of using it to the best advantage as a car factory.

One of the lessons learned had been quantity or "massed" production, but the system could only be used with effect if the finished products could be turned out in sufficiently large numbers. He decided therefore to concentrate upon the manufacture of one model – the Austin Twenty. Although an extremely good car which became very popular, it was a big vehicle, and as time went on the demand for smaller and cheaper cars grew. In October, 1921 the Austin Twelve, a scaled-down version of the Twenty, was introduced.

Problems associated with labour, the supply of raw materials and a general slump in trade led the Austin Motor Company into financial difficulties. The demand for cars fell, particularly for those costing over £500, and investors ceased subscribing to motor stocks and shares. It was against this sombre background that the Austin Seven was conceived.

1922

A New Chapter in Motoring History

"It is no use attempting to sell a worker anything that is not genuine. The British working man will not stand any nonsense. It is not a fancy trade." *Sir Herbert Austin in his speech to the press at the introduction of the Austin Seven at Claridges on 21st July, 1922.*

During the early part of the summer of 1920 Austin began working secretly on designs for a completely new light car. Every night after dinner at his home Lickey Grange, just off the tree-lined road down from the Lickey Hills, he would retire to the billiard room to mull over his ideas, and to make preliminary sketches. As his plans evolved, and detailed drawings became necessary, a junior draughtsman from the Longbridge factory, named Stanley Edge, went over to the Grange and helped Austin with the drawings.

Stanley Edge left school at 14 in August 1917 and joined the car drawing office at Longbridge at the end of 1918. As the assistant to Jack Clarke, the engine designer, Austin got to know him quite well, and must have been impressed with his knowledge and the standard of his work. One day in September 1921 A. J. Hancock, the chief designer, called Edge to his office and asked him to sit down. This he did with trepidation, thinking that an invitation to sit down was likely to lead to an invitation to quit the company. When he was asked to leave to go and work at Lickey Grange, which was now Sir Herbert's home, he was not at first reassured, but when Hancock went on to say "Sir Herbert has asked me to find out for him, and if you agree he will give you all the details himself", Edge agreed, and next day Sir Herbert asked him to see him at his home on Sunday morning. He stayed there working for the next eight months. Arrangements were made for him to lunch and dine at the house, and to sleep at the lodge during the week.

Edge found that at Lickey Grange Austin was a completely different character from the tornado which used to tear around the works and offices at Longbridge. Austin gave him instructions by a few sketches and word of mouth, but as his own drawings of the Seven took shape it was these which were discussed and modified again and again. The sketches – rough full-

*1. Lord Austin of Longbridge —
the originator of "Motoring for
the masses", from a photograph
taken early in the 1920's*

sized semi-freehand drawings but nevertheless reasonably accurate and containing a fair amount of detail – must have been prepared by Sir Herbert himself, perhaps on the billiards table which was large enough for a full size drawing of a small car. This may account for the billiards table legend, but Edge never made a drawing or a sketch on the table all the time he was there.

These drawings at the start did not resemble the final Seven; they more nearly resembled the Rover 8 with its air-cooled horizontal twin engine and worm-drive rear axle, probably the most popular and successful light car of 1921. Sir Herbert had borrowed a Rover from the chief cashier at Austins and had gone over it very carefully taking measurements. Between September and December 1921, Edge spent twelve or more hours a day on the drawings. Austin was not at home every evening, but when he was they would pore over the drawings, sometimes starting before dinner then breaking for the meal and continuing afterwards until about 10pm. Edge found Austin's alertness to design problems after having spent all day at the factory, coupled with his ability to concentrate well into the night, remarkable.

No finalised designs were available by January 1922, and many possibilites had been explored; for example four wheels in a diamond pattern and rear-wheel steering. For a time after abandoning the horizontal twin, Sir Herbert wanted three cylinders, and this was studied from all possible viewpoints. Stanley Edge knew Austin better than almost anyone else who worked at Longbridge, and gives this interesting insight into their relationship:

"I feel sure that at that particular period I was as up-to-date as Sir Herbert on engine matters because I read everything which was available, Government publications, the *Automobile Engineer*, papers by Harry Ricardo etc, but on how engines could be connected to road wheels, how the whole lot were put into a frame and a body mounted thereon I was educated by Sir Herbert. In his teaching he was always painstaking and kind, and when I felt I had something worth while he would always listen. In fact our whole relationship was an extension of my first Sunday morning at Lickey Grange. My picture of him at this time is of a portly gentleman, wedged against my drawing board, talking and sketching with a stub of a pencil, or looking straight at me while I tried to say what I thought. Often after dinner he would ask whether I had enjoyed it, and at times he would bring in some chocolates or crystallised fruits.

At sometime early in New Year 1922 we had decided on the sort of car to be made, and from then on the production of the detail and final general arrangements lay with me. Sir Herbert would at times have second thoughts and make modifications, but my general attitude was to say, "If you wish me to complete these drawings we must stick to what we have decided upon."

If Sir Herbert and I had parted company in 1921 my picture of him would have been of a man of abounding energy yet nevertheless essentially a kindly father figure, but as I have said there were people who saw him in a different light. As my work continued into 1922 I came to know these different aspects. I had a sensitive disposition, but this is perhaps putting it too delicately. A lot of people I knew then were inclined to call me "a touchy devil" and although I think I have grown more mellow with age – some people still do. Therefore, I may have fancied changes in his attitude, where none existed. In any case, I had probably overworked for four or five months without being truly aware of it, and goodness knows what pressures may have been exerted on Sir Herbert. Be that as it may, he came to ask the question in the evenings more and more as to when would I be ready with the drawings.

The first few months sketching and scheming were comparatively carefree, but the responsibility for correct details was entirely my own and I intended to be doubly careful in avoiding errors. In due course I completed details in batches, of engine, gearbox, rear axle, front axle, steering, frame work and finally the body. He kept saying, "We really must get these finished you know", which began to sound more like, "You must get a move on." I still had no idea of what we were going to do with the drawings and I tentatively suggested that first the engine assembly details and then the other assemblies could be issued for manufacture as I completed them. In this way I think we could have started about the end of February. However, just before Easter I was finished completely and then he told me to bring all the drawings to the factory on the Tuesday after Easter and this must have been his target all the time. I found that men had been engaged on preparing a "boarded-up" section of the works and North works superintendent McLellan, who had been put in charge, had been receiving the same exhortations as myself at Lickey Grange.

All the time I was with Sir Herbert I never saw him make a design calculation, nor did he ever give me results of calculations. I know he was keen on estimating weights and he would work out costs, whether correctly or not I do not know, but when I proposed a certain compression ratio for the engine he just said "All right", and when I said the bore and stroke which we have settled on will give 696cc he simply said "Will it?" Things like the inertia of the reciprocating parts, or the inlet and exhaust gas speeds he just wasn't bothered with. Again, because I considered myself an engine expert, I did not worry. Similarly I was quite capable of settling gear ratios, clutch dimensions and all calculations dealing with transmission of engine power, but there were questions of gear-box and axle construction, steering and brakes of which I had no experience, and in the main I scaled these down from larger cars. But even then the parts generally came out too large, and Sir Herbert would say, "Make it like this", generally cutting down my transmission and chassis dimensions.

After Easter 1922 I worked in the private boarded-up section of the Longbridge works where the first Sevens were built. A separate office in this section had been set aside for me and my drawing board, and Mr. McLellan also had a desk in there. He had been in his superintendent's position during the war years and those immediately following; an older man than Sir Herbert, I have never seen his name mentioned in the accounts of Austin affairs, but I think Sir Herbert had good recollections of Mac's work with him in the past and so selected him for the job. He was a rough and ready type, but notwithstanding had tact which was invaluable. He and I got along together very well and here I pay tribute to him because it was largely due to his overall guidance the Sevens were built according to requirements, which were to have three cars ready for Whitsuntide. I am not writing here about the work done in making the Sevens, except insomuch as this throws a light on personal relationships. Now that I was established in this works office Sir Herbert still spent considerable time at my board, but I had to share him with the rest of the section. He was not able to give his undivided attention to the designs in hand.

When Whit Monday arrived we had cars to show for our labours and I intended to enjoy the festivities, but some work cropped up and I spent most of my day in the office. During the afternoon Sir Herbert must have slipped away from the official function. He came into the office and was surprised to see me there. After a brief glance at what I was doing he told me that everything was going well and he outlined plans he had for variations on the Seven theme. This was nearly the last time I had a heart to heart talk alone with Sir Herbert. We spoke together many times afterwards of course, but there were generally others present. It was either on this afternoon or one shortly afterwards while we were talking alone, that a young man, who looked not much older than myself, came unannounced into the office and addressed Sir Herbert familiarly saying, "So this is where you hide yourself away." Sir Herbert replied courteously if somewhat stiffly, and they carried on talking about the car, myself supplying an arrangement drawing for Sir Herbert to illustrate a feature from time to time. Towards the end the young man spoke pontifically saying, "My dear sir, the public will just not stand for this", and Sir Herbert replying with equal dignity, "My dear sir, I am educating the public." I learned afterwards that the visitor was Mr. "Billy" Rootes of Rootes, Maidstone, who were then important Austin agents."

When the design and the full general arrangement drawings were ready, perhaps not unnaturally in view of the poor financial state of the Austin Company, there was opposition from Austin's fellow Directors on the Board, some of whom were by no means convinced that a new light car would be the answer to the firm's current problems. A rumour persisted about this time that Austin was tendering for the Wolseley factory at Adderley Park, Birmingham, which was then for sale, and which would have been ideal for Austin to produce the Seven independently had the Austin Board decided to veto its production at Longbridge. Be that as it may, there is no doubt that the Seven project was only accepted grudgingly and that it was put into production under protest. The prototype Austin Twelve, the production of which had been financed by funds received from the sale of surplus plant and stock, was in the Board's opinion much more the sort of car to attract the typical potential buyer; how could they expect to sell a "bath on wheels"?

Austin had provisionally patented those of his own ideas which were incorporated in the design of the Seven, and so the Board, faced with the choice either of having the prototype produced at Longbridge when the design was sufficiently far advanced towards the end of 1921 or of losing it altogether, finally let Austin have his way. However, Austin extracted from them an agreement giving him a royalty of two guineas on every Seven the Company sold.

Sir Herbert chose a most inappropriate time and place at which first to announce the future production – at the Annual Dinner of the Birmingham Motor Cycle Club which took place in January, 1922. He had a profound contempt for motor cycle combination makers, and had expressed this in jest after the First World War when he told the chief engine draughtsman that he considered them "only a step above perambulator makers". As one of the guest speakers at the dinner he made an announcement to owners and prospective owners of light cars, and went on to refer to a new Austin which would, he prophesied, perhaps rather tactlessly in view of the fact that he was in the company of so many ardent motor cyclists, and at least one well-known sidecar manufacturer, "knock the motor cycle and sidecar into a cocked hat and far surpass it in comfort and passenger-carrying capacity". He continued by saying: "I cannot imagine anyone riding a sidecar if he could afford a car", a statement that so enraged the correspondent to the *Irish Cyclist* that this worthy wrote, in a February issue of the magazine: ". . . this seems to us to indicate the frame of mind of the person who thinks that everyone should like what he likes".

For reasons difficult to determine in the light of what has been said subsequently, none of the writers to the motoring press of the period had a harsh word for the Austin Seven in print. They could have had little fear that any critical views that they might have expressed would cut down their revenue from advertising because Austins had no spare money to spend on such luxuries in the early 1920's. Yet the general view at the time – as Edgar N. Duffield's notes on the subject show – appears to have been that the intro- duction of the Seven, however good its design, would be the end of the Austin Motor Company. Many foresaw complete disaster and felt that sufficient people would be unlikely to buy it to make its production a profitable proposition. How wrong they were, and how right Herbert Austin was proved to be. The amusement and contempt with which the car was regarded by some was in no way detrimental to it, and because of its success, the humorists soon found that they must ridicule the new class of motorist for whom it provided such a practical and cheap means of transport for the first time in motoring history, rather than waste their efforts on the vehicle itself.

The first prototype Seven, registered as OK 2950, was built in the Longbridge Experimental Department workshop in the early part of 1922, and although it was reported as having been seen running in the vicinity of the factory and surrounding district in March, it was not until the following

July that details were released to the press. The Austin Company, like Daimler and Vauxhall, usually announced their new models just prior to the autumn London Motor Show, but Sir Herbert disliked the idea of waiting to make an announcement to coincide with Olympia. Another Seven had been completed by July and bore the registration number OK 3537; this car and OK 2950 were shown in all the early advertisements and catalogues. Initially production was slow because a complete section of the factory had to be reorganised, and it is doubtful if more than a few Austin Sevens were on the road by the end of 1922. The original cylinder bore diameter of 2·125 in. was increased in March, 1923, to 2·2 in. starting at car number A1-101. The two prototypes were numbered CHA1-101 and CHA1-102 and the first production tourer was numbered A1-1, from which it would appear that the first car with the 2·2 in. bore built in March, 1923, was the 103rd Seven produced.

A typical reaction to the new venture followed the press luncheon which Sir Herbert gave at the official "launching" at Claridges on 21st July, 1922, after which the *Financial World* reported:

"Holders of motor car manufacturing shares are well aware that we have persistently and enthusiastically advocated investment in the light car issues. We are glad to note, therefore, that Austins have (at last) made up their mind to enter that field.'

Although preliminary descriptions and photographs of the first car appeared in the major weeklies earlier in July, the luncheon at Claridges, and the examination of OK 3537 which was on view in the firm's Oxford Street Showroom gave the correspondents a chance to discuss aspects of the new model with Austin. He said that he was convinced that there was a large market of would-be motorists in England at the time who wanted some form of automobile that would give better weather protection than the sidecar and yet was not so expensive to buy or run as a contemporary conventional car. The individual at whom he was aiming was the "man in the street" whose car must be:

"A decent car for the man who, at present, can only afford a motor cycle and sidecar, and yet has the ambition to become a motorist. It is also for the vast host of motorists who realise that, owing to taxation and the high cost of living, they are paying ridiculously for the privilege of using their car."

Sir Herbert went on to say that:

"In evolving this car we have endeavoured to meet the requirements of those who cannot afford motoring other than that of the cheapest kind. The powerful car, with its heavy running expenses and extensive garage requirements, is beyond the reach of many who, nevertheless, enjoy motoring quite as much as those possessing more cash, and so we have designed a car which will be put on the market at £225, or perhaps a little less."

Although motor cycle combinations could be bought for between £160 and £180, the best available models could cost £200 fully equipped; for as little as an additional £25 the motor cyclist could have a complete motor car.

Many questions were raised ranging from the diminutive size of the 696 c.c. engine to the four-wheel braking system. When it is considered that even the *Light Car and Cyclecar* reported that the Seven was one of the smallest cars that they had ever seen, it is not surprising that Sir Herbert was asked why he had adopted such a small engine. A 2·125-in. bore was exceptionally small for the time, but his reply to the question, like his reason for the small size of the engine was simple:

"It is all that is necessary with so small a car."

As the rate of taxation was at £1 per horse power, calculated on the R.A.C. Formula that takes no account of crankshaft stroke, but only the diameter of the cylinders, this measurement was a very material factor in keeping down running costs. It was one thing to build a cheap car, but quite another to ensure that it was cheap to run. The Company claimed a fuel consumption of fifty miles per gallon with a top speed of fifty-two miles per hour. Appearance was also important, the Seven bore a close resemblance to the Twenty and Twelve horse power Austin models and looked a real scaled-down version of these two well-known and popular cars. Customers were offered something with which they were familiar – the traditional post-war Austin outline.

One revolutionary feature was the four-wheel braking system, a refinement hitherto obtainable only on high-priced racing cars or fast touring models directly derived from them. Sir Herbert pointed out that as the Seven necessarily had a narrow track, and was at the same time equipped with an engine that gave it speed and liveliness on the road, he had come to the conclusion that a better than normal braking system was required. The brakes on all four wheels guarded against any danger should one rear tyre become deflated. In order to fit front-wheel brakes he had discarded the usual semi-elliptic front springs, which when used for front axles fitted with hubs carrying brake drums and shoes, had to be made very heavy to cope with the resultant additional torque and so stiffened up the front suspension and made riding uncomfortable, he chose a single inverted transverse-mounted spring and radius arms instead. With regard to cost, by careful design he had so arranged things that no more parts were used in the four-wheel braking equipment of the Seven than would have been necessary if rear-wheel brakes alone had been fitted. He believed that front-wheel brakes would soon be universally adopted, and that it would be only a matter of time before drivers became accustomed to them. In the Austin Seven design the front wheels were braked by operation of the centrally mounted brake lever. His own words when asked the reason for this were:

> "In this particular design I am using the hand control for the front brakes because I think that one is not inclined to apply that when negotiating corners, therefore the risks of anything going wrong through mistakes in braking are avoided because the driver would apply only the foot brake on the rear wheels when actually negotiating a corner, and would use the hand brake as well only while on the straight approaching it."

After road tests of OK 3537 in July, 1922, glowing press reports appeared. The *Motor* was first to record impressions of the car on 11th July; they considered it to be "a real bid for the simple car market", but they were just too early to include the photograph of the test car so they printed a side view of Sir Herbert in the first prototype without lamps or registration number plates. They found the road performance astonishing. Because of the high power-to-weight ratio it was remarkably lively, the engine showed up to the greatest advantage when hill climbing. With two up the car ascended the factory test hill on second gear at 20 m.p.h. and beat an Austin 20 on acceleration from a standing start. An article in the *Light Car and Cyclecar* on 15th July was the most informative technically and is reproduced as an Appendix.

It was not long before the new car was given a chance to demonstrate its hill-climbing ability. On 29th July Lou Kings, the Company's chief tester, took the prototype OK 2950 to its first sporting event, it having been entered in the Midland Automobile Club's Hill Climb at Shelsley Walsh in Worcestershire. He also drove an Austin 20 in the same event and won the "Open" class on Formula with a time of $70\frac{1}{5}$ seconds. The Seven was naturally much slower, taking $89\frac{4}{5}$ seconds for the climb, but even so this was better than the times achieved by many cars with engines as large as $1\frac{1}{2}$ litres. It could not hope to compete against Frazer Nash on his special G.N. "Kim", a Bugatti and the Aston-Martins but nevertheless was placed third on Formula.

On 22nd September a Mr. George Evans drove up to Scotland in one of the prototypes for the Cairn O'Mount Hill Climb. The car started well but began firing only on three cylinders when half-way up the slope and was beaten by an Amilcar, a 7 h.p. Wolseley, a Charron-Laycock, a 10–15 Fiat and a Morris Cowley. First Prize on Formula in the Open Trade event went to an Austin Sports Twenty which was beaten on time only by a 30/98 Vauxhall and a Sunbeam.

During the last month of 1922 it was decided to introduce a number of minor changes in design; running boards were to be used on the production cars and in November the prototype OK 3537 was fitted with those shown as Type A in the illustration. Other alterations which were to be standardised on the tourer during the 1923 season were fitted to this car because it was to be shown in most of the early advertisements and catalogues. The windscreen was also modified by lengthening the uprights and setting them in a more vertical position than that of the single-piece screen, and a top cross-tube was added upon which a short movable section was used in place of the celluloid flap which previously had been fixed to the hood. Following Sir Herbert's visit to America, which was undertaken in order to ascertain how the motor industry there was able to produce cars so economically that they could be sold at a good profit and at a price that in this country we should have to pay for materials alone, the price of the Seven was reduced drastically in December from £225 to £165. By this time some cars were already being delivered to agents for demonstration purposes and although orders were being taken for them it was not expected that deliveries to retail customers would be possible until the following spring.

SPECIFICATION OF THE FIRST AUSTIN SEVEN
Published in July, 1922.

Dimensions	Overall length, 8 ft. 8 in.; Overall width, 3 ft. 10 in.; Wheelbase, 6 ft. 3 in.; Track, 3 ft. 4 in.; Weight, 6½ cwt.
Engine	Four-cylinder water-cooled detachable head.

Bore, 2⅛ in. ⎫
Stroke, 3 in. ⎬ 696 c.c., R.A.C. rating 7·2 h.p.

Brake horse-power, 10 at 2,400 revs per minute.
Ignition, Magneto.
Oil circulation by pump.
Cooling, thermo-syphon with film radiator.
Roller crankshaft bearings.

Clutch	Single plate.
Gearbox	Three speeds forward and one reverse: ratios (approx.), 4¼, 8¼ and 14½ to 1; 17 to 1 reverse. Ball bearings throughout.
Rear axle	Semi-floating, with differential and torque tube. Ball bearings and thrusts throughout. Final drive by shaft and helical bevel; metal universal joints.
Springs	Semi-elliptic cross spring in front. Quarter elliptics at rear.
Steering	Worm and sector, having provision for taking up wear.
Front axle	Forged "H" section.
Brakes	On all four wheels; compensated and instantly adjustable. Hand brake to the front wheels. Foot brake to the rear wheels. (All parts of the brakes are interchangeable.)
Wheels	Special wire detachable, fitted with 26 in. × 3 in. non-skid tyres. One spare wheel with tyre.
Controls	Of magneto and carburettor on steering wheel.
Petrol tank	Four gallons.
Lighting	By gear-driven dynamo, with accumulators.
Carriage-work	Two bucket seats, for driver and passenger, instantly adjustable and detachable. Rear seat to carry two or three children. Ample tool box accommodation under seats. Spare wheel carried on back of car. Hood, double screen, and full side curtains (those over the doors open with them). Electric horn operated from the steering wheel. Road clearance, 9 in. The panels are stove-enamelled for durability of finish and ease of cleaning.

Edgar N. Duffield, a well-known motoring journalist of the 1920's gave the following impressions in 1950 about the introduction of the Austin Seven:

When we first saw the Austin Seven at Olympia very few of us gave it more than perfunctory inspection. Its appearance, its size, its price, all suggested that it was the sort of thing at which we would look seriously later on – when we had time. It would have been outstanding at a Motor Cycle Exhibition; but in a Car Show, and alongside such things as the other occupants of the Austin 1922 Olympia Stand – well, as I say, we decided that we would have a real look at it later on.

It was treated as a joke and, the Show over, you could not walk into a smoke-room without hearing somebody say:

"Did you see that little Austin? Interestin' but rather surprisin', don't you think, for a serious bloke like Austin to show a machine like that? Of course, he'll sell a few, to youngsters, people who want to play at motoring, or run a car for the womenfolk's shopping and that sort of thing, but . . . well it beats me, even at £225."

Very good judges, who should have known better, were unimpressed. It seemed childish to fritter away production resources on a thing like that; and for a firm like Austins to do so, instead of putting all their energies into really serious propositions, was ridiculous. But Austin had always been a dogged sort of chap, quite satisfied to satisfy himself. His business, anyhow! And that was that. Yet not quite.

At the first opportunity, and I mean just that, I borrowed a Seven from the Company's London Showroom. Mr. Edgar Wren smiled as I – being only sixty-six inches in length and 120 pounds in weight, all on – got into it and emerged into North Row, and thence across Park Lane and into Hyde Park. I had a photographer on the staff of the *Auto Motor Journal* and his stand camera and bag were stowed in the rear. I drove out of London towards Surrey, took photos, dropped the photographer at the office and put in a solid hour seeing what could be done with an Austin Seven in between Great Queen Street and the Austin Depot in Oxford Street. Wren was out at lunch when I returned but a member of the staff whom I knew said "Well, Mr. Duffield, what do you think of our Baby? Isn't so much of a joke as you thought, is it?" I assured him that it was not.

On my way back to my office, on foot, I began to analyse my impressions. To begin with the unfavourable; while it might be amply powered for the stated load of 32 stones or 4 cwt. (obviously the weight of four eight-stoners!) to describe it as a four-seater was certainly extravagant. I owned an Austin Twenty at the time, you see, one of the first delivered, an open tourer, and the abundant roominess of that, a biggish car judged by any criterion, and an absolute giant in relation to the Seven, made more striking than otherwise would have been, the description of the original "touring" Seven as a four-seater. One did not see why it should not carry 4 cwt. of either live or dead weight, but having been told that it was a four-seater, one automatically said "Yes, seating four; but four what or whom?"

We soon began to see the Seven used to carry four fully grown adults, particularly in rural districts, on market days; and I decided, privately, that here was one more of the cars called four-seaters which were very good cars for two grown-ups and two children, or two grown-ups and a lot of light touring baggage.

The world, particularly the English-speaking world, had been saying for ever so long that it wanted a motor car reduced to its least complicated, something made for use, not ornament, mere means of transportation, as comfortable as was practicable, waterproof; but above all simple and economical. Sir Herbert had heard this demand expressed so often and widely that he believed that just for once the public really knew what it wanted. That was what he had given them. If they wanted frills, they must add them to his product. How many people bought them "just for the wife, you know, to use when I am using the car".

It created a new market for itself. Whether or not he thought of it originally in relation to sport and competition work is not known – people saw in the Seven something whose engine lent itself to tuning. It is doubtful that more sports cars have been produced from any other touring model chassis than were made up from Sevens.

There are better things than sporting success, more useful things; but there is no less costly form of publicity than successful racing, particularly if it is done wholly at the expense of one's customers, and they have not an exaggerated idea of the contribution they are making to the manufacturers' prosperity. For one or two purchasers to do a little racing is just one of those things, and one which can be as productive of headaches as of material advantage to the manufacturer; but when whole droves of would-be winners of Trophies put up for anything from kilometer sprint events to 200-mile races, get really keen, and they are all willing, whether or not they are able, to do their own tuning, and organise their own participation in every event in the calendar, the manufacturers' anxieties evaporate, and he can sit back and bask, more or less, in reflected glory.

When asked by other senior executives who wanted some of the great deal of floor-space devoted to the Seven for their own schemes, Herbert Austin said:

"I think you'll find, if you go into the matter, that the Seven earns its little bit of floor-space. Or do you suggest that we should discontinue the Seven and produce more, and bigger, and therefore arithmetically more lucrative models?"

He knew that it was easier to sell half a million pounds worth of Sevens than the same value of cars costing a great deal more.

A man who bought a Seven was a potential customer for something bigger. S. F. Edge said that Austin's creation of the Austin Seven from a blank sheet was the greatest thing ever done by a British automobile engineer – even though Edge himself had never been associated with such a small car. Edge never saw anything funny in the Seven. As early as 1925 when his own business was in a bad way he said:

"I'd rather have given the world the Austin Seven, my dear fellow, than have won the Gordon-Bennett race for England a dozen times over, and in twelve consecutive years. Hang it, you don't realise what Austin has done. I wonder, indeed, if Austin himself realises what he has done? Ford had a unique market, on his own doorstep, for the Model T, one which had never existed previously and will never exist again. Austin had not. Austin's case was an instance of that very uncommon phenomena, a supply creating a demand, and filling it to the last ounce and penny piece."

When this was repeated to Lord Austin ten years later his only comment was "That was nice of S. F."

The Austin Seven

From the *Light Car and Cyclecar*, 15th July, 1922

The Austin Seven is one of the smallest motor-cars that we have ever seen. Yet it is certainly a sound job and its performance on the road is perfectly astonishing. From its front view it is obviously an Austin, solid and perhaps a trifle squat, but following closely the lines of the 12 h.p. and 20 h.p. models of the same make.

So small a car needs a small engine. The dimensions of the water-cooled four fitted to the Seven are 55 mm. bore and 75 mm. stroke, which makes the capacity 696 c.c. The monobloc casting is only $11\frac{1}{2}$ in. long and some 5 in. wide, yet the unit develops 10 h.p. at 2,400 revs per minute and may be speeded up to over 3,000 revs per minute. The car unladen weighs 6 cwt. and it is, therefore, not surprising to learn that its power-to-weight ratio is even better than that of the Austin Twenty. Evidence of this is forthcoming by standing start tests on both cars on Rose Hill, a fairly long ascent near Birmingham terminating with a gradient of about one in six. On this hill the Seven actually beat the Twenty!

Indeed, the liveliness of the tiny four is one of its principal attractions. With a $5\frac{1}{4}$ to 1 compression ratio and gears of $4\frac{1}{2}$, 8 and $14\frac{1}{2}$ to 1 in conjunction with 26 in. $\times$ 3 in. wheels, its nippiness up hill and down dale is remarkable. Rose Hill, for instance, was climbed with two up on second gear, and only near the top did the estimated speed fall below 20 m.p.h. On the level at 30 m.p.h. the engine runs like a turbine, no period in its range of speed being noticeable.

The actual dimensions of the wheel base and track of the car are 75 in. $\times$ 40 in., and yet the two separate and adjustable semi-bucket seats provide a perfectly comfortable and natural position for driver and passenger. Behind these seats there is a back seat for children, who, of course, must be lifted into position unless one of the front seats is removed. Another feature of note is the great width of the two front doors, which measure 20 in. across and permit the easiest access to the driving compartment, a point often overlooked on small cars.

The car is intended to compete directly with the family sidecar and will be listed at about £200. The equipment is remarkably complete and includes four-wheel brakes, all-weather hood and curtains, electric light and detachable wire wheels. What more could the man of moderate means want for his money?

Going into greater detail, it is seen that the engine closely follows the design of the popular Austin Twelve and Twenty, the principal alterations being the sweeping forward of the exhaust piping to avoid the undue heating of the driving compartment and the fitting of the sparking plugs in the centre of the detachable cylinder head. The latter, which is provided with priming cocks is held to the block by means of fourteen nuts and studs, the block itself being secured to the base chamber by eight bolts and nuts, three of which are located on the near side of the casting inside the valve stem casing.

The valves are arranged side by side and, as the two breathers from the crankcase communicate with the valve stem chamber, both stems and adjustable tappets are lubricated by oil spray. The inlet and exhaust manifolds are formed in a single casting, the exhaust pipe being connected up to the front end of the manifold and leading thence downwards and rearwards.

The timing gear is located in the usual position in front of the engine and drives the magneto through the medium of a vernier coupling on the off side of the unit, the magneto lying parallel with the casing and being held to its platform by means of a metal strap. A generator driven from the forward end of the camshaft by a spiral gear provides current for the electric lighting, which is to be standardised, whilst on the rear end of the same shaft is found a vertical extension to the gear-driven oil pump which supplies the camshaft bearings with lubricant. Oil is then led round the back of the engine to a gallery on the off side of the case, from two points of which it drips into wells cut on the crankshaft. Through these wells it finds its way to the big-end bearings and is splashed on to the aluminium pistons. The latter are provided with two rings above and one below the gudgeon pin, which is clipped to the small end of the connecting rod.

The crankshaft runs on two bearings and the oil sump contains three pints of lubricant, the whole engine, with the gearbox, being four-point suspended in the frame. Cooling is effected on the thermo-syphon principle, the radiator containing some two gallons of water. The petrol tank, containing four gallons of fuel, or a supply which should be sufficient for close on 200 miles running, is located on the engine side of the dash, a sloping wide-neck filler enabling the approximate amount in the tank to be calculated by sight. The bonnet, which is hinged to form three sides, can be lifted off as a single unit and the engine then appears to be very accessible.

The flywheel and single disc clutch are contained in an aluminium cover, the back half of which is formed in one with the gearbox casting, thus neatly completing the power unit.

A central change is adopted, the gear ratios being $4\frac{1}{2}$, 8 and $14\frac{1}{2}$ to 1. The propeller shaft is built in two portions, the forward end of the front one being provided with a small ring type coupling where it adjoins the gearbox, whilst the rear half which is splined to the rear end of the other piece, is enclosed in a torque tube attached by means of a spherical joint to one of the two main cross-bracing members of the frame. The final reduction on the axle is by means of a spiral bevel encased with the parallel pinion differential in the central aluminium casing to each side of which are attached the steel tubes containing the driving shafts.

The thin ends of the rear five-leaf quarter-elliptics are threaded through clips on the under side of the axle casing, the lowest leaf, which is wider and thicker than the others alone being held rigidly in the clip. The thick ends of the springs are fixed in the butt ends of the side members of the frame, where they are neatly housed by the inverted U section. The rear brakes, like those on the front, are of the internal expanding type and are operated by pedal through the medium of a single cable passing through suitable compensating gear. A somewhat similar arrangement is adopted for the front-wheel brakes, which are operated by hand. Each end of the single control cable is attached to the brake proper, immediately under the pivot, and as the cable passes round a compensator, which is, in turn, controlled by the brake lever, further complication is unnecessary.

The front axle is a very strong job and is carried well below the front hubs, thus increasing the stability of the car on the road. A transverse spring

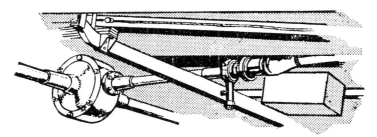

Fig. 1. 1922 rear axle and propeller shaft.

necessitates the fitting of radius rods, which lead from the extremities of the axle and unite in a ball-and-socket joint anchored to the forward cross-member of the frame.

The 26 in. × 3 in. wire wheels are of Austin design and are quickly detachable and interchangeable, the spare being carried on the back panel of the car. The wheel is secured to the axle by means of three studs and nuts. The hub shell flange on the wheel is drilled with slots, with which the studs register, the axle being locked home by its washers and nuts when the wheel is moved round slightly to bring them to one end of the slot. To disengage, the nuts are removed, the wheel turned back so as to bring the studs opposite the other end of the slots, the washers removed and the wheel pulled off.

The steering column follows standard practice, it being a simple matter to adjust the worm and segment and also the rake. The wheel measures 15 in. in diameter and is set in a convenient position in relation to the driver's seat. An oil pressure indicator is mounted on the dash and the horn is carried under the bonnet.

The frame is roughly A shape in plan, although the front is somewhat rounded off in order to accommodate the anchorage of the front transverse spring. There are two cross-members and the butt ends of the side members serve, as already stated, to house the thick ends of the rear quarter-elliptics. The frame is of the inverted U section, suitably strengthened at the points at which the cross-members join it.

The most interesting feature of the body is its great capacity in comparison with the diminutive appearance of the car. The front semi-bucket seats are really comfortable. The cushions are 7 in. deep and their backs are well padded and provide plenty of support for the body. They have a 3-in. range of adjustment, the seats being automatically locked in one of three positions and covering two large lockers for the storage of tools and spares, whilst an additional and larger locker is provided under the rear seat for the same purpose. The side curtains, made of Duratex, like the hood, can be folded in pockets at the back of the bucket seats when not required. When erected they convert the car into a comfortable all-weather vehicle in which all passengers are properly protected. The hood is normally kept in a cover, but when erected is found to incorporate with its leading edge a narrow glass panel, which completes the adjustable windscreen.

The convenience of the body can be judged from the fact that it measures some 40 in. across, whilst the two front doors are no less than 20 in. in width. Metal panelling, to be produced on the huge Austin presses, is continued right round to the sides of the radiator, the lower run of panelling on each side of the engine supplementing the bonnet.

It is on the road that the wonderful qualities of this tiny car are evident. It will climb the Austin test hill, which has a gradient of 1 in 5 to 1 in 6, from a standing start and will very nearly take the same hill with a short run on its 8 to 1 second speed. One can start the engine literally with one finger and it then ticks over as sweetly and silently as could be desired. The acceleration on the lower gears is quite astonishing and the seats are set at such comfortable angles that the effect compares favourably with an armchair. The car has received the personal attention of Sir Herbert Austin for the last two years and is the development of an idea he has long had in mind. If it can be produced at the price contemplated it should certainly make an outstanding mark in the annals of economical motoring and for this reason its appearance will be widely welcomed.

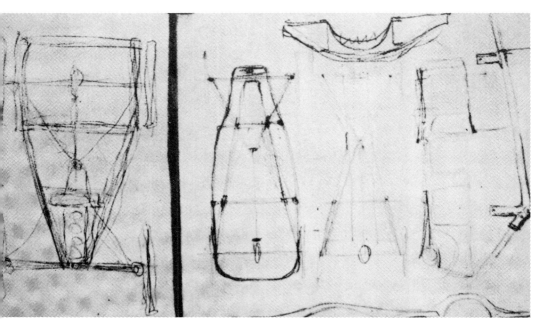

2. A page from Lord Austin's
sketchbook showing the drawings made for the prototype
Seven in 1920-21

3. A very early car
without running
boards

4. The 1923 press
handout

5. OL 166 early in
1923

1923

The Races Begin

"I told Sir Herbert that I was convinced that the only way to make the public accept the Austin Seven was to race it from the beginning."

E. C. Gordon England.

Early in 1923 a light two-seater fabric-bodied car with a white radiator shell was prepared at the factory and registered OK 7095. After a few test runs around Birmingham Captain Arthur Waite, Sir Herbert's son-in-law, drove it to Brooklands to compete in the Easter Monday meeting on 23rd March. It started from the limit mark in the Small Car handicap, completing a standing lap at 56·64 m.p.h. and flying lap at 62·64 to beat the cycle-cars with ease, at an average speed of 59·03 m.p.h. Captain Waite then drove it back to his home in Bromsgrove, 116 miles away, covering 190 miles in the day at an average speed of about 32 m.p.h. without the slightest trouble.

Satisfied that the car was reliable, Waite then asked permission to take it to Italy for the Italian Cycle-car Grand Prix race which was to take place at the Monza track on 29th April, his idea being that if it was unsuccessful at least it would have disgraced itself at a sufficient distance from home to avoid creating adverse publicity. Any fears that he had were proved unfounded for he won the 250 km. race in the 750 c.c. class at nearly 57 m.p.h., his fastest lap being at over 64 m.p.h. One of the first to congratulate him after the race was Signor Anzani whose very fast car driven by Ordorici finished second. Earlier he had offered Waite garage facilities and was very impressed by the fact that the Austin, with its side-valve engine, could give a better performance than a car with overhead valves. The duel with Anzani lasted for 130 miles, but Waite gained a lap lead when his rival stopped to change a sparking plug.

The successful Seven, in accordance with Austin's policy, was built up from standard parts. As was the case with the first two prototypes it used a 4·5 to 1 final drive ratio in place of the 4·9 to 1 ratio that was standard on the touring cars. It ran on Shell fuel and Speedwell oil, Pirelli 26 in. × 3 in. tyres, had a Watford magneto, K.L.G. plugs, Hartford shock-absorbers, and a Cox-Atmos carburettor. A great deal of interest followed the Austin's success as it was the first British car to win an event on the Continent since before the war; the newly formed British Broadcasting Company even made an announcement about it over the air.

E. C. Gordon England had become associated with his father's firm, George England Ltd., after the war and had been successful in tuning an A.B.C. car, which had already competed in the 1921 and 1922 200-miles races. In 1922 he returned to an earlier interest, gliding, and built a machine in his spare time which he entered for the *Daily Mail* Glider Competition. By an error of judgment caused by his long absence from the air, he crashed on the last day of the trials. The result was a broken ankle that put him in hospital where he had plenty of time to meditate on motoring problems. After studying the details of the new Austin Seven he came to the conclusion that it would make a good racing car, so he wrote to Sir Herbert stating that he realised that to get the public to accept such a small car would not be easy, and that in his opinion the only way to do so and to get the car recognised as a practical proposition, would be to race it from the outset. He concluded by saying that he wished to discuss the matter. Sir Herbert replied expressing willingness to see him.

As soon as England was able to leave hospital, and whilst still forced to use crutches, he went to Birmingham by train. Arriving at the Longbridge Works before the appointed time, he took the opportunity to speak to members of the staff about the Seven. As he had thought might be the case, none of those to whom he spoke had much faith in the Seven's prospects and it was regarded generally with what seemed like some embarrassment.

At length he was taken to Sir Herbert whose opening words hardly sounded encouraging – "What the hell do you want to see me about?" England then told him that Austin's own staff were not taking the Seven seriously and were even opposed to it, and that the only way to get it launched as a commercial proposition would be to establish it first as a racing car and that he, Gordon England, was the man to do it. Looking at England's crutches Sir Herbert retaliated: "You'll make a bl——y fine racing driver." With this the ice was broken and Austin said "Done", and thereupon agreed to prepare a suitable car for England free of charge. "And I'll get it to you before your leg is out of plaster." He was as good as his word and the special car arrived by train before England was fit enough to drive it.

The next series of events in which OK 7095 competed were at the B.A.R.C. Whitsun meeting at Brooklands where Waite was joined by Gordon England in his new single-seater. The Works' car did not finish in the Small Car handicap, but in the 75 m.p.h. short handicap covered the standing start lap at over 63·5 m.p.h., a flying lap at nearly 70 m.p.h. and finished second.

England completed his standing start lap in the Small Car handicap at 59·58 m.p.h., covered the second lap at 70·05 m.p.h. and beat the cycle-cars at an average speed of 67·75. He took third place in the other event, after he had been rehandicapped on the results of the previous race, although his car went faster than the Works' racer with laps at 69·36 m.p.h. and 71·15 m.p.h. respectively.

Two more fabric-bodied Works' cars were prepared for racing; OK 8945 and OL 166 which were driven by Waite and Cutler at the B.A.R.C. Summer and August Meetings.

Waite, still with OK 7095, and Kings and Cutler with the two other cars which had raced at Brooklands during the summer, went to Boulogne in September, 1923 accompanied by Sir Herbert. Twin Cox-Atmos carburettors were used feeding through long riser pipes to enable a three-branch exhaust to be fitted. The engines had high lift camshafts but were otherwise standard, and were capable of attaining 5,000 revolutions per minute. Eleven gallon fuel tanks were carried in the scuttles and the spare wheels were slung beneath the tails of the bodies. K.L.G. plugs and Palmer tyres were fitted, and to save weight dynamos were omitted. The results of the race were disastrous for the Austins and the fate of the cars is described in the following extract of a letter written by Sir Herbert and published in the *Motor* on 11th September, in which he also reveals his attitude towards the production of cars designed specifically for racing:

"Racing enthusiasts tell us that racing improves the breed, and teaches us a lot about efficiency, control, materials, etc., while its opponents say that all these can be obtained by other means.

There is something to be said for both sides. Racing has undoubtedly hastened our knowledge and experience. It has given us data in a few weeks that would have taken years to obtain by any other means. It has also provided sport of an exceptional interest and character; but has it done all it might have accomplished? It has always seemed to me that the building and racing of special or freak cars is a mistake, except for amateurs unconcerned with the responsibilities of the production of standard cars for public use. I have, therefore, never attempted to go outside equipping a standard car with some small change in the various organs that did not affect its design as a vehicle capable of being sold to the public in large quantities, in the belief that any help or information of value must of necessity follow this procedure. I am still of that opinion, and I think it is more important today than it has ever been before. Now that we are reducing the dimensions of our motors all round, and getting the power by increased revs rather than by bore and stroke, it becomes an important question that, for the motor particularly, its main features should be embodied in the design used for the car to be put to the test in racing.

This does not seem to be the practice followed by most of the other concerns who have taken part in road or track racing. They build cars entirely different from those they produce for sale to the public, and it is, I think, for this reason that the public takes so little interest in our racing events compared with the size and extent of the capital investment in a track like Brooklands, or the expense of the race just held at Boulogne; the small attendances point to lack of interest. If the great body of the buying public takes little account of the races, then what is the use of building special racing cars? Why not – if we are to support the expense, and it is the makers of cars who foot a large part of the bill – confine our efforts to getting the most value we can for the benefit of our everyday products, and, if possible, at the same time, increase the public attendance and interest?

As an instance of the futility of building pure racing cars one has only to examine the times made by cycle-cars in the Grand Prix de Boulogne and compare them with the voiturettes fitted with engines of twice the capacity. Up to the seventh circuit, when our third driver, Cutler, was leading his class, and was still going strong, his time was only 28 minutes 11 seconds behind the best of the voiturettes for a distance of 261 kilometres over a difficult and hilly course, his total time being 2 hours 58 minutes 16 seconds giving an average speed of 88 km ($55\frac{7}{8}$ miles) per hour. This for a standard touring car chassis, fitted with a special camshaft and exhaust and inlet manifold, and driven by a man who had never taken part before in a road race, and only once at Brooklands proves, in my opinion, that one can get sufficient speed out of a standard chassis to make the race interesting, and that the test will find out the weaknesses quickly, and therefore give valuable data for manufacture in quantity at a reasonable cost. Our cars all broke down for the same reason – viz., the method of lubrication to the connecting rods, which, although satisfactory in ordinary use, is evidently not good enough to withstand the heavy strain of continuous running for several hours at over 5,000 revs.

If we manufacturers could, therefore, agree to race only standard car chassis, fitted with special parts, as allowed by suitable regulations, we should derive much more benefit from the expense and, I am confident, get the public to take a more lively interest in our contests."

These failures occurred because the oil for the big ends was fed in at the front end of the crankshaft after entering a hollow "nose cap" that enclosed the rear end of the starting handle shaft and the starter dog. After passing through the number one journal the pressure had to overcome centrifugal forces that were considerable at high engine speeds to get across to journals number two and three. By this time the pressure was considerably reduced and it was found that the number four (rearmost) big end was "starved".

Sir Herbert, with his alert brain, soon showed how the effects of centrifugal force on the oil pressure could be eliminated, and designed tubes to attach to the crankshaft to carry the oil circumferentially between numbers one and two, and numbers three and four journals respectively. These tubes were available later for fitting to engines already in use. Eventually some crankshafts were produced with circular webs thus making the tubes unnecessary. Occasionally on the pressure-fed engines small chippings from the starting handle shaft and starting nut were taken through into the crankshaft with disastrous effect on the bearings.

S. F. Edge, whose pen seemed always poised ready to attack or support a manufacturer voicing his opinions on motor racing, wrote a letter agreeing

Fig. 2. Adjustable panel attached to hood peak.

with Austin. Warwick Wright, however, thought that Sir Herbert was "putting the cart before the horse", and that it was wrong not to give credit to pure racing cars. He pointed out, perhaps with his tongue in his cheek, that if the Sevens had been developed in the first place as racing cars the engine lubrication problems, in all probability, would have been corrected at a much earlier stage.

Between Whitsun and September Gordon England made a number of modifications to his racer. Specialloid pistons were fitted, a high lift cam-shaft, stronger valve springs, Celerity valves, a new cylinder head giving a higher compression ratio, forced feed lubrication to the big end bearings, twin carburettors and a modified exhaust system. Apart from the 4·5 to 1 rear axle the car remained a standard production chassis. In this 7½ cwt. single-seater with its uncowled radiator England set out at Brooklands on 6th September to capture as many of the class L records as possible.

He covered the 5 miles at 79·62 m.p.h.

10 miles at 78·57 m.p.h.

10 laps at 75·95 m.p.h.

50 miles at 76·51 m.p.h.

100 miles at 64·79 m.p.h.

an (1 hour at 73·59 m.p.h.

A two-seater body was built weighing about 20 lb. – less than the weight of the filled petrol tank – and Gordon England obtained Austin's permission to enter it in the 1100 c.c. class of the J.C.C. 200-mile race at Brooklands on 13th October. Thirteen cars started, three of which were Salmsons, in this test of speed and stamina.

The French Salmson trio took the lead almost at once and held their positions until one had to retire after fifty miles; then another pulled into the

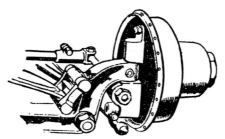

Fig. 3.   1922 front axle.

pits but was soon off again, although it had to stop for water after every two laps from then on. Only six cars now remained in the race; the Austin in second place, lapping at 79 m.p.h. consistently, and speeding down the straight at 85 m.p.h., Bueno's Salmson came in first having taken the fifty mile record at 87·85 m.p.h., but hardly had spectators' attention turned once more to the track than Gordon England flashed over the finishing line, amid rousing cheers, leading the next Salmson by nearly three miles, after a non-stop run with an average speed of 76·84 m.p.h.

Work on the Austin had been completed only twenty-four hours before the race. England and Hall took it for a test run on the track late on the previous afternoon and did two laps at over 76 m.p.h. Long Tom, the well-known Brooklands bookmaker, went over to see England and asked him if he would like to make a bet on his chances the next day; England suggested odds of 100 to 1 for a place, but Long Tom would only agree to 33 to 1, which Gordon England accepted, handing over a pound note stake. After the race Long Tom gave him £34 and told England that he had never parted with such a sum more gladly, saying: "Mr. England you've made my day." Sir Herbert was probably just as pleased but did not show it with similar gallantry, his reply to Gordon England when the latter telephoned to Longbridge to give him the good news was, perhaps, typical of the man: "Why didn't you bl——y-well win?"

England's success was due to the ability of the Austin to complete the race without a stop. The car behind him had made the fastest lap at 92·57 m.p.h. but in spite of its being much faster it lacked the stamina to sustain this performance over 200 miles. Such an unexpected success for Gordon England and his Austin naturally attracted the attention of the press, and a reporter

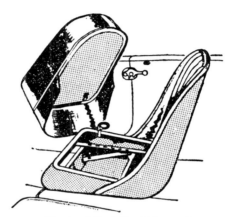

Fig. 4.   Adjustable driving seat.

from the *Light Car and Cyclecar* spoke to England just after the race and was told:

"If you want to know what sort of a chance I thought I had, I don't mind telling you that I backed myself for a place; it was a marvellous performance and nothing short of staggering. For a little engine of 748 c.c. to lug two grown-ups round a track, which for surface isn't exactly as comfy as a bed of roses, non-stop for 200 odd miles at a speed of just under 80 m.p.h. – well, as I said, it's staggering, and, mark you, it wasn't all-out at that, and had as much power on the last lap as on the first."

When asked if it was difficult to hold the car at 80 m.p.h. he replied:

"Coming off the banking it was, just a trifle, but it was my own fault, as my Hartfords wanted tightening a little at the outset."

In a letter to the *Light Car and Cyclecar* he described his tactics during the event; how the car was driven throughout very well throttled, the reason being that he decided it would be impossible for such a small car to win under normal conditions. It was heavily handicapped by the small capacity of its engine, and so it was decided to run at a predetermined speed to ensure that it would complete the course non-stop, and finish the race, so clearly demonstrating its reliability. In his own words:

"We assumed, in laying our plans, that having regard to the previous history of the 200-miles race, a schedule speed of about 75 m.p.h. would bring the small car well within the first few to finish, and we considered, bearing in mind the special racing jobs that we were up against, that this would be all that we could reasonably expect to accomplish.

In practice, the car had indicated that it could lap easily at 80 m.p.h. with two up, and as a matter of fact, as soon as I had obtained a lap speed of 80 I stopped all further efforts at tuning because I was firmly of the opinion that this was as high a speed as we could reasonably hope for, and that, having regard to the fact that the car was a standard job, to try to get further increase in speed might overstrain certain parts, and as time was so short it was decided to go steady rather than see what was the utmost of which the car was capable. In the race the car never gave a moment's trouble from start to finish, the engine revolutions varied between 4,500 and 4,700, according to the throttle opening given, and it is interesting to know that as the race went on, so the speed of the car was gradually increased. Our first laps were in the region of 74 m.p.h., our final laps 78 and 79 miles per hour.

I am sure that it will be of particular interest to those who assume that small cars are difficult to handle at high speed to know that this car has the standard steering and that it was quite easy to handle up to 80 m.p.h. Going past the Vickers' sheds at a speed of about 85 m.p.h. the bumpiness of the track at this point made it a little difficult, but the car was never either uncertain or ever likely to get out of control.

As I completed my final lap in the race I opened the throttle for the first time fully, and the revolutions immediately went up to the maximum we had ever attained in practice, showing that the engine had not lost the slightest bit of its tune. The maximum speed of the car on the level was actually 86 m.p.h.

The springing on this car was so good that neither I nor my mechanic were at all shaken, or bumped about during the whole of the race."

During the race England set up the following class records:

100 miles at 75·65 m.p.h.
150 miles at 76·44 m.p.h.
200 miles at 76·84 m.p.h.
1 hour at 73·90 m.p.h.
2 hours at 76·48 m.p.h.

I have described the early races in some detail as the successes provided a firm foundation for the growth of the Austin Seven's popularity, and because from the cars which took part in them two new standard versions of it were developed and offered for sale in January, 1924: the Sports model, and the Brooklands Super-Sports model. Appearance rather than performance was the main attraction of the two-seater Sports models, which had perfectly standard chassis with the exception of a more raked steering column angle and a longer gear lever. The increase in speed over and above the standard cars was achieved mainly by a slightly advanced ignition setting. All cars were stove-enamelled in Kingfisher Blue and weighed 8½ cwt. Electrical starters

Fig. 5. The hand-operated mechanical starter.

were standard, and the equipment included a speedometer and front and rear shock-absorbers. The top half of the windscreen was detachable for "speed work" and at a price of £175 the first car of the batch, A1-3126, was sold in March, 1924. In mid-1924 a standard Sports car was taken on a twenty-four hours' run at the Aspendal Track in Victoria, Australia. One three-lap section, including stops, measured 141 miles and was covered in three hours, at an average speed of 47 m.p.h.; unfortunately, with less than three hours to go, one of the nuts on a connecting rod worked loose and the test ended prematurely after the car had completed 887 miles in twenty-one hours at an average speed of 43 m.p.h.

In his letter to the press some months before, Gordon England had said that within a very short time he hoped to offer for sale replicas of his record-breaking Seven. These were the Brooklands Super-Sports models and an entirely different proposition from the standard Sports cars. They retailed at £265, excluding wings, hood and screen, and, according to the first catalogues, each car was sold with a Brooklands Certificate of 75 m.p.h. The chassis were delivered from Birmingham to George England Ltd., who built them up with their polished aluminium three-ply framed bodies with undershields, and fairings over the front axles. A tool locker was provided behind the two bucket seats, one of which was staggered back 9 in. behind the other. Hartford shock-absorbers were used on both axles, and the equipment included a speedometer and radiator thermometer. Engine details that differed from standard were the high compression cylinder head, special timing gears, high iift camshaft, modified tappets, Celerity valves and double valve springs. Twin Zenith 30HK carburettors fed into a special induction manifold. The transmission included a fabric-type front universal joint, and the rear axle a 4·5 to 1 ratio bevel and crown wheel (later a 4·09 to 1 ratio final drive was offered as an option).

The exhaust system was carried outside the bonnet and terminated in a detachable fishtail. In the light of previous racing experience the lubrication system was modified to provide direct force-feed lubrication to the big ends.

With the exception of an attractive little 2½ cwt. delivery van which was introduced in October, 1923 at £180, a commercial travellers car, an experimental single-seater taxi shown at the Commercial Vehicle Exhibition, and the Sports cars, Austin produced no other standard models during the early years. Certain developments and modifications which were made to the more expensive range were gradually applied to the standard tourers. At the 1923 Motor Show the chassis, with a mechanical starter, cost £130, and with electric starter £138. The tourer was listed at £165, with electric starter obtainable at £9 extra.

1924

Gaining Experience

Commencing at Car Number A1-101 in March, 1923 the engines were bored to 2·2 in., which increased the capacity to 747·5 c.c. Fans and starters were not provided, there were all-metal sliding universal joints at both ends of the propeller shaft, and the stepped scuttle and square doors with catches on the inside were to remain for some time, as were the adjustable, non-tilting, bucket seats. Children could get into the rear compartment either by squeezing between the front seats, or by being lifted into the back by the driver, or his front passenger, from the side or the rear of the car.

The word *Chummy* is almost synonymous with the Austin Seven. Originally used to describe a particular type of coachwork, it was soon to become applied exclusively to the Austin Seven tourer. Popular small cars of the period were generally provided with bodies having two seats, both of which were under the hood, but a four-seater on a light car chassis usually had but two of them under the hood, with the two additional seats, or dickey seat, as it was called, outside the hood, and when not in use hidden under the boot lid. Such accommodation was cold, wet, generally uncomfortable, and dangerous for children, and so by 1922 some manufacturers had begun to extend the coachwork to include all four seats under the hood; the dickey declined in popularity, and the "occasional" four-seater – already being referred to as a *Chummy* by October – became increasingly common.

Cars as small as the Seven were not designed to carry four adults in comfort, as to do so would have imposed too great a load on a car weighing only 6½ cwt. or so, and to quote the Company's own literature:

"The space at the back of the driver's seat has intentionally been restricted so that any attempt to overload the car with too many passengers will be militated against by the discomfort attached thereto."

43

Any discomfort there may have been, however, did not prevent owners from overloading their cars. Although intended for children or light luggage, and not two adults additional to those in the front seats, four full-grown people were carried only too often, and in a relatively short time several weaknesses in the design were disclosed.

The Service Department recorded daily, from customers' letters and reports from the Repair Department, all complaints concerning the various models. These were classified under different headings covering the several models, and the various components of the respective vehicles, and lists were compiled weekly, typed out, and circulated to Sir Herbert and the heads of the departments responsible for the design, production and inspection. In this way those concerned were kept informed of all faults that developed in service, whether from design, material or manufacture, not to mention those that were due to the customers' own neglect or misuse, and so were able to take steps to eliminate them. The management were also able to determine whether or not any modifications made had proved successful in preventing repetition of the trouble.

One of the first series of complaints concerned cracks developing in the bodies f the tourers at the bottom rear corners of the door openings, and also to a lesser extent at the "toes" or front corners at the base of the scuttles. These cracks were mainly caused by overloading the rear compartment as the back of the body was unsupported by the chassis which terminated only just behind the rear spring anchorages. Accordingly, pressed steel extension pieces were designed for fitting to the early chassis. These were arranged to be held in place by the front clips of the quarter-elliptic rear springs, and were issued to customers or could be fitted in the Longbridge Repair Department. The body was also deprived of some support when the original type of door catches, which actually held the body sides to the doors, were superseded by spring latches. The latter enabled the doors to be slammed shut, but the originals were much more practical as they prevented the doors from opening accidentally.

Difficult starting from cold, before the electric starter became standard, was found to be due mainly to a particular make of magneto – not of British manufacture – that was fitted as standard equipment to the first batch of cars. This type of magneto was most satisfactory and reliable once the engine started, but gave a feeble spark at low speed. When replaced by another make the starting trouble was overcome. To some extent cold starting was rendered uncertain by sticking valves, and a slight modification to the upper ends of the valve stems at the base of the radius below the valve head overcame this difficulty. Starting difficulty probably did much to bring about the discarding of the mechanical starter, first referred to in advertisements as early as May, 1922, which was later superseded by the electric starter which was fitted in conjunction with a heavier capacity battery and larger dynamo in December

1924. It is only fair to say, in defence of the mechanical starter, that it was not intended for use in cold starts, but only as a convenient means of restarting the engine should this be inadvertently stalled in conditions that made it inconvenient to get out of the car to use the starting handle.

Heavy oil consumption and oiling up of the combustion chambers were

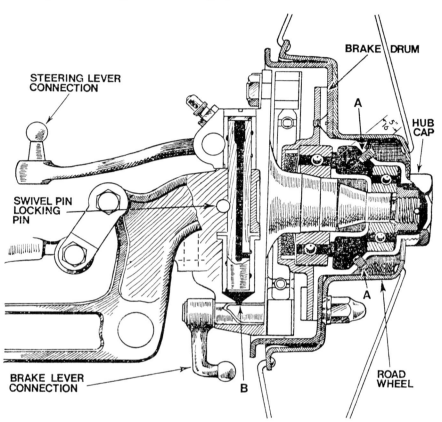

Fig. 6 Front hubs with taper bearings.

other troubles that afflicted early Sevens, and were not quite so easy to correct. In bad cases the Repair Shop staff used to remove cylinder blocks and lap the bores and rings (fitted to "slave" pistons) with a very gentle abrasive to obtain a perfect finish and this usually proved effective. Later, and experimentally, they began fitting stepped type scraper rings in place of the taper section scrapers that were standard. The stepped rings were produced from standard compression rings by turning away some of the bearing surface, so increasing the radial pressure on the remainder. Later, and when the new type proved successful they became standard and were obtained from the piston ring manufacturers in the ordinary course of business. The original design of taper scraper rings suffered from the fundamental defect of becoming progressively less efficient as they wore and the bearing surface became wider. Austin Seven engines were always "oily", unless one of the oil jets became choked!

At first the cars were fitted with oil gauges, but it was found that owing to the great drop in oil pressure when the engine heated up, and the lubrication system was working satisfactorily, there was a tendency for drivers to be misled. The uninitiated were apt to think that the pump was failing or that all was not well somewhere. They should in fact have been apprehensive only if the gauge had registered a sudden increase in pressure as this would have shown that one or both of the crankcase oil jets had become restricted or choked entirely. To have continued in such circumstances would have been to risk running a big end, or seizing a piston. A rise in pressure when the engine was hot required the immediate clearing of the jets by poking them clear from above with a length of wire inserted through the small plugged holes provided. Also many gauges failed due to the great variation between the cold and hot pressures, and leaked badly, and so gauges were superseded by a simple indicator with a black button that protruded from its surrounding plated bezel when the oil pump was working. The knob receded slightly when the engine became hot and the oil less viscous, but the difference in position was less noticeable than an easily read needle indication of actual pressure drop. It was still necessary, however, to warn owners that a sudden, and otherwise unaccountable, protrusion of the button in normal running showed that it was essential to stop the engine and clear the jets at once before continuing. The jets were readily cleared after the $\frac{1}{4}$ in. plugs above them were taken out from the top of the crankcase.

Rear axle trouble in the form of teeth stripping off pinions and crown wheels persisted for some time, and several modifications were made to these two parts. Ultimately it was decided that the alternations in load on the thrust bearings on the pinions, as the loading changed from drive to over-run, was the main cause. To reduce the extent of the alternations the "hand" of the spiral of the teeth was changed to concentrate the load in one direction.

In the early stages of production two other factors were contributory causes of rear axle trouble: lack of rear shock-absorbers, and the very short clutch pedal travel. The latter made it difficult for even experienced drivers to get a smooth take-off from rest, and novices, of which there were many, usually got away in a series of violent jerks which the totally undamped rear springs accentuated by making the body of the car bounce up and down, which was most disconcerting. The fitting of shock-absorbers as standard equipment did much to cut down transmission trouble, but control of the clutch was always somewhat tricky.

The designer's intention had probably been to provide for the lubrication of the rear hub ball races from the main axle casing from grease that worked its way past the felts at each side of the differential casing. The Company did not recommend gear oil for axle lubrication, but always specified "a mixture of yellow grease and engine oil", and insufficient of this worked along the axle tubes and entered the hubs so that many bearings ran dry, rusted, and eventually disintegrated. To eliminate this defect the hubs were drilled, the modification coming into force in February, 1924, to enable an adaptor to be screwed in so that grease could be injected direct to the hub bearings by grease gun. At first two holes, tapped ⅛ in. B.S.P., were drilled diametrically opposite to each other in each one, and when greasing, the hole opposite to that in which the adaptor was fitted was left open so that when the hub was full the excess began to exude from it. Later on, only one hole was drilled and a modified adaptor was issued. This had flutes right across the threaded section up which excess grease issued when filling was completed.

Early front and rear hubs were fitted with ball races having tapered inner rings fitting over tapered seatings on the stub axles and rear axle tubes respectively. Trouble was experienced with these inner rings splitting, possibly due to over-tightening of the lockrings securing the rear ones. The splitting was confined to the rears although over-tightening of the stub axle nuts might have been expected occasionally to have happened with the fronts. Following many complaints the seatings were modified and bearings with parallel bored inner rings became standard. These gave no trouble.

Hartford shock-absorbers were offered as extra equipment by the Service Department for chassis not originally fitted with them, but provided with the necessary brackets. These shock-absorbers worked well if looked after and not over-tightened, but if neglected sometimes stiffened up to such an extent that the leverage of the very long arms put severe bending stresses on the brackets at the rear of the chassis with the result that these broke off. A temporary expedient of bracing the rear cross-member by short tubular struts, stopping it from being bent forward at the bottom, did not prevent the fractures.

As many owners were guilty of very much over-tightening the adjustment of the shock-absorbers, the Austin-designed type that superseded the Hartfords in June, 1925 had no adjustment. Coil springs provided the pressure on the friction linings, and the only way in which this could have been increased would have been to turn back the shoulder of each centre pin and so decrease the installed length of the spring, or to fit stronger springs. Customers were unlikely to go to so much trouble, and except for an occasional faulty coil-bound spring due to manufacturing errors the Austin shock-absorbers were satisfactory. Complete freedom from bracket breakages was not achieved, however, until the rear of the chassis was modified to incorporate brackets of better design, and at the same time extensions to support the rear of the body were included.

As the Seven became more popular enthusiasts found that the already good

performance could be improved by a moderate advance in ignition timing.
Having gained a little in maximum speed, far too many owners thought that

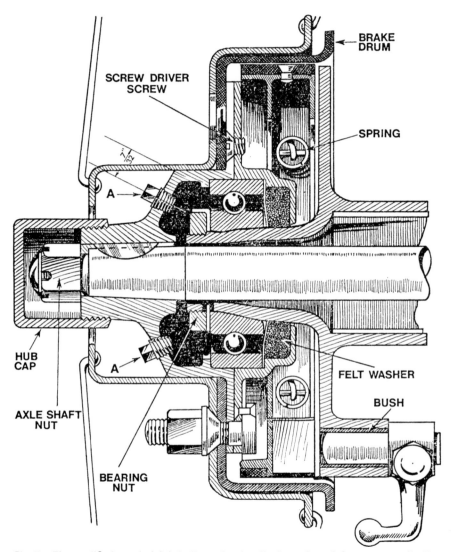

Fig. 7.   The modified rear hub lubrication, showing the two plugs A for grease application.

by doubling the extra advance given they would double the increase in speed.
One result of over-advancing the ignition timing was to make the engine very
"rough". The Seven engine did not "pink", but the roughness affected the

6. A contemporary view of one of the first Sevens taken in 1923, which shows the horn button and C.A.V. switch panel on the extreme right of the dash

7. 1923 – the first Austin Seven 2½ cwt. van

8. The single-seater taxicab shown at the 1923 Commercial Vehicle Exhibition

Features:
4-cylinder Engine.
Water Cooled.
Detachable Head.
Automatic Lubrication.
Three-speed Gearbox.
Bevel Drive.   Differential.
Brakes on all Wheels.

Equipment:
Electric Lighting.
Electric Horn.
Hood and Double Screen.
Side Curtains.
Spare Wheel and Tyre.

Price at **£165** Works

Write for " The Motor for the Million,"
——a delightful booklet illustrated.——

THE AUSTIN MOTOR CO. LTD.
NORTHFIELD, BIRMINGHAM.
And 479-483, OXFORD STREET, London, W.1.

9. OK 3537, the second prototype with running boards fitted and top section of screen sketched in, as used for an advertising postcard in March, 1923

clutch which was caused to slip because of vibration set up in the flywheel in extreme cases.

Clutch trouble of a different kind resulted from the shearing of the two taper pins securing the declutching levers to the clutch pedal shaft. This occurred because the clutch thrust race housing completed its travel, and was unable to move further, before the clutch pedal travel had ended. Thus the full pressure from the driver's foot came on to the declutching levers and the taper pins came under very heavy shear stress. As an immediate means of preventing this the Service Department issued, free of charge, small plates cut from steel sheet and drilled to fit over the off side rear engine fixing bolt. After fitting, the plate was set to form a stop for the pedal, and when correctly adjusted the bolt was tightened. As soon as the castings could be modified a permanent stop for the pedal was arranged by a suitable boss formed on the crankcase rear engine bolt lug.

Some cases of broken crankshafts were reported, and were attributed to over-driving with over-advanced ignition, particularly when the rear end roller bearings were worn and considerable crankshaft whip took place. One or two fractures were traced to faults in grinding the big end journals, the process having left chamfers at each end of the journals instead of the designed radii.

In June, 1924 after some 4,500 Sevens had been produced, and in preparation for the 1925 season, the new and slightly longer type "C" touring body was introduced. It had wider doors with sloping rear edges, a vertical windscreen frame, flat scuttle sides and modified bonnet, but retained the original internal door catches. There was more space in the rear compartment, in conjunction with which modification the back part of the hood was raised to give additional head-room. A speedometer was added to the dashboard, which now carried the oil indicator button, the magneto switch, dimmer switch, horn push button, air strangler control and the black circular C.A.V. three-button switch panel. The Patent Plate was fixed above the steering column clamp. The chassis, which already had a Hardy-Spicer fabric front universal joint, mud excluding flanges on all brake drums, and a radiator cooling fan, was listed at £120, and the Tourers and Sports models were reduced to £155 for the standard model, stove enamelled in Kingfisher Blue, and £170 respectively in October.

Following the many racing and record-breaking successes, alternative styles of light Sports coachwork by outside manufacturers, available on the standard Austin Sports chassis, were first produced late in 1924. There was the two-seater pointed-tail Sports body designed by Thomas Hughes & Son of Sparkhill, Birmingham, panelled in polished aluminium and fitted with six-inch domed mudwings and a Vee windscreen; weighing only $1\frac{1}{2}$ cwt. it had a polished mahogany instrument board and a hood. Upholstery was available either in leather or leather-cloth. Another, perhaps less attractive body was

4

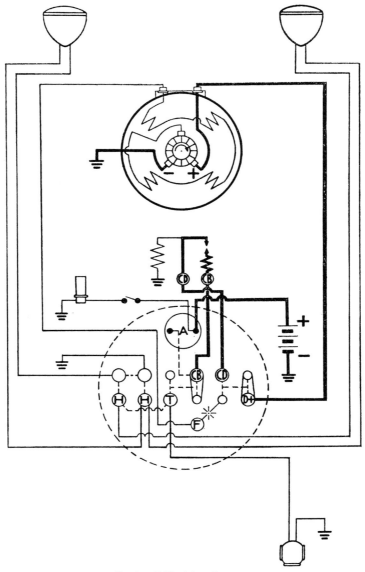

Fig. 8.   1924 wiring diagram.

designed and manufactured by Wilson Motors of 7 Eccleston Street, London, S.W.1, and called the Burghley. It was built up of steel panels with a boat-shaped rear section decked over with satin walnut planking secured by copper nails.

In dark grey with scarlet wings and scarlet Rexine upholstery, the car was listed at £195 but was reduced to £185 in January, 1925. This model, however, was a prototype with an upright screen, and the Burghley was redesigned and modified in February, 1926 with a longer tail and larger mudguards. The two-door body was finished in grey and the hood also in grey material. Running boards were of aluminium, there was a hinged three-piece bonnet, and aluminium wheel discs were included. Alternative windscreens were available, a metal framed Vee type, or a fixed single-panel type with slight rearward slope.

During 1924 474,000 private car licences were issued in Britain, 91,000 more than in the previous year. Motor-cycles were declining in popularity, and for the first time the number of two-wheeled vehicles in use was less than the number of cars. Having started at practically the same level in January, by the end of the year cars outnumbered motor-cycles by nearly two to one. Taxation figures also confirmed a tendency towards the smaller-engined cars, whereas by the end of 1922 the average tax paid, based on the R.A.C. formula rating was £17 12s., the figure fell a year later, and by the end of 1924 it stood at £16.

An Austin Seven could be bought for as little as £59 deposit and repayment of £9 per month which included interest, but it was not the only small car on the market in the £150 category capable of 40–50 m.p.h. with a fuel consumption of 50 m.p.g. There were the popular Rover 8, the Jowett, Mathis, Peugeot and the 7 h.p. Citroen. The Austin was both shorter and narrower by several inches than any of these competitors. Austin and Citroen were engaged in a minor price-cutting battle at this stage; the Citroen was reduced to £145, in response to which the price of the Seven tourer was dropped to £149. As soon as the French company heard this they offered their two-seater at £130. The Austin still had the advantage in this country because it had gained for itself a fantastic reputation. Demand exceeded the supply in spite of the fact that two night shifts were being worked at Longbridge. There were 7,000 employees and early in 1925, 150 to 200 Sevens were being completed every week.

High-pressure beaded-edge tyres combined with rather stiff springing – the shock-absorbers contributed to this – made long journeys over the inferior roads of this country after the war rather uncomfortable. The Americans were by this time fitting low-pressure tyres on well-base rims, and Dunlops produced a special wired-edge type " Balloon" tyre size 26 in. × 3·50 in. for the Austin wheels. This change was announced in February, 1925 and the new tyres became standard equipment on all Sevens produced from March that year.

Many more sporting achievements were made in 1924. On 15th April Arthur Waite set up two Brooklands class H records; the flying kilometre at 85·97 m.p.h. and the flying mile at 84·29 m.p.h. Two months later R. E. O.

Hall took one of Gordon England's cars to the track at Weybridge where he broke a number of records, amongst which were the standing-start mile at 61·8 m.p.h. and the flying half-mile at 83·64 m.p.h. Waite continued increasing the speed of the Works' car and was joined by Captain Samuelson, Major Gardner and Dingle. The best lap in a B.A.R.C. event was made by England at 83·7 m.p.h.

Three of the firm's cars were taken to Le Mans to compete in the 750 c.c. class of the Grand Prix des Voiturettes, Waite in car number 8 finished third, and Roddis came fourth. Six more class H records fell to Waite at Brooklands on 15th August; the standing start kilometre at 60·26 m.p.h. and the previous mile record held by England was increased to 65·73, the flying start 5 kilometre to 82·13, the 5 mile to 81·33, the 10 kilometre to 81·04, and the 10 miles to 81·14 m.p.h.

Waite's biggest disappointment was at the Swiss Grand Prix race in Geneva at which he was one of about half a dozen entrants in the 750 c.c. category. When he took the car out for a practice run the other competitors took fright and scratched, leaving him alone in the race, which the authorities promptly abandoned. He was then approached with the offer to race in the 1,100 c.c. class and in spite of the handicap, he decided to compete. Much to his surprise he was four minutes ahead of the field after 170 miles, but, unfortunately, with only ten miles to go the clutch gave out. The excitement was not yet over because the only other car came in with its mechanic out of action with a cut eye caused by a stone breaking his goggles. This meant that no one would get the prize unless another mechanic was found, so Waite sent out his own man to finish the race with his rival.

The J.C.C. 200-miles race on 20th September was run in three classes; for cars up to 1,500 c.c., 1,100 c.c. and the new 750 c.c. category which had been added since the previous year. As the six-cylindered 750 c.c. supercharged Vagova failed to appear the Austin Sevens were left to struggle amongst themselves in the smallest class. Three cars were entered in Waite's name and driven by Waite, Kings and Cutler, and there were six other private entries that were to be driven by Dingle, Hall, England, Hendy, Samuelson and Selbie-Bigge, whose car was prepared by George England Ltd. This car had twin Zenith carburettors, larger ports, modified engine lubrication system, and all four brakes operated by pedal. Unfortunately this and Samuelson's car failed to start. Hall made an excellent get-away, closely followed by Waite and Kings. Cutler retired in the second lap, Dingle in the tenth, Kings in the twenty-first, and Hall in the sixty-third. Gordon England won yet again, after a non-stop run, attaining an average speed for the race of 75·61 m.p.h. – a little slower than his 1923 average – with Hendy second at 68·69 m.p.h. England broke three records during the race: 1 hour at 75·77 m.p.h., 100 miles at 75·99 m.p.h., and achieved the fastest lap at 80·33 m.p.h. The retiring Austins failed owing to inadequate engine lubrication, and towards the end of the race even England's engine was not firing on all cylinders. He had sufficient time in hand however to win on three cylinders, and so decided not to stop to change the plug that he suspected to be at fault. It was not until the head was removed the next morning that fragments of the connecting rod were discovered in the oil sump. There was no trace of the piston!

Montlhéry, the French racing track, was opened in 1924 and Gordon England took over one of his Brooklands models with which he won the 750 c.c. class by covering 108·5 miles at 73·25 m.p.h. Hall came second, a fifth of a second behind, Waite was three-fifths of a second behind him, and Dingle two-fifths of a second behind Waite. The report in the *Autocar* stated that Waite, in his pea-green car, sportingly entered the 1,100 c.c. class and was only beaten by the Salmson team.

In this first full year of racing the speed of the Austin Seven had been progressively increased from 62·5 to over 84 m.p.h. The little cars received 173 awards in sporting events in Britain alone, and 20 more were gained elsewhere in Europe. Gordon England accounted for most of the year's records at Montlhéry on 16th October, when in an unsuccessful attempt on the twelve hours' record he set up the following records in the 750 c.c. class:

Standing Start;   1 hour at 78·77 m.p.h.
                  2 hours at 79·89 m.p.h.
                  3 hours at 78·77 m.p.h.
                  4 hours at 79·89 m.p.h
                  50 miles at 80·36 m.p.h.
                  100 miles at 80·72 m.p.h.
                  200 miles at 78·60 m.p.h.
                  300 miles at 80·00 m.p.h.
                  5 km. at   72·15 m.p.h.
                  10 km. at   77·10 m.p.h.
                  50 km. at   80·47 m.p.h.
                  100 km. at   80·47 m.p.h.
                  300 km. at   77·14 m.p.h.
                  400 km. at   79·32 m.p.h.
                  500 km. at   79·89 m.p.h.
                  600 km. at   79·32 m.p.h.

Flying Start;   5 miles at 74·38 m.p.h.
                10 miles at 78·26 m.p.h.
                Fastest lap: 84·10 m.p.h.

1925

Racing Successes Continued

Gordon England's 1924 record-breaking successes had proved unbeatable. He held every Brooklands class record from half-mile to 200-miles and this may well have prompted Waite's next move. The Company's little booklet *The Supremacy of the Austin Seven* which was produced in October, 1927, gave a list of Austin Seven records, and whether by accident or design, although his speeds were given England's name did not appear. In addition, due to a misplaced date heading, anyone reading it would gain the impression that eight of Waite's 1925 records were made in 1924.

Whilst the practice of supercharging was still in its infancy, and following the success of a similar device applied to a twin overhead camshaft 746 c.c. Peugeot, Waite decided that the only way to achieve his new goal – to obtain 100 m.p.h. from a 750 c.c. car – was to experiment with a Rootes blower on one of his Sevens. The French had been able to get 42 b.h.p. at 5,600 revs per minute from the Peugeot. In bench tests during the first few weeks of 1925, Waite found that by placing a small $7\frac{1}{2}$ in. $\times$ 7 in. Rootes type triple impeller supercharger, lubricated by mixing a small quantity of oil with the petrol, between the 33 mm. Cox Atmos carburettor (which replaced the standard 24 mm. instrument) and the engine he could feed in 60 cu. ft. of air at 5 lb. pressure which was most effective at engine speeds between 4,000 and 5,000 revolutions. At 5,000, supercharging raised the power from 25 to 43 b.h.p. When the engine was put into a modified chassis with underslung springs, a canted radiator and lowered steering, which combined to give a considerable reduction of the superficial area of the body, the maximum speed was increased from 80 to 88 m.p.h. With the supercharger operating the petrol consumption went from 32 to 22 m.p.g. and without a supercharger the most effective compression ratio was 6·8 to 1, but the increased volume of gas when blown burst the cylinder head and experiments showed that a ratio of 4·8 to 1 gave the best results.

Waite took the car to the 1925 Easter Monday meeting at Brooklands but was unable to get the best from it owing to a sticking throttle cable. However, on 15th April he returned to the track with the single-seater which, with the rear of its body made from aeroplane fabric stretched over an ash frame, weighed less than 7 cwt., to attack the International class H records. He managed to cover the two-way flying start mile at 84·29 m.p.h. and the kilometre at 85·97 m.p.h., reaching 92·44 in one direction. The car proved that a supercharged Austin Seven was a practical proposition, although the Company found that it was extremely difficult to achieve the extra 8 m.p.h. to reach the coveted hundred.

The cheapest Sports model available at this time was the Works' standard car at £170 and fun though it was, it was quite useless for competitive racing. Gordon England had a firm hold of the sporting model market with his Brooklands Super-Sports model which cost £265, probably the only car sold in quantity with an independent certificate that it had accomplished its guaranteed speed before delivery. Many dealers were unwilling to encourage purchasers of sports and racing models because the cars often gave trouble and owners were inclined to demand an extensive after-sales service. England, on the other hand, found that once he had sold a Brooklands Seven he seldom had any trouble from the customer and, in fact, the cars were splendid travelling advertisements for themselves. When parts were required he had adequate stocks which were cheap because the specification was so similar to that of the standard models. 80 m.p.h. did not prove so much that it overtaxed the chassis and engine.

Introduction of a supercharger, however, presented a different proposition. In Gordon England's view it posed so many new problems in design that by the time all the difficulties had been overcome, the cost of experimenting and the modification of the engines would put the cars out of the reach of most small manufacturers and practically all the amateurs for whom his Brooklands model was designed. As an example of how racing costs went up with the use of superchargers, due mainly to the time needed to prepare the engine, Gordon England estimated that it would cost at least £200 extra to supercharge a Seven engine and, even then, the purchaser would have been told by England that he had no faith in its reliability, although it was feasible to guarantee a speed of 95 m.p.h. To ensure complete reliability, the additional cost would be at least £800. Not unnaturally all the development work was done in the Austin factory by the Works' racing team, as it was only there that the costs could be absorbed. Some years passed before supercharged Sevens were offered to the public.

Between 350 and 400 Brooklands Super-Sports cars were made altogether, most of them in Gordon England's factory at Felsham Road, Putney. The specification underwent a few minor improvements during the production run. It was never intended for ordinary road use, in fact Gordon England produced a special "Cup" model, a fabric two-seater with a domed back containing the spare wheel, which first appeared in August, 1925. With regard to the Super-Sports models, standard Austin Seven chassis were sent down from Longbridge by rail and the engines were modified and tuned. Few alterations were necessary, valve ports were polished, a high-compression cylinder head, light pistons, high lift camshaft and modified timing gears were fitted. Special K.E. valves were needed to cope with the sustained high engine speeds and these were provided with special tappets and double valve springs. Valve clearance adjustment was made by varying the thickness of the tappet head by grinding off the required amount, exhaust valves were set at 0·010 in. and inlet valves 0·006 in.

Early models used twin Zenith carburettors, but a single 30 mm. Solex

Wife (proudly) : Thank goodness we were able to afford a four-seater.

with an improved induction pipe was adopted later. This instrument used a 22 mm. choke, 110 main jet, 50 pilot jet and a 47 gramme float. For racing, a 24 mm. choke and 130 main jet were recommended. A special crown wheel and pinion gave gear ratios of 14·5 to 1, 8·17 to 1 and 4·4 to 1. Lubricated with Castrol "R" and using Aviation petrol maximum engine speeds were in the region of 5,000 revs per minute and every car sold still had a Brooklands certificate that it had accomplished 75 m.p.h. It was found that the best results were obtained with an ignition setting at which the magneto points broke contact at 2½ in. before piston top dead centre, measured on the flywheel rim, with the contact breaker in the fully advanced position.

One of the most important modifications to the engine was to the lubrication system. A problem with the earliest Super-Sports models was to ensure an adequate supply of oil to number three big end with sustained running at high speeds. At first, the oil pressure was increased but this proved ineffective because it caused the sparking plugs to oil-up too frequently. Ultimately it was found that the centrifugal force of the crankshaft at high

10. Arthur Waite at the wheel of OK 7095 on the day that he won the Easter Small Car handicap at Brooklands in 1923

11. The 1924 Gordon England production Brooklands Super Sports model. Guaranteed speed – 80 m.p.h.

12. The 1924 standard Sports model

13. One of the three racing cars that went to Boulogne in August, 1923

14. A late 1924 Burghley Sports model, made by Wilson Motors of Victoria, S.W.1

15. Late 1924 polished aluminium body by Thomas Hughes of Sparkhill Birmingham

16. 1926 Chummy
with headlamps in the
forward position

17. An experimental
Works' coupé–March,
1926

18. P. Brough in a
Gordon England Cup
model, in which he
won the disabled
drivers' handicap at
Brooklands in April,
1926

19. Samuelson in
Gordon England's
car, which was used
in the 1925 200 and in
which Samuelson
won the 750 c.c.
Short handicap at
Brooklands at the
1926 J.C.C. Spring
meeting

20. 1927 fabric saloon

21. H. B. Parker taking over from Chase (standing on the left) during the successful attempt on the twenty-four hours' record at Montlhéry on 7th June, 1928

22. A group of Austin Sevens (kept in order by an Austin Twelve) snapped in 1928

engine speeds overcame the oil pressure in some of the crankshaft ducts. This was corrected by using the pipes mentioned in an earlier chapter so that the centrifugal force assisted the oil flow. By employing this method it was possible to reduce the oil pressure by 10 lb. per square inch, it also resulted in less oil consumption.

Bodies for the first sports cars were made specially for Gordon England by Weymann and were of three-ply on a white wood frame, panelled in aluminium. In later cars this panelling was varnished. Two hundred men worked at the Felsham Road factory, turning out a wide variety of coachwork for most well-known cars, with three or four Brooklands Models a week, six "Cup" Models and a contract to provide twelve England saloon bodies a week for delivery to Longbridge. There was no room for expansion in Putney and the lease on the premises was to expire in 1927, so England decided to move. When the Empire Exhibition finished at Wembley in October, 1924 the buildings were bought by a financier named James White whom England, accompanied by one of his fellow directors, went to see in an attempt to obtain a lease on part of the Palace of Industry. They had great potential and a good income but lacked capital and although they could afford to pay a small rent, all their cash would be needed to expand the business. After listening attentively to and being obviously impressed with these go-ahead young men, White replied: "Well, look here you boys, I like you and I'm going to let you have the premises you want." Shortly afterwards Gordon England went to White's solicitor to draw up a provisional agreement and learnt that White had given instructions for the first year of the tenancy to be rent free with a nominal payment for the next two years, after which the situation was to be reviewed. Unfortunately, in June, 1927 and half way through the negotiations White died, but the executors of his interests decided to honour his agreement with England and allowed him to be tenant at will. Later it will be seen how wise White had been in seeing a great future for England and his ideas.

With the standard Seven chassis at £120 (reduced to £115 in September), the tourer at £149, the Sports model at £170 (reduced to £159 in September), the Startin-built van at £180 (first listed in August, 1925 and reduced to £170 later in the year), and the new coupé which was introduced in March, 1925 at £165 and of which only a few were made, there was very little competition from other light car makers in the baby car field. During 1925 the British Motor Industry built 28,000 cars rated at 10 h.p. and below, more than a quarter of which were Austin Sevens – 7,043. This was almost double the production for the previous year; between November, 1923 and the end of 1924 only 4,700 Sevens left Longbridge. Minor modifications continued to be introduced during the year, by far the most important being the introduction of balloon tyres and well-based rims, referred to in the last chapter, which commenced at car number A1-8150. The horn switch was placed on the centre of the steering column in September at chassis number 12,328, and for the October Motor Show both the drivers' and passengers' seats were made to tip forward.

> "I have been working for some time past on the possibility of incorporating two Austin Sevens for racing in the 1½-litre events next year. There are, however, many difficulties to overcome, and while I am confident of very satisfactory results, the actual tests, I feel, are going to be carried out against the better judgment of a much more able engineer than myself."

I am not sure to whom Waite was referring in this letter which he wrote to the press, but I assume it was Sir Herbert because the result was that the engine of one of the cars was merely bored out to 57 mm., which raised the capacity to 775 c.c. so that it could compete in the 1,100 c.c. class in the 200-miles race at Brooklands on 26th September.

It has always been thought that there was only one supercharged car running in 1925, but the evidence shows that there were two. The bored-out car had its first trial at the Brooklands August Bank Holiday meeting. Depper drove a standard supercharged car to third place in the 75 m.p.h. Short handicap in which Hendy and Cutler also competed, the latter in Gordon England's car, but the 775 c.c. Austin ran in the 75 m.p.h. Long handicap race for the President's Gold Plate. Parry Thomas won at 96·89 m.p.h. and Waite lost second place to Campbell by only 600 yards. Cutler and two other Sevens also entered, but without much success. On the other car, Depper also achieved another third place in the 100 m.p.h. Long handicap.

The main race of the day was the *News of the World* 100-miles handicap, a thirty-seven-lap event in which only fifteen cars were permitted to start. Gordon England was allowed a 20 minute 10 seconds start and owing to the fact that three cars had scratched, Waite was able to enter but retired in the sixth lap with universal joint trouble. Still in the lead at the half-way mark, England began to slow down with pre-ignition trouble, he continued in the lead until the race was three parts over when Parry Thomas flashed by. England's car was still running and in sixth place when the event finished, but he failed to complete the thirty-seven laps.

On 5th August Waite took the streamlined car to Brooklands again and succeeded in taking the following class H records: Standing kilometre at 60·26 m.p.h., standing mile at 65·73, flying 5 kilometres at 82·13, flying 5 miles at 81·33, standing 10 kilometres at 81·04 and the standing 10 miles at 81·14 m.p.h. Two longer distances were captured from England on 23rd October, the standing 50 kilometres at 83·45 and the standing 50 miles at 83·74 m.p.h.

Waite and England, with his wife as passenger, entered for the George Boillot Cup handicap race at Boulogne on 30th August, England's car being a prototype for the new "Cup" model. The two Austins set off together on the 327-miles journey with a start of 1 hour 6½ minutes; Waite gave up and England failed to finish in the stipulated time.

More than 30,000 spectators watched the 200-miles race at Brooklands. A different course from the previous year was chosen: this time competitors had to enter the straight section of the course and double back to the main track at the fork; this hairpin bend made the race slower but more interesting both for the drivers and the crowd. Waite's supercharged red bored-out car entered in the 1,100 c.c. class in an unsuccessful attempt to challenge the three Salmsons; he retired in the forty-fifth lap with transmission trouble. Five Austin Sevens entered in the 750 c.c. class – Depper, in the other supercharged Works' car, Gordon Hendy, A. Grey, and R. E. O. Hall and England driving two of the latter's streamlined cars. Both used the engines which had been prepared for the previous year's race, but with only one carburettor. On both, standard Austin chassis frames were cut through at the spring anchorages and the springs arranged to lie parallel instead of at an angle. They were mounted on special cross-members and attached to the axle by modified linkages which allowed the seats to be slung well below the torque tube. The streamlined bodies were three-piece shells which enclosed everything but the wheels, made of three-ply on a light wooden framework, the weight of the complete body being only 45 lb., including bonnet and undershields. Nine gallon petrol tanks were fitted and reserve oil supplies were carried. Both these cars suffered from overheating and Hall's was slowed down to such an extent that he only completed fifty-five laps. At one stop he spent twenty-two minutes replacing the cylinder-head gasket. After the twenty-eighth lap A. Grey, who had experienced tyre trouble earlier on, was travelling at about 75 m.p.h. low down on the banking near the Members Hill, when there was an explosion of a tyre bursting. The car swerved and then somersaulted, landed on the track upside down, bounced in the air again and finished up on its wheels in the ditch. Grey received head wounds and concussion, and his mechanic, J. Pares, was taken to hospital in a critical condition. Depper had to call in at the pits with clutch trouble and Hendy was the only driver in the class to make a non-stop run, but Gordon England, true to form, won the race again at 61·16 m.p.h. Hendy was only a fraction slower at 61·15 and Depper came third at 60·29. Positions in the overall classification were eighth, ninth and tenth.

Shortly after this exciting race the bored-out supercharged Works' car went to Brooklands again for the Essex Motor Club's meeting. Waite lent it to George Duller for the 50-miles handicap and, much to everyone's surprise, Duller won with a fantastic average speed of 89·90 m.p.h.

1926

Goodbye, Gordon England

1926 began with the introduction of the first production Austin Seven saloon body, built under contract for the Company by Gordon England Ltd. Two inches longer in body space than the tourer, there was sufficient room for comfort and to allow for very wide doors with sliding windows, which were also used in the sidelights for the rear compartment – still more suited to carry two children than for adults. The fixed windscreen was provided with a suction windscreen wiper and the fabric exterior of the coachwork could be obtained in a choice of three shades, red, grey or dark blue, all with black above the waist lines. Wings were also black. For the first time the lamps were moved forward from the screen pillar to a much more convenient position between the wings and the bonnet and separate side lamps were mounted on the wings. Pneumatic, cloth-covered ribbed upholstery was used on the two front adjustable bucket seats and for the rest of the interior trim; the near side seat slid forward and tipped for easy access to the back. Radiator shells were nickel plated and fluted louvres were cut in the body side to keep the heat from the engine compartment away from the enclosed interior. This excellent little saloon weighed only 8¾ cwt., slightly less than the Chummy, and cost £210. A de luxe model with leather upholstery was also listed at £230. In addition to this new car, the England range still included the Super Sports model and the new "Cup" or "Semi-Sports" model at £185.

It was not an easy matter to provide a small saloon body combining the essential features of comfort, protection and appearance with lightness, strength and cheapness. Maximum comfort could only be achieved in the 1920's by making a coachbuilt body that would have been far too heavy for the Seven chassis. Fabric-covered bodies were developed to overcome the weight problem; a simple, well-designed framework was built up over which a cellulose-based fabric was stretched. This principle had been used by the aeroplane manufacturers but in the form in which it existed there proved to be several disadvantages. Sir Herbert always referred to them, rather scornfully, as "rag" bodies and he was quite correct when he remarked later on that there would be very little future in them. Although the Gordon England body was fabric-covered England had spent four years in developing a technique of construction which made his Saloons better than many of the patented fabric bodies available at the time. England's bodies were solid plywood shells and not skeleton frameworks covered with fabric as in the Weymann designs. Construction was in the form of a hollow box girder of plywood around the base of the body. This was attached to the frame at three

Fig. 9. "*Please, Sir, there's a gentleman outside wants to know if you can go for a trial run in an Austin Seven*".

points, two at each side approximately where the front doors were hung and one centrally at the back, by small bolts and Hardy fabric universal discs. Dash and instrument boards were mounted independently of the body and the floor boards, and seats were placed on the chassis. The whole purpose was to make the body an umbrella resting on the chassis by three-point suspension. When the chassis was distorted, either on the road or permanently for demonstration, the body on top of the twisted frame retained its form completely and each door could be opened and closed as easily as if the body were standing on the ground. One complete body, built, trimmed, fitted and finished and the chassis road-tested, was turned out in five days for each five men on the payroll.

Returning to figures, the Austin Seven's share of sales in the class rated at under 10 h.p. rose to nearly half the combined output of the entire British

Motor Industry. Production figures were double those of the previous year and totalled 14,000 Sevens in 1926, in spite of industrial unrest and the loss in output caused by the General Strike.

In February, a number of minor improvements were introduced and the standard tourer body was re-designed slightly to give greater width, length and more knee room, and the bottom section of the windscreen was curved around the scuttle. The first vehicle with this new type "D" touring body was car number A2-7074, chassis number 17,074, and it became standard from car number A2-7340. Both interior door latches were replaced by spring catches with handles to enable the doors to be opened from the outside with the new folding side screens in position. An alteration in the shape of the frame allowed the hood to be furled without taking the screens down.

Saloon bodywork was becoming increasingly popular and pictures of a new standard Austin metal saloon first appeared in the middle of 1926; this was the prototype car, car number A2-137, chassis number 20,032 which was produced in May and registered ON 2448. It was priced at £169, the Gordon England saloon was immediately reduced to £195 and the tourer and saloon were reduced by £4 each to £145 and £165 respectively in mid-September in preparation for the Motor Show in which there was more serious competition than before. As well as the Ford, Trojan, Jowett or the Morris – a two-seater Cowley cost only £148 10s. – there was the new Singer Junior at the same price. A Longbridge-built van was introduced at £170 in June. Brake drum diameters were increased at car number A3-3727 in September, the first car with the four-piece bonnet was A3-4725, screen wipers at A3-5345 and the Lucas switchboard at A3-5700 all in time for an announcement just prior to the Motor Show.

To prevent dazzle and in line with all the Gordon England models the lamps on all Austin Seven cars were moved forward from the scuttle to the more convenient position between the wings and the bonnet.

As an example of what could be expected from a Chummy, certainly the cheapest car available at the time which was capable of sustained hard work, let us look at a mid-1924 model which was driven for eighteen months, covering 13,000 miles. Its top speed was 50 m.p.h. and averages achieved in fast runs on good roads were 160 miles at 32 m.p.h., 80 miles at 35 m.p.h. and one over 10 miles at 44 m.p.h. The only faults which showed up were loose engine bearer bolts and fracture of the petrol feed pipe to the carburettor. This was prevented in later models by coiling the pipe to absorb the engine vibration. After 2,000 miles there were frequent punctures in the 26 in. × 3 in. beaded edge tyres, at 3,000 new ones were needed. With the low-pressure covers it was possible to obtain 10,000 miles without trouble. Replacements consisted of two valves and a set of top compression rings, rear brake linings, a fan belt and a speedometer belt. Overall running costs totalled a mere penny-farthing a mile.

1926 produced even more Austin Seven sporting successes than before. Waite took the 747 c.c. supercharged car to the opening B.A.R.C. meeting on Easter Monday; he entered for several races but was unsuccessful in securing a place. Gordon England sent two of his 200-miles race cars along, one was driven by F. H. Samuelson and the other by R. T. Spenser who won the 75 m.p.h. Short handicap at 73·34 m.p.h. This was soon followed by an announcement from England that he had decided to give up racing on account of his business activities and that his 200-miles race car was for sale at £350.

All the well-known Seven racers turned up again at Brooklands for the

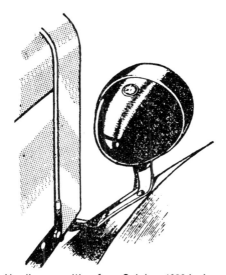

Fig. 10.   Headlamp position from October, 1926 to January, 1927.

Junior Car Club meeting on 17th April. Duller, Waite and Gordon Hendy entered for the Short handicap in which Waite, in spite of a lap completed at nearly 90 m.p.h., could only drive to third place. These three were joined by F. Samuelson, S. Bassett and Calcott Reilly – Sales Manager of Gordon England Ltd. – in the 750 c.c. Short handicap which Samuelson won at 71·97 m.p.h. Only five of the Austins competed in the final race, the 50-miles handicap, and Hendy came third.

Abroad, Zubiaga was third home in the 1,100 c.c. class at the Targa Florio Race which was run in Sicily on 27th April. He covered 201 miles without trouble. In the same car he won the 750 c.c. Class of the Grand Prix des Voiturettes by three laps. Samuelson drove to fourth place in the 1,100 c.c. Class at the Boulogne Grand Prix using a Brooklands model, BP 9520, which he had bought from Gordon England nearly three years before. These successes on the Continent attracted useful publicity abroad at a time when Sir Herbert was making his first attempt to contact a firm in France to build Sevens under licence.

Another important J.C.C. event took place at Brooklands towards the end of July, the Production Car Race. Seventeen cars started but only eight finished. Samuelson's car caught fire, Gordon Hendy retired early with big end failure and Walther, driving Boyd-Carpenter's car, put up the best average for a Seven at 51·23 m.p.h. Waite's car was the only other Austin to finish, at an average speed of 46·54.

Finally, another exciting 200-miles race. Gordon England had already threatened to retire from racing but it was not merely to add another class win to the two which he already held that made him decide to contest again. His motives are explained in the following letter which he wrote to the press in September:

"So many people have asked me how it is my name figures in the entries for the 200-miles race after I had definitely stated I had given up racing, that it would seem that I ought to offer some explanation for such reprehensible conduct.

The 200-miles race has always been to my mind the most sporting race organised in this country, and it has a peculiar fascination for me. This is perhaps understandable when it is recalled that I have competed in every 200-miles race. I have always succeeded in finishing, and for the last three years have always gained an award, so it almost might be said that the 200-miles race has become a habit with me, and habits once acquired are very hard to break.

Owing to the lack of entries there was the danger that the 750 c.c. class might have to be abandoned, and I considered that this would be a very great pity, for this country at present holds the lead in this class of car against all comers. It does not seem too much to expect that in a few years time 750 c.c. will be the limit in engine size for international races, so this class in the race should be encouraged and maintained. It was just this little extra reason which overcame my already tottering resolution not to race again.

My family and my co-directors remain opposed to my continuing an active part in this excellent sport, and so that future temptation may be removed from my path, it is proposed to auction my trusty Austin after this race. Sad as I shall be to part with such a sterling little car, it will be some satisfaction to feel that whoever buys it will get a fine little racer which is still capable of giving a very good account of itself in competition. This car is ideal for modern long distance races where there are plenty of corners and much gear changing and braking."

Only three drivers had entered for the 750 c.c. class, Gordon Hendy, C.

23. A 1928 Gordon
England fabric
Sunshine saloon

24. Gordon England's
1929 fabric saloon

25. A 1928 commer-
cial. Morgan Bros. of
Swansea covered 250
miles a week with
this van, delivering
radio batteries

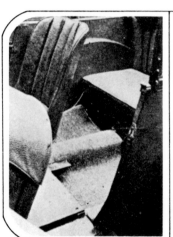

26. Views of a 1928 tourer

Walther and Hall in Boyd-Carpenter's car. Four were needed for a class award to be presented and to allow the smallest class to be run, so Gordon England drove and the result was his third successive 200-miles race win, this time at an average speed of 58·28 m.p.h. The car used half a pint of oil and averaged over 33 m.p.g. Hendy came in close behind at 58·25. Hall had retired after seventy laps, unfortunately being flagged off the course in error; Walther gave up with magneto trouble in the fiftieth lap. Waite had entered the bored-out car in the 1,100 c.c. class but had to give up after 51 laps owing to a broken body support.

Although he had not been particularly successful at Brooklands Waite was amply compensated by holding thirteen of the twenty International class H records:

1 km. standing start	96·983 k.p.h.
1 km. flying start	138·355 k.p.h.
1 mile standing start	66·33 m.p.h.
1 mile flying start	84·29 m.p.h.
5 km. flying start	132·168 k.p.h.
5 miles flying start	81·33 m.p.h.
10 km. flying start	130·125 k.p.h.
10 miles flying start	81·14 m.p.h.
50 km. standing start	134·3 k.p.h.
50 miles standing start	83·74 m.p.h.
100 km. standing start	132·755 k.p.h.
100 miles standing start	83·61 m.p.h.
1 hour	83·66 m.p.h.

Camuzet held the 3, 6, 12 and 24 hours, 500 km., 500 miles and 1000 km. records with a Peugeot.

Waite's name fades from racing for the time being as he sailed for Australia on 8th January, 1927 to work for Austin Distributors Pty Ltd., a branch of Cheyneys.

1927

The Seven Goes Abroad

It was very difficult for Britain to develop her motor export trade in the 1920's; British products were more expensive than many American cars and the difference was accentuated by the high import duties and restrictions imposed by all countries in which there was a potential market. Even in the Colonies, where one would expect there to have been preferences for British goods, the situation was far from satisfactory. Only some 20 per cent of the cars imported into Australia came from this country. As another example, the registration figures for Ceylon in 1926 showed that only a quarter of all the cars in use were of British manufacture. In both these cases the American car predominated.

Overseas countries were not alone in imposing duties to limit the entry of foreign goods in order to protect their own manufacturers. During the war, and throughout most of the 1920's, the motor industry in this country was protected by the McKenna duties which levied a $33\frac{1}{3}$ per cent surcharge upon a wide range of goods, including motor vehicles. The Ford company overcame this by setting up a manufacturing plant in this country. No British motor organisation in similar circumstances could afford to do this on a large scale but it was possible to induce foreign manufacturers to build British cars themselves under licence. Citroen had already tried with some success in Germany, the result being the Opel, built at Cologne on the lines of the well-known French car.

Reuter news agency circulated information to the press in February, 1927 that an agreement had been concluded with Gotha Waggonfabrik of Eisenach to make and sell the Austin Seven under licence in Germany and Eastern Europe, and that the product was to be known as the Dixi. Sir Herbert was questioned immediately and added that a plant was being built to allow for production on a large scale, at the rate of three hundred cars a week to begin with; the works were being extended and the German company was increasing its capital to cope with the enormous demand that was expected to follow the introduction of the first small car into that part of the world. What had happened, in fact, was brought about by the merger of a number of German companies under a scheme instigated by Herr Chiraupo. The Germans found that one of the firms involved owned a large derelict munitions factory so they decided to use it for the production of motor-cycles. Later, it was felt that there would be scope for a small car in Germany, a country in which only one in four hundred of the population owned cars, so Herr Chiraupo came

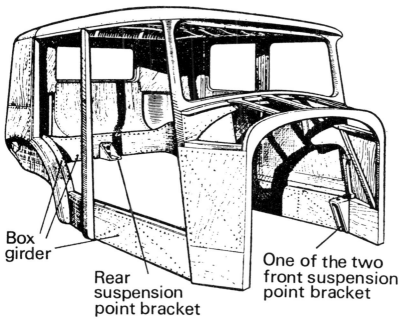

Box girder

Rear suspension point bracket

One of the two front suspension point bracket

Fig. 11. Gordon England's patented fabric body construction.

to an agreement with Sir Herbert for the manufacture of the Seven to be undertaken under licence at a royalty of 2 per cent. German materials and labour were to be used and the cars would be sold only in Germany and Eastern Europe at a price which the manufacturers would determine themselves.

Without any further serious rivals in the light car range until the Triumph Super Seven appeared in September at £149 10., production of the Seven at Longbridge continued to increase and in 1927 approximately 22,500 cars left the Works. With some 50,000 Sevens now on the roads giving excellent service and proving that the modifications which had already been made were sufficient to keep the specification up to date, only a few minor alterations were found to be necessary during the year.

Towards the latter part of 1926, from car number A3-4572 to A3-6753, the combined head and side lamp units were repositioned between the wings and the radiator. The legality of this was questioned by the Hampshire Police who considered that mounting the lamps at the front gave no indication of the full width of the car. Unable to obtain a definite ruling from the Ministry of Transport it was decided, in January, to revert to the original position on the screen pillars. The alternative would have been to place separate side lamps on the wings, as was the case with all the Gordon England models, but this would have meant extra expense.

In preparation for the 1928 season, the gear levers on saloon models were lengthened and cranked. This commenced in July, from chassis number 41,001. Belt-driven speedometers were discontinued and during September and October the drive was taken from the gearbox; the first car with the improved fittings was car number A5-1675, chassis number 45,016. A further change took place in the speedometer and its drive from chassis number 46,920. These alterations necessitated a modified gearbox casing and a different third motion shaft.

From 28th August prices were reduced yet again, the chassis to £99, the tourer to £135, saloon to £150, van to £140, and two new models appeared, the Mulliner fabric saloon at £150 and the Austin fabric saloon at the same price. Gordon England, now established in the new premises at the Palace of Industry, Wembley, was able to revise his prices in September; the fabric saloon was now £170 and the "Cup" model £150. Standard Gordon England colours for 1927/8 were orange, dark blue, maroon, brown and green. Larger bucket seats were used, brown hide pneumatic upholstery and improved door locks; it was also found necessary to replace the fixed glass panel with a hinged windscreen.

More special bodies appeared in 1927 than ever before to satisfy the growing demand for a light two-seater of sporting character. In May the first Swallow Austin Seven, known as the saloon-coupé and made by the Swallow Sidecar and Coach Building Co., appeared. The prototype was registered FR 7995. It was built on sporting lines and panelled in aluminium, having a polished cowled radiator with a wire mesh stone guard over the air intake and domed aluminium cycle-type wings. The spare wheel, battery and luggage space were in the tail section, to which access was gained through an aperture behind the seat squab. A sloping vee windscreen and rigid metal-framed side screens were provided. A detachable coupé top made from aluminium panels and lined with Bedford cord was hinged behind the front seat and was pulled down by spring catches at the top of the windscreen. This could be removed and substituted by an ordinary hood. Upholstery was in leather and there was a mahogany instrument board. External finish was cream with dark crimson lake wings, wheels and coupé top. The car sold for £175 with an extra £10 for the detachable top. Donald Doughty, who has researched

Swallows in some detail, has discovered that a Sports 2-Seater was made late in 1926, although not announced to the public until May of the following year. Swallows continued in production until October 1932; the Mk 2 Sports 2-seater running from 1930 until the end, the Mk 1 Saloon from October 1928 to September 1930 and the Mk 2 Saloon from October 1930 until June 1932. No records seen to exist of the total production, although it is known that about 100 Swallows still exist.

H. Taylor & Co. Ltd., 49–53 Sussex Place, London, S.W.7, produced an attractive two-seater mounted on what they termed a "special sports chassis", for £175.

In November, Cole & Shuttleworth Ltd., of 407–411 New King's Road, Chelsea, introduced their two-seater, again at £175. It had an aluminium body mounted on a chassis with long extensions, raked steering, a number of extra instruments; the spare wheel was carried in the rear locker and the hood folded into a slot in the body.

Duple Bodies and Motors Ltd., Edgware Road, London, N.W.9, made a semi-sports two-seater finished in a two-colour scheme, the section above the deck line being painted a darker colour to match the wings. The body was of ash covered with steel panels, upholstery was in leather cloth and the price for the complete car was £165. Leather upholstery could be fitted for an additional £3. This firm also offered an unusual tourer which could be converted into a flexible sided delivery van for £177.

Another two-seater was sold for £177 by Jarvis & Sons Ltd., Grove Works, Morden Road, London, S.W.19. Yet another, rather clumsy, two-seater known as a "coupette", costing £175 was made by the Arc Manufacturing Co., of Hyde, Manchester.

The New Avon Body Co. Ltd., Wharf Street, Warwick, sold a low-built two-seater body with a tapered tail having a deck shaped top for £52.

Granville Motors of Broadway, Walham Green, London, first advertised the flexible fabric "Wydor" saloon in September. The ash-framed body was built out over the rear wings and covered with a material called "Fabricoid", the doors were carried down to the running boards for easy access and the light construction allowed for exceptionally wide doors. There was a single piece windscreen, dummy hood irons, and the steering wheel was lowered four inches. Standard colours were blue, brown, maroon and primrose with the upper parts in black if desired. This model cost £172.

In support of the contention that there must have been two supercharged Works' cars in use during 1926 there was one interesting press report which appeared in conjunction with Waite's move to Australia in January 1927, which is the only occasion on which both cars were mentioned. It was stated that one was shortly to be sent to Australia if it was found that the tracks out there were suitable for racing, and that the other was to be sold to a customer in Spain.

A car was undoubtedly shipped to Waite later but he claimed that this was a prototype for the "Ulster"; anyway it bore no resemblance to either of the cars in question. Nothing further is known about the Austin Works' car which was supposed to have gone to Spain, but it is certain that the well-known supercharged record-breaker of 1926/7 was sold – without its original engine – to J. Pares an Austin Agent, who entered it to be driven in numerous events by Coldicutt. It became very well known subsequently as "Slippery Ann".

Gordon England had, to all intents and purposes, given up racing. He did, however, enter an England fabric saloon in the J.C.C. High Speed Trial in June and obtained a gold medal, but the famous 200-miles race car was bought by Boyd-Carpenter.

In conjunction with S. J. Bassett, J. P. Dingle ran a repair shop specialising in the tuning of Austin Seven engines in Beavor Lane, Hammersmith, called Maintenance Ltd. The standard Bassett-Dingle "hotting up" cost £7 10s.

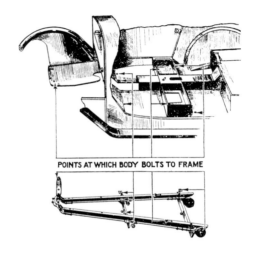

POINTS AT WHICH BODY BOLTS TO FRAME

Fig. 12.   Removing a 1927 body.

and included widening and polishing the valve ports and fitting double valve springs and a special induction manifold. A 30 mm. Solex carburettor was used with increased compression ratio which was achieved by removing $\frac{3}{64}$ in. from the cylinder head. Clutch pedal travel was increased by modifying the withdrawal mechanism and the hand and foot brakes were coupled. With regard to performance, 19 m.p.h. could be obtained on first gear, 42 in second and at least 54 in top.

Boyd-Carpenter and Thompson took over Gordon England's West End Lane service garage in Hampstead to specialise in Austin Seven tuning and in addition to similar processes carried out by Dingle, they also provided a different final drive ratio which gave speeds of up to 50 m.p.h. in second gear and 65 ir top.

On 25th August Boyd-Carpenter and C. K. Chase took a modified Gordon England "Cup" model with twin Solex carburettors, which they called "Mr. Jo Jo", to Brooklands in an attempt to capture the long distance 750 c.c. records held by Camuzet's Peugeot. They took them all with the exception of the 24 hours.

Speeds were: 3 hours at 63·50 m.p.h.
500 km. at   62·60 m.p.h.
500 miles at 62·83 m.p.h.
1000 km. at   62·97 m.p.h.
6 hours at 62·97 m.p.h.
12 hours at 62·53 m.p.h.

During the 12 hours the car averaged 42·4 m.p.g. A. Walter increased the 3 hours record to 63·75 m.p.h. on 10th November.

Boyd-Carpenter entered the 200-miles race car in two events during the Brooklands Easter Monday meeting but was outclassed by the larger cars. At the Surbiton Club's meeting on the following Saturday he put up an outstanding performance by winning the first race, a short handicap, at 74·22 m.p.h. Again, in the third race, he won easily at 76·39.

In May the J.C.C. held its spring events, but this time there was more competition, some of which was from private owners with no trade connections who saw better opportunities now that Gordon England had retired, and with the Austin team showing no further interest in competition work. F. Maunde Thompson and C. U. M. Walther raced in the two lap Novices handicap; Walther was third. Later there was another two-lap event for 1,100 c.c. cars which Gordon Hendy won from Boyd-Carpenter at 71·05 m.p.h.; Maunde Thompson and H. W. Edwards had also driven. The main race of the day was the fifteen-lap Junior Grand Prix and three Austin Sevens competed in the 750 c.c. class: Gordon Hendy who finished third at 47·79 m.p.h. in a Brooklands model, J. S. Wilson who was placed sixth at 45·52 and Boyd-Carpenter's ex-Gordon England car which was driven by J. S. Wilson and overturned in the thirteenth lap whilst in third position.

A six-hours endurance race was staged by the Essex M.C. at Brooklands on 7th May for standard cars to which only limited alterations were permitted. In the 750 c.c. class cars had to run for a minimum of 234 miles. Dingle, in a "Cup" model, registration number YR 2548, covered 250·57 miles at an average of 41·70 m.p.h., to win a special Gold Medal. P. J. Calvert drove one of the early Brooklands types in which the spare wheel was carried in the tail and protected by a hinged streamlined cover. The wheel would not stay in position so the mechanic, after several unsuccessful attempts to hold it from his seat, decided to carry it in his lap after it broke away from its support. In spite of his efforts to ensure that he was able to continue without breaking any rules, the car was forced to retire after completing 196 miles.

In July a daily newspaper, *The Sporting Life*, ran a Brooklands meeting for the first time. This is of interest as far as Austin Sevens are concerned because Gordon Hendy entered a green supercharged car, the only one to appear in 1927, which cracked its cylinder head in the "Drivers' race" and also ran in the 100-miles handicap. Chase retired early in the latter event in Boyd-Carpenter's car which E. Phillips drove earlier in the 90 m.p.h. Long handicap. The only place was gained by J. S. Wilson, who was third in the 1,100 c.c. Spectators' race which was not surprising because only four cars ran.

Dingle entered a Brooklands model, PD 4930 in a fuel consumption race organised by the Surbiton M.C. in September which he won at 52·11 m.p.h. on 4¾ gallons of petrol averaging 37·5 m.p.g.

At the Brooklands autumn meeting Boyd-Carpenter came second in the 90 m.p.h. Short handicap and won the 90 m.p.h. Long handicap at 78·38.

The famous J.C.C. 200-miles race was held on 15th October. In the 750 c.c. class Samuelson, who usually appeared on the track driving an Austin Seven, entered a Ratier; the other six cars were all Austins – Gordon Hendy, Walther, J. S. Wilson, Boyd-Carpenter and Chase and someone driving under the pseudonym "El Bolivar" in a car entered by A. E. Walter. Hendy was the first in trouble, his engine broke a crankshaft in the second lap. Walther retired following a crash and "El Bolivar" fell out towards the end of the race. Chase in the "Cup" model "Mr. Jo Jo", and Boyd-Carpenter in "Mrs. Jo Jo", and Wilson were all still running when at 5.15 p.m., the scheduled finishing time, they were called to a halt. None had covered the necessary 73 laps, Chase completed 68 at an average speed of 58·14 m.p.h., Wilson 68 at 57·91 and Boyd-Carpenter 65 at 55·40 m.p.h. Hardly the sort of success to which Gordon England had led people to expect, but Boyd-Carpenter felt that his two "Jo Jo's" had done themselves justice for he put them both up for sale immediately after the race.

Finally, Hendy in the supercharged car and Boyd-Carpenter in "Mrs. Jo Jo" entered in two races at a meeting at Brooklands in November.

On 28th December Austin sailed to America on the Aquitania to discuss the marketing of the Austin Seven in that country, for which preliminary negotiations had been going on since May; his object was to find a manufacturer who would produce under a seven-year licence. His travelling companions were Morris and the sales director of the Triplex Safety Glass Company. They arrived in New York early in 1928.

1928

Is There a Motor War?

"Some people seem to think that my idea is to crush the Austin Seven off the market – which is absurd. But I can say this, the price of my new car will not be higher than that of the Austin Seven."

W. R. Morris.

"I do not regard Mr. Morris's new development as a challenge, and I don't like the suggestion of a fight. The public will decide whose car they like best."

Sir Herbert Austin.

Whatever Morris may have said, there is no doubt that the Morris Minor, which he announced in May, 1928, was intended as a direct competitor to the Austin Seven. His own statement that "It has been apparent to me for some time that there is a growing demand for a miniature type of car, and the new model has been designed to meet this demand", defines his intention quite clearly.

One of the most interesting questions arising when considering cars of the 1920's relates to Austin being permitted to continue for so long without any serious, successful competition from other manufacturers in the seven horse power range. Admittedly, he had anticipated the demand when he pioneered the small, light economy car in 1922, but one would have thought that by the middle of the decade there would have been a flood of imitators. This unexpected delay may have been due partly to the fact that Morris, his most serious rival and the largest British motor car producer, was probably the only manufacturer with sufficient capital to introduce a reliable new model on a scale large enough to ensure success. Why did Morris wait until 1928? Although there is no record of his own views at the time, the factors which made him wait for so long and finally to chose 1928 as the year in which he would set out in earnest to capture potential Austin Seven customers must

73

have been based upon his appraisal of the situation. The cheapest Morris cost £142 10s. in its most austere form and Morris car sales, 61,632 in 1927, were far in excess of Austin's because he was producing the best, cheapest car in, what was then, the most popular horse power range. If Morris had introduced a light car before 1928 at a time when the demand for cars of this type was at only about 20,000 a year it is certain that he would have taken some of the Austin Seven market, but he could well have produced a car which would have created direct competition to his own Cowley. Some other reasons may have induced him to hold back. He had transformed his organisation into a Public Company in 1926 and had just taken over the Wolseley Company which extended his activities beyond Cowley near Oxford, to the Adderley Park factory in Birmingham. In addition, he had changed the appearance of his famous Bullnose by introducing the flat radiator for the 1927 season.

In 1927 the Ministry of Transport departed from previous policy by providing statistics of vehicles registered for the first time, as distinct from total registrations. When these records were published in 1928 it was seen that of the 190,900 British and foreign cars accounted for, 30,900 (16 per cent) were exported, 28,300 (15 per cent) were imported and the balance, 131,700 (69 per cent) were retained on the British market. It is interesting to note that of the 162,600 British cars produced in 1927 over 100,000 were made either by Austin or Morris.

Cars in the 12 h.p. category accounted for 21 per cent of all new cars licensed in 1927 against 25 per cent of the total number licensed in 1926. By the same token, the 8 h.p. class saw a much more spectacular increase from 5 per cent to 14 per cent.

It is difficult to gain an accurate assessment by comparing 1927 figures with those of previous years but the numbers can be looked at in another way; in 1926 a maximum of 176,000 12 h.p. cars were in use at any one time, this increased by only 15 per cent in the following year. With 8 h.p. vehicles, however, the total doubled from 35,400. Of these we know that 14,000 were Austin Sevens and Austin also accounted for 22,709 of the 71,000 old and newly licensed cars in 1927. Allowing for wastage, it is not unreasonable to assume that about seventy per cent of the small cars newly licensed in 1927 were made by Austin.

This trend towards the smaller car was aided by the 1928 Budget in which the Chancellor, Mr. Winston Churchill, upset the motor industry by imposing a duty on petrol of 4d. a gallon. All these points must have been considered by Morris and influenced him to choose May, 1928 as the month in which to announce the Morris Minor.

Half of Austin's output consisted of Seven h.p. cars and he certainly could not afford a set-back now. The Company's gross profit had doubled between 1925 and 1927, the capital structure was more or less in order and Sir Herbert had to ensure that his best seller remained the most popular car in the range. Chassis price was still £99, the tourer cost £135 and the saloons £150, but there were other cars to contend with. Probably the 848 c.c. Singer was the most popular because the firm was the third largest motor manufacturer in the country with an annual output of some 11,000 cars; their cheapest model was only £140. Apart from the foreign competitors, there were also the 7·9 h.p. Triumph at £149 10s., the Trojan and the Jowett.

Not to be outdone by Morris, Frank Smith the managing director of Clyno – certainly a poor relation as a motor manufacturer with sales of about only 9,000 vehicles a year – showed that he could be just as effective with publicity as his larger rivals. His announcement for the new Clyno 9 in June followed the Morris pattern and explained how the tests had been cloaked in mystery and how all the staff had been sworn to secrecy. Unlike Morris, he could not manage headlines as the one in the *Daily Mail* which claimed that "Only his wife knew of his secret plans", but everyone was aware that Clyno was to join in the light car war. A member of the firm told the press that they would be in production at the rate of three hundred cars a week by the following month in the new factory at Bushbury near Wolverhampton, which had just been equipped with £120,000's worth of machinery. An estimation of the cost at £115 was quite accurate as the new car, the "Century" or the "long man's little car" appeared at the Motor Show in the autumn at £112 10s. Neither Austin nor Morris seemed to be worried particularly; Morris said: "There are already a number of 9 h.p. cars on the market", but did not add that none could be bought for £115, and Sir Herbert was equally unperturbed and repeated what he had said when Morris made his move, but added: "There are other cars at a lower price than ours, but ours is still in great demand."

S. F. Edge was not to be left out; he prophesied that a 5 h.p. A.C. would be selling at 100 guineas by 1929. He did not, however, take the risk of producing such a car at his Thames Ditton factory; no doubt he felt that it was rather hard to see all these other firms obtaining so much publicity without getting into print himself.

Everyone in the industry was talking about inevitable price increases and by the time pictures of Morris beside the first two-door fabric Minor Saloon were appearing in June, he had decided to increase the price of his cheapest model by £5 with corresponding rises throughout the range. This was what everyone had been waiting for; Clyno's envisaged a 5 per cent increase all round and the entire industry stood in readiness to put prices up before the Motor Show. They had forgotten one thing – Sir Herbert had not yet spoken. Obviously he had to do something drastic and his action made everyone think again with the exception of Morris for whom it was too late to retract. In the midst of an atmosphere of rising prices, Austin made the same brilliant stroke, albeit on a much smaller scale, that Morris had employed earlier. He brought the price of the Seven chassis down to £92, the tourer was reduced by £10 to £125 and the saloons £15 to £135; all the special body builders followed suit, the new price of the Gordon England "Cup" model being £140 and the saloon £160. Morris fell into line with the Minor, the four-seater tourer was to sell at the same price as the equivalent

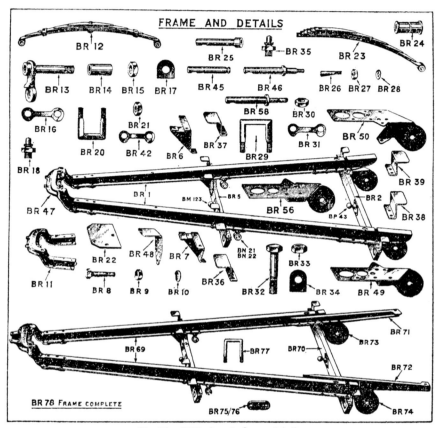

Fig. 13. 1928 chassis frame details.

Austin and his four-seater fabric saloon was also £135. On the face of it, the Minor had a number of advantages over the Seven, an overhead camshaft engine with an extra 100 c.c. and yet still with the same horse power rating for taxation purposes. In addition it was larger and employed conventional suspension.

The motor war had begun. To keep in the battle all contestants had to introduce improvements, bring prices down and yet still make profits for their companies; very few could meet all these requirements, as time was to tell. As a more profitable alternative the American principle of amalgamation could have been adopted and, in fact, this was suggested on a number of occasions, but the industry in this country was controlled by so many men with strong personalities who wanted to remain in command of their own situations that mergers were uncommon in England in the 1920's. Even on the Continent Rosengart had merged his company with three other French firms, Chenard-Walcker, Donnet and Delahaye to prevent competition between each other. Austin would have liked to have joined forces with Morris but it was not until 1952 that the two great concerns amalgamated to form the British Motor Corporation.

M. Lucien Rosengart decided to resign from the managing directorship of the Peugeot Company in May, 1928 in order to concentrate upon the production of the Austin Seven in France. He employed M. E. Salomon, the engineer responsible for the design and construction of the first Citroens, as his chief engineer and designer and it was on his advice that Rosengart decided to adopt the Austin and to manufacture it under licence in France as the 5 h.p. Rosengart.

The French edition differed only very slightly from the English version as far as the chassis was concerned, but the body was a three-seater cabriolet with two separate front seats and a third set crosswise at the back. Construction was of a metal and fabric combination with steel panels up to the waist line. There was a locker in the tail, disc-covered wire wheels and no running boards were fitted; this was the only passenger model planned initially but there was to be a light delivery van later on. Rosengart hoped to build 60,000 vehicles a year and had already made a few test cars by June, in fact he drove one himself for some months and found that he could attain a speed of 45 m.p.h. and average more than 30 over some of the better French roads. By October a saloon had been developed and this, priced at £137, was shown with the three-seater coupé which sold for only £120, at the Paris Salon; the crowd around the stand on which "Le Bébé" was exhibited was so great that at one time the police had to be called in to keep everyone in order. In the same month a supercharged Rosengart Sports model lapped Montlhéry at 77 m.p.h.

Rosengart's factory had been erected just outside Paris by the Bellanger Brothers during the war and it covered an area of 538,000 square feet; the Peugeot Company took it over in 1919 and Rosengart purchased the site and the buildings from them. He had double this capacity available, however, because his interests extended over a wide range of motor activities. Chenard-Walcker, for example, were to assist him in marketing the new cars. The new organisation was registered in Paris as the Société des Automobiles L. Rosengart with a capital of ten million francs; the Board of Directors consisted of Rosengart, Henri Bancel, the Chenard-Walcker Co. and Sir Herbert.

In Germany the other continental Austin, the 3–15 Dixi, was being built by the Dixi Werke Company at the rate of about fifty a day. Its first public appearance was at the Copenhagen Motor Exhibition at which it was listed at £129 15s. As with the Rosengart the sporting potential was not overlooked and three sports models were competing in German events by September. Sir Herbert went over there himself at about that time to discuss details of the absorption of the original company by Bayerische Moterenwerke, better known by the initials B.M.W. At that time 6,000 Dixis had been sold. Austin received a 2 per cent fee on all Continental sales which was divided equally between the Company and himself.

As far as the English Austin Seven was concerned, at the beginning of the year and starting from chassis 50,901 an additional support was provided for the body by an extension to each of the frame side-members. With this modification the rear shock-absorber frame bracket was redesigned and simplified and the tubular steel strut used in connection with the brackets was no longer required.

After March, 1928 (chassis number 56,890) shock-absorbers carried a brass disc at the friction pivoted point at each side of the frame member to separate them from the friction discs; this resulted in greater efficiency and they were less affected by the intrusion of dirt and mud. Additionally, rubber bushes replaced the wooden ones normally used in the arm anchorages to the axles. Each brake drum was secured to the hub by three screws, thus preventing the drum from being removed with the wheel. The starting handle was extended to facilitate swinging the engine with a radiator muff in position at chassis number 59,275 in April. A more accessible position was also found for the radiator drain tap and the oil filler orifice was redesigned.

The introduction of the Minor led to a number of alterations which changed the appearance of the Seven to some extent; unfortunately it lost much of its character in the constant endeavour to keep a step ahead of its competitors. These changes were made gradually between July and September. Most noticeable of all were the higher radiator with its new nickel-plated shell and redesigned wings which were first applied to car number A6-9330, chassis number 67,024. Coil ignition was used on most cars after car number A7-1280, chassis number 68,814, engine number 69,000. To conform to the new dash-board with two cubby holes, the speedometer was moved to a position in the centre of the panel. A flat steering wheel replaced the deeply dished type and the lamps were moved forward again, this time the casings were larger and two separate bulbs replaced the double filament type which seems to have satisfied the legal requirements. For some unknown reason the door handles of the tourers were made to point toward the ground. Scuttle ventilators were fitted to some models at the Motor Show to provide a flow of cool air into the body, necessary because the saloons were given a single-piece windscreen. The last "Top Hat" Saloon, of which some 5,000 had been sold, was made in August at about car number A6–8822 (chassis 66,458). It is possible that a few more were made after then, possibly up until December when the wide-door RK Saloons were introduced, some of which were built before the last "Top Hats". From September, some of the aluminium saloons were sold with fascia-board glove boxes and the modified oil-pressure indicators. From the evidence of existing cars, most narrow-door saloons made after September seem to have been fitted with scuttle vents, and retained the two-piece screens. This gradual introduction and overlap at the time of a model change on the production line shows some of the complications when trying to date a car, or to decide upon its originality. More often than not, alterations were brought in haphazardly, as they are in modern car factories. Special body builders had been so successful in the past with their two-seater Austin Seven bodies that it was decided to offer a standard Works' coupé, which was priced at £135 with rep or Bedford cord upholstery and an anti-glare visor above the windscreen. It was slightly lower than the fabric saloon and had raked steering, the body was of metal with a fabric top.

1928 was another good year for the special body builders and the following list gives all the models available in February:

Maker	Name of Model	Price
Alpe & Saunders	Coupé	£164
Arc	Drop Head coupette	£160
Burghley	Sports	£165
Cole & Shuttleworth	Sports	£175
Duple	Semi-Sports	£155
Gordon England	Cup	£150
Gordon England	Fabric	£170
Gordon England	Sunshine Saloon	£170
Gordon England	Van	£135
Jarvis	Sports	£177
Mulliner	Fabric Saloon	£150
New Avon	Semi-Sports	£152
Swallow	Detachable-head Coupé	£190
Swallow	Open Sports	£175
Taylor	Semi-Sports	£165
Granville Motors	Wydoor Fabric Saloon	£160

William Lyons' Swallow Sidecar and Coachbuilding Co., now at Coker Street, Blackpool, introduced a number of modifications to their coupé early in the year. The new model had a fixed head in place of the hinged type fitted previously, which gave much more head room and it was no longer necessary to provide a hinged roof in order to enter the car. The roof was provided with a hinged ventilator and an adjustable roof light. Formerly only one colour scheme was offered, now there was an alternative – suede grey with green wings, chassis and top. Although the coupé top was no longer hinged it could be taken down by removing two bolts by which it was fixed to the body at the rear, and by a snap fitting at the top of the windscreen. A folding hood could be substituted. The more famous Swallow saloon came out in time for the Motor Show and sold for £185.

By May, K. C. Bodies of 407–11 New King's Road, S.W.6, were offering another very smart two-seater for £175; the New Avon Company added the "Swan" sliding head fabric coupé to their range in July priced at £165. Boyd-Carpenter & Thompson Ltd., of 47 West End Lane, Kilburn introduced the only real sports model in August which they hoped to put on the market shortly for about £190. The prototype was based on experience gained in racing and employed flattened springs, a low-built body, cycle-type wings, modified clutch, twin carburettors, lightened flywheel and coupled brakes. All bright metal parts were copper oxidised and lacquered with the exception of the radiator shell which was copper plated. Taking this car as an example it can be seen that Austin Seven special body building could be a reasonably profitable occupation; the standard chassis cost £99 retail, add to this a delivery charge of a few pounds and deduct about 15 per cent discount, leaving a purchase price in the region of £85. This left Boyd-Carpenter with £105 to build a body and to modify the chassis, and when one considers that Austin allowed himself only about £24 to build a tourer body – admittedly on mass-production lines – the profit margin was more than reasonable provided that production could be undertaken in quantity. Gordon England

Fig. 14.   October, 1928.   Modified gear lever and gear-driven speedometer.

was in this happy position; no less than 2,000 Austin Sevens had passed through his works by the end of 1927 which enabled him to sell the "Cup" model at a very competitive price and yet still to make a fair profit for his company. He was able to fit a clock and a dash-mounted fuel gauge on to the Sunshine saloon but he was criticised in some circles for the fact that the diagonal bracing members in the roof were untrimmed and soon rotted when the roof covering, which was only held to the body sides by press button, let in water. The stories about sending men down to the docks to collect old

27. Austin Seven bodies available in 1928. Jarvis, Gordon England Cup, Arc and Swallow

28. Wydoor, Gordon England Sunshine, Chummy, Duple, Taylor, standard saloon

packing cases for his body-building shop are not true; his cars were certainly built as cheaply as possible but there was nothing shoddy about them – had there been he would not have sold so many. Two new Gordon England Austin Sevens were introduced at Olympia, the "Wembley" saloon which looked something like the Swallow and the "Stadium" semi-sports two-seater, a slightly larger version of the old "Cup" model.

Trials, racing and record-breaking continued to attract Austin Seven owners throughout 1928. The late Gunnar Poppe, captain of the London Welsh Rugby fifteen, who joined the Austin racing team later on, made a fantastic rush journey from London to Edinburgh and back in March. He used a standard tourer which was normal in all respects except for a $13\frac{1}{2}$ gallon petrol tank. In order to cover the 394 miles to Scotland in ten hours and at an average speed of a little under 40 m.p.h. he had to exceed the legal speed limit throughout most of the journey. But as the motoring correspondent of the *Polo Monthly* remarked: "Of course such a thing is hopelessly illegal, but since the law is itself so hopeless an anachronism no one in their senses would take the least exception to a wonderful exploit." Fifteen minutes after he had reached his destination, Poppe set off again and arrived back at Rootes' showroom in Piccadilly 20 hours and 56 minutes after he had left.

In April, Arthur Waite sent Sir Herbert the following cable from Australia: "Austin Seven (Waite) first against all classes up to 2,000 c.c., 100 miles, 68 angle bends, bad roads; 1 hour, 46 mins., 40 secs. Created furore." This related to his success in the first Australian 100-miles Grand Prix which he won in a car with a sloping pointed-tail two-seater body, twin aero screens and a radiator filler extension, which Austin had sent out to him. Nothing is known about the car but Waite claimed afterwards, in 1955, that it was a prototype for the famous "Ulster" Sports model and although it bore a resemblance to the cars which appeared later in the year, there is no record as to whether or not it was supercharged. If it was, then it is surprising that the Company did not use the success in its advertising programmes for the announcement of the first supercharged Seven to be offered to the public in late July. This was known as the Super-Sports model and was to sell at £225, produced mainly from standard parts but with several alterations to cope with the increased power and speed. Pressure from the Cozette blower was not particularly high and the instrument was placed on the exhaust side of the engine, gear driven from a train of gears in the timing case. Modifications included a specially large balanced crankshaft, different valve gear, camshaft, manifold and cylinder head, a pressure fed lubrication system of the type described earlier, a water pump and lower front suspension; the road springs were cord bound. Speeds up to 7,000 revs per minute could be achieved with an output of 27 b.h.p., at 4,500 increased later to develop 33 b.h.p., and the maximum speed in top was in the region of 70 m.p.h. Standard gear ratios of 16, 9 and 4·9 to 1 were employed; doors were not provided and the body sides were cut low for entry. Pneumatic upholstery was used for the two small bucket seats.

Two prototypes were taken to Shelsley Walsh on 28th July by Gunnar Poppe and S. V. Holbrook, the son of the Austin Sales Manager. Boyd-Carpenter and J. D. Barnes and Coldicutt in the veteran "Slippery Ann" were amongst the other Austin Sevens competing in perfect weather before an enormous crowd, one of whom was Mr. Stanley Baldwin, the Prime Minister. Holbrook managed to climb the hill at about 32 m.p.h. in 63·6 seconds Barnes crashed on his first attempt but at the second try raced to the top in 62·40 seconds. The fastest 750 c.c. car, however, was "Slippery Ann" with a time of 57·4 seconds. Holbrook and Poppe were much more successful when they took the two cars to Pendine Sands in August, obtaining a first and a second place with laps at 60 m.p.h. and top speeds of 84 on the straight.

Going back to the beginning of the year, it was in March that Chase, a director of Boyd-Carpenter and Thompson Ltd., decided to prepare a car to

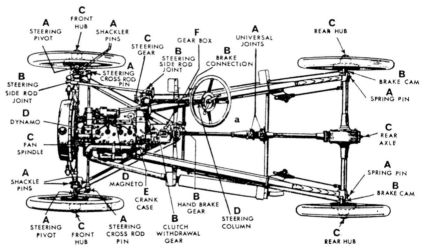

Fig. 15. 1924 chassis lubrication. A, grease weekly; B, oil weekly; C, grease monthly; D, oil monthly; E, keep oil level in engine sump up to "full" mark on dipstick; F, periodically check level of oil in gear box.

take to Montlhéry to capture the 24-hours record which was the only one remaining in the class not held by an Austin Seven. He took H. B. Parker and H. D. Bland as his co-drivers to beat the Peugeot speed which stood at 40·86 m.p.h. Basically, the car was the same vehicle in which Chase had won the 1927 200-miles race, but with the engine tuned by Thomson and Taylor and a special light body which had been built by Hoyal of Weybridge in three days. Minor troubles delayed the journey to France and eventually the car was loaded on to a lorry at 6.15 a.m. on a June morning to arrive at Folkestone in time for the afternoon boat. It took fifteen and a half hours to transport the little car from Boulogne to Montlhéry and at 4 p.m. on Thursday, 7th June, after preliminary tests, Chase set off. He drove for two and a half hours through a series of hailstorms and at the end of his three hours' run he had managed to keep up an average of 67·25 m.p.h. Parker took the wheel for the next two hours and Bland for another three. Chase returned again at midnight and at 2.30 a.m. narrowly escaped disaster when, in his own words:

"After two and a half hours of driving through the rain I suddenly went completely blind and the car swerved towards the inside edge of the track, missing the red lights and the edge of the concrete by inches. The temporary blindness passed – luckily for me – and I managed to regain control of the car and reach the pits; but on getting out I collapsed on the concrete road and found that my sight had practically gone again. Bland sportingly took over for the remainder of my watch, completing the twelve hours and establishing intermediate records."

Parker took the wheel again and by 7 a.m. Chase had recovered and was able to drive once more. After fifteen and a half hours running, the existing 750 c.c. 24 hours distance record fell to the Austin at an average of 64·75 m.p.h. There were still eight and a half hours to go so Chase decided to increase the speed, averaging over 80 m.p.h. for the last four laps. Over the 24 hours the car's speed was 65·98 and it covered 1,584·32 miles with stops amounting to only 35 minutes 40 seconds. Other records broken during the run were:

12 hours at 64·4 m.p.h.	1000 miles at 64·75 m.p.h.
1000 km. at 63·7 m.p.h.	2000 km. at 65·60 m.p.h.

On 28th April, J. S. Wilson and Gordon Hendy, the latter in his super-charged car, entered in the 850 c.c. class in the second J.C.C. Grand Prix. Twenty-five laps had to be covered and they held first and second places for the first six before the handicapped cars overtook them. Later, on Whit Monday, Hendy won a 75 m.p.h. Short handicap at 80·20 m.p.h. and Spero was third in a Long handicap in one of Boyd-Carpenter's "Specials". J. P. Dingle and R. B. Waters, the latter in a "Cup" model called "Felstead II" and registered PF 6886 with a skull and cross bones emblem on the radiator grille, ran in the 150-miles speed and economy race organised by the Surbiton Club at Brooklands in which 750 c.c. cars had to average 33·3 m.p.g. The Club could not allow an Austin Seven to win its 1928 event so easily as Dingle had done the year before. With their previous experience the promoters cut down the fuel allowance and provided a less generous handicap for the smaller cars. Dingle's "Brooklands" model missed the chance of a place by falling out with engine trouble after completing only six laps; he had to push the car from the fork back to the Paddock. The Austin was by no means alone, six of the other light car starters failed to complete the course. Waters had covered only thirty-seven laps when J. Taylor's Austro-Daimler crossed the line to win, but the Austin used fuel at the rate of only 46·39 m.p.g.

The Essex Motor Club held its second Six-Hours Endurance race at Brooklands on 12th May. Cars were allowed to be modified to a minor extent and superchargers were permitted only if they were standard on the production models. This event was a test which provided valuable data for the manufacturers and good or bad publicity, dependent upon the results of the race. In order to qualify for an award, competitors had to cover a minimum distance which, in the case of the 750 c.c. car, amounted to 240 miles. The winner was judged the car which covered the greatest distanct in six hours above the minimum required in its class. Dingle, with J. H. Wilson as his co-driver, was the sole Austin entrant and in spite of clutch trouble they completed the course at an average speed of 51·16 m.p.h. and were awarded a special gold medal. The overall winner was Ramponi on an Alfa-Romeo which completed an additional 87·45 miles whilst Dingle was second with 66·4 miles to his credit.

Always the most exciting motoring day of the year, the eighth 200-miles race in the series began by Hugh McConnell in 1921 was run at Brooklands on Saturday, 21st July. Only seven Austin Sevens entered in the smallest class, Gordon Hendy taking advantage of the limit being extended to 850 c.c. by emulating Waite and boring out the engine of his supercharged car to 57 mm. Unfortunately he withdrew before the start.

Other competitors were Coldicutt in "Slippery Ann", A. E. Walter in a car with a sloping radiator entered by J. Rawson & Sons of Kent, H. C. Spero in "Mrs. Jo Jo", Dingle in the "Six-hours" car PD 4930, R. F. Walker in XU 1581, and Chase in the 24-hours record-breaker. Seventy-three circuits of the course had to be completed and the six Austins all got away well in the massed start. Walker made the first pit stop twenty minutes after the start to cure a leaking oil tank; Spero went to the other extreme and ran non-stop until he had to refuel on his sixty-fourth lap. Most of the troubles experienced were confined to the cylinder heads. "Slippery Ann" needed new plugs at nine laps, the magneto then had to be changed and finally a new cylinder head gasket was fitted but this failed to cure the trouble and the car retired after sixteen laps, by which time "Mrs. Jo Jo" was running well on its thirteenth. Walker ran out of water after twelve laps and had to retire, again with cylinder head trouble. At lap twenty-eight water leaked into Dingle's engine and he stopped for a new gasket. At forty laps the order was Spero, Chase, Walter and Dingle bringing up the rear. Spero ran very consistently averaging 58 m.p.h. for the first twenty laps and just over 59 for the remaining fifty-three, his average never varying more than a few decimal places.

Chase was most unfortunate; on his seventy-first circuit he was running second in the 750 c.c. class when his oil pump spindle fractured and hot oil was forced out of the sump filler hole, pouring over the driver and burning his arm severely. He coasted as far as he could, then had to push the car over a mile to his pit; the sump cap was replaced because this was thought to be the only trouble as the oil gauge needle had stuck. Chase had no indication that there was no oil pressure but halfway down the railway straight the engine seized. Being under the impression that he was in his final lap because his scorer had inadvertently torn off two numbers, he made a fantastic effort and pushed the car two miles round the course in the blazing heat and in agony from his injured arm. He arrived at the finish only to find that he had completed but seventy-two laps and was flagged off because the time limit had expired.

Spero won the class award at 59·95 m.p.h., coming eighth in the general classification; A. E. Walter was second and tenth respectively at 55·90 m.p.h. Spero's car had run in no less than five 200-miles races. Gordon England used it in 1924, 1925 and 1926. He sold it to Boyd-Carpenter who gained third place in 1927 after giving it the name "Mrs. Jo Jo".

At the B.A.R.C. autumn meeting in September Spero came third in the thirty-third 90 m.p.h. Short handicap, being only just beaten for second place by Clive Dunfee's 3-litre Austro-Daimler. Spero also competed in the Long handicap and came second, just beating a Bugatti which was quickly overhauling the Austin in a most exciting finish with only a fifth of a second between first and second and second and third. Both these races were won by G. E. T. Eyston with his 1½-litre O.M. The outstanding event of the day was a handicap race over 3¾ miles for the Taylor Cup. Spero held the lead until the end when Bouts in a Sunbeam and Taylor in a Delage passed him almost at the post at 100 m.p.h. to win a dead heat for first and second places.

Road races were not allowed on the public highways in Britain so the R.A.C. ran most of their road competitions in the Isle of Man, but in 1928 it was decided to return to Ireland to the scene of the old Gordon-Bennett events of the past, and to stage a mammoth Ulster Grand Prix on Saturday, 18th August. The race was over thirty laps covering a total of 410 miles. 750 c.c. cars were given a five-lap start leaving a distance of 341 miles in all. The brothers J. D. and F. S. Barnes were provided with ER 3410, a non-supercharged version of the Company's new sports model and Sir Herbert went over to Ireland himself to judge whether or not it would be a good idea to enter an Austin Works' team for a future race. Forty-four cars started, of which only twelve finished; the Austin crashed early on after J. D. Barnes had been leading for five laps and although his brother took over they fell back to sixteenth place after ten laps, their lap speed of only 48 m.p.h. was far too low to keep up with the faster cars. Austin learnt a valuable lesson as we shall see when he entered his full team in 1929.

1929

The Future Cannot be Foreseen

"I cannot honestly recommend the purchase of motor car shares. The whole industry is in a state of flux, and the future cannot be foreseen. In view of the next Budget I advise the sale of all motor shares."

Advice from a financial journalist in 1929.

First Urchin   (surveying small car standing by the kerb):
            "It's an Austin, I tell yer."
Second Urchin: "T'aint, it's a Morris Minor."
Third Urchin: "S'neither, – it's got pedals."

Contemporary joke.

The depression of the early 1930's was already reflected to a small extent in the dropping off in trade in the motor industry as early as 1928. During that year only 154,500 cars were produced, considerably less than in both 1926 and 1927. Austin was fortunate because more than 22,000 of them were Austins Sevens, and as trade deteriorated so demand for the smaller, more economical car increased. Naturally, this situation could not continue. It did so for longer than expected, however, and in 1929 26,992 Sevens were built, a total which was only exceeded in one other year – 1935. The greatest demand was for saloons in the 8 h.p. category and the taxation figures for the first quarter of 1929 showed that, of the 37,000 new cars registered, no less than 30,500 were saloons. There were 7,268 new registrations in the smallest class compared with 5,265 in the previous year. For the first time, 20 per cent of the British motor industry's output consisted of 8 h.p. cars. This augured well for the motor manufacturers, but the trend, in a country with more than a million men on the dole, had little chance of continuing.

Chiefs of the oil industry met in March and decided to increase the price of petrol by 2¼d. a gallon. This came at a very bad time for those who had to sell motor cars because most buying was done between the beginning of

86

March and the end of July at that time. Winston Churchill, who was busy preparing his Budget, was also concerned because then, as now, petrol prices affected so many other things and contributed towards inflation. Manu-facturers of small cars were not at all depressed. Increases always tended to stimulate the demand for their products, albeit only temporarily. Churchill's Budget did nothing that could help the situation which existed in the country and the Conservative Government was defeated at the General Election in May. Ramsay MacDonald became the Labour Prime Minister. His first threat, not to renew the McKenna duties which had afforded protection for industry for so long, and provided the Government with an income of £m3½ a year, caused a great deal of worry and uncertainty. Unofficial strikes swept the country. Longbridge had to close down for several weeks in March

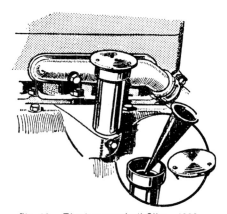

Fig. 16.   The improved oil filler—1928.

because of a dispute over methods of paying for piece work, and production was not resumed until Sir Herbert threatened to dismiss those who remained out after a certain date. This had the desired effect and the strike collapsed. There was no alternative with a million unemployed waiting for work.

Those concerns which were poised ready to put their prices up in 1928 had been prevented from doing so by Austin's reductions. They did not have to wait very long, because Sir Herbert soon realised his mistake and put up the prices of the Seven, Twelve and Sixteen with effect from 29th January. The Seven chassis was now £94 10s., the tourer £130 and the coupé and saloon £140. There had to be an excuse, so by way of explanation the Company sent out this letter to all its dealers:

"During the last Olympia Show and subsequent thereto, there has been a constant demand on the part of the buying public, strongly supported by our agents throughout the country, for detail improvements quite distinctive from the general design, efficiency and finish always recognisable in the Austin product. Furthermore, the directors of the Company, appreciating the general desire on the part of the present day motorists for refinement and superior quality have supported the policy of constant improvement. Recently all our coachwork has been substantially improved and generally strengthened in construction on scientific lines without addition to weight – a better quality of upholstery, both leather and cloth, has been introduced – more efficient door hinges and locks, and Triplex glass included in front screens as standard on all cars. To meet a part of the added cost of this new additional equipment, the Austin Company are making extra charges throughout the range."

Morris now had the upper hand. The Minors were £5 less than the equivalent Sevens and Morris followed a different policy. If a purchaser wanted something that was "quite distinctive from the general design, efficiency and finish" recognisable in the Morris product, then he paid more and bought a de luxe model. But the basic price of the Minor was less than the Seven.

Alterations in the design of the Seven continued to be made throughout 1929, culminating in what were called "major improvements" at the time of the Motor Show to ensure that the 1930 cars at least looked different. Competition was serious, and for the first time there were sufficient reliable alternatives to attract buyers away from the Austin Seven. The answer was to change the outward appearance of the car slightly each year, a practice which became increasingly popular amongst manufacturers throughout the 1930's. At car number A8-367, chassis number 77,801, new pistons were introduced with three compression rings in $\frac{3}{32}$ in. grooves instead of the two formerly used, in order to correct the tendency for the engine to over-oil. At about the same time the cheaper die cast F.Z.B. carburettor became standard. Commencing from chassis number 84,001 in May the rear axle and torque tube were altered. After this, it was possible to adjust the crown wheel without parting the axle case and tubes, the torque tube was arranged to screw into the axle case instead of being flanged and held by set screws which allowed the pinion to be set correctly with greater ease. A new silencer and exhaust tail pipe was used on all cars after chassis number 84,691, a type which had been fitted previously to the coupés. In September, the Austin-made radiators first came into use with the larger filler cap and chromium-plated shell. From chassis number 90,030 all front springs were made with eight, instead of five, leaves for greater flexibility. At chassis number 96,201 it was decided that the over-oiling problems had been aggravated rather than cured by the last modification so it was decided to revert to the original piston design with two compression rings and one oil ring in $\frac{5}{32}$ in. grooves. The oil ring in the piston skirts was stepped at the bottom edge, an idea which had been tried

Gordon England, Mulliner, Cole and Shuttleworth, Burghley, New Avon, Alpe
Saunders

30. The 1928 Motor
Show coupé which
went to the 1929
New York Show

31. An American
Bantam

32. A 1928 three-
seater Rosengart

– 33. Dixi saloon ; Above – 34. A 1929 demonstration chassis

35. Views of a saloon made in late 1929

experimentally on a few engines in mid-1928. In October 1929, the car number prefix letter was changed from A- to B-, and at B-257 the diameter of all crankshaft bearings, except the front one, were increased and the webs were stiffened. The alteration involved new connecting rods, bolts and pegs, new rear bearing housings and bolts, and a shorter oil jet to clear the enlarged shaft. A wider taper at the rear end of the shaft necessitated a modified flywheel. In place of the ineffective felt oil retaining washer an oil return reverse thread was machined on to the shaft; this was also applied to the gearbox first- and third-motion shafts. Ball-change gearboxes were used on all cars from chassis number 99,001, but one or two chassis had been converted

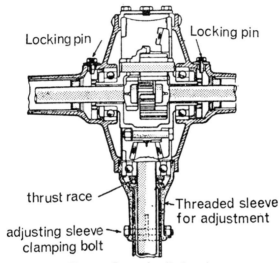

Locking pin   Locking pin

thrust race

Threaded sleeve for adjustment

adjusting sleeve
clamping bolt

Fig. 17.   Rear axle adjustment.

before October for experimental purposes in which the first and reverse gear positions were reversed.

Sir Herbert's successes in France and Germany made him even more determined to conquer the American market. No small cars were made there and, in fact, the Americans seemed to be so set against miniature vehicles that none were being built even in their own overseas factories. Both Ford and General Motors had manufacturing plants all over the world, in many places where the greatest demand was for small cars, but it was not until well into the 1930's that even in those ideal situations they accepted the fact that there was sufficient demand to enter the field themselves. There was not then, and there has not been since, any real desire in the States for a light economy car. In the late 1920's this was a generally accepted fact to most people but Austin, as all who became associated with the American Austin project were soon to discover for themselves. The New York magazine *Town Topics* provided this typical reaction:

> ". . . one considers very seriously whether there is any real hope of success with the car among us. Many attempts have been made here to put over the baby type of machine, but they all have passed on. The big stumbling block is, as always, a temperamental kink among Americans which sets them against the Tiny Tim machine; the standard of living and luxury with us doesn't seem to leave much room for the Austin size of car. With all due respects to this machine, when you ride about in one in our congested traffic you feel as though you were hemmed in by elephants and Juggernauts on all sides. It will take some powers of persuasion to convince Americans that they should take the baby type of car to their bosoms."

Foreign cars appeared for the first time in a major American exhibition at the 1929 National Automobile Show in New York; Britain was represented by Vauxhall, Daimler and Austin. Sir Herbert and Lady Austin arrived in New York on the *Berengaria* on 3rd January after a storm-tossed crossing, accompanied by four Sevens, one of which was a little coupé similar to the one which had been shown for the first time at Olympia three months before. Austin was there in a dual rôle, firstly to represent the Society of Motor Manufacturers and Traders at an international motoring conference and secondly to follow up his previous unsuccessful visit to Detroit in 1928 to see what could be done to market the Austin Seven in America. His object was to discover an American concern prepared to produce the car under licence which he would grant, together with the necessary designs and a team of experts to assist with the preparations for production, in exchange for a directorship and the customary 2 per cent. He set up his headquarters in the Commodore Hotel, ready to meet applicants for the franchise and advertised in all the major newspapers that "The Austin Motor Company desires to get in touch with either an individual or group of individuals who are willing to undertake the manufacture and sale of the Austin Seven in America and Canada."

The first serious approach came from Manchester, the largest city in New Hampshire. Speaker Foster, an administrator of the town, had appointed a Committee earlier in the year upon the authority of the House of Representatives and their preliminary findings were that the necessary finance would be beyond the city's resources. Not completely satisfied with this, the Board of Aldermen asked Mayor Arthur E. Moreau to look into the matter. Moreau held a long conference with Sir Herbert in New York and took away detailed plans of the car to show the Manchester businessmen because he felt that they would be sure to favour the idea of having an automobile plant to bring added work and prosperity to the district. Sir Herbert told Moreau that he had already been approached by other manufacturers and organisations and that one actually had made a firm offer which had been referred to the English board of directors because it suggested different terms from those which had been proposed. Austin promised that no firm arrangements would be made with the other groups until Moreau had looked into the question of financing the project in Manchester, and sailed for home again at the beginning of February, 1929 to await developments.

As Foster had already discovered, Manchester could not find a million dollars and Moreau reluctantly had to admit defeat. On 28th February arrangements were finally concluded with the other group of Americans and the result was the formation in Wilmington of the American Austin Car Co. Inc., to acquire an exclusive licence to manufacture and sell the Austin

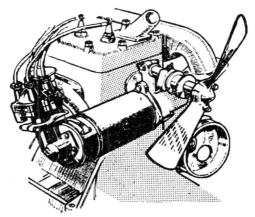

Fig. 18. 1929 coil ignition distributor.

Seven in the States for the next ten years, terminable if they failed to produce a minimum number of cars. Particulars of the deal were given in this country in August with a view to the stock being introduced on to the London Stock Exchange. The new company entered into a contract with the Standard Steel Car Co. of Pennsylvania for the purchase of a factory in Butler for $250,000 in cash and 25,000 fully paid shares; $100,000 was payable on the execution of the Deed and the balance in five years. Authorised capital amounted to a million shares of no par value of which 350,000 were for immediate issue and, in addition, on 1st August Bulkley, Vallance & Co. agreed to purchase 300,000 at $9 each. Of these, 100,000 were deposited with the Guarantee Trust Co. and reserved for the London market. Although the American issue had been oversubscribed at $12.50, prospects were not thought of very highly over here and the *Investors Review* under the heading "Prospectuses criticised" said: "The Austin Seven is an excellent engineering product, but conditions obtaining in America are, of course, very different to those prevailing in this country, and the proposition must naturally be classed as speculative." Sir Herbert and the Austin Motor Co. Ltd. had a joint option extending to 15th September, 1932 of buying 50,000 shares at $9 each on the provision that they held them for twelve months; Sir Herbert was also given a seat on the board.

Arthur J. Brandt was chosen to direct the affairs of the company but finding it impossible to recruit technical staff for development work in Butler, he went over to Detroit. As the American magazine *Automotive Industries* pointed out in the title to an article on the new car in 1930, the "American Austin design differs radically from British". This was certainly true as far as the coachwork was concerned. Count Alexis de Sakhnoffsky was given the task of designing a miniature interpretation of the current American popular car, and the Hayes Body Corporation tooled-up to produce a body style then quite unknown to the American market. The designer's requirements presented the body-builders with some apparently contradictory requirements:

(1) Body lines had to flow smoothly to conform to current American practice, and yet they had to allow for adequate seat width.

(2) In spite of the short wheel base of 75 in., the maximum leg room had to be provided.

(3) The car had to be unusually low and yet they still had to provide ample head room, and to keep the body proportions in balance.

(4) Due to relatively low horse power, the weight of the body had to be kept to an absolute minimum and yet be inherently strong.

In order to achieve the first and second requirements the Hayes Co. had to restrict itself to two types of body, a two-seater coupé and a two-seater saloon; the so-called four-seater body, whilst acceptable in England, was not a practical proposition as far as the American public was concerned. The all-steel body weighed 245 lb. without trim and glass, of which only 40 lb. was timber, and was the closest approach to an all-steel design that had been produced in the United States on a commercial basis. Outside body stampings contributed at least as much to the strength of the complete structure as the scanty chassis members and by extending this principle to greater limits than was usual, inherent strength with low weight could be achieved.

With regard to the A-shaped chassis, whilst of the same basic design, the triangular frame was extended to the rear axle in order to support the body beyond the point at which the chassis finished, which was achieved on the English version by short chassis extensions. The same type of construction, with quarter-elliptic springs to the axle, was employed in the American design but from the point of the attachment of the rear springs the frame side channel was extended up to continue to the rear of the body. Cross-bracing was provided by the one-piece welded-in floor of the body which meant that the shock absorbers had to be repositioned. By welding everything to the chassis frame the body became an integral part of it and, to all intents and purposes, the American Austin Seven was constructed on the same principle employed by manufacturers today.

Left-hand drive was used and there were front and rear bumpers, which were already an essential feature in America, eight-inch brake drums, disc wheels; arrangements were in hand to adapt all the thread sizes from Whitworth to the American S.A.E. pattern and a contract was placed with the Warner Gear Co. to build ball-change gearboxes. Very little happened in 1929 and we will return to the story again in the next chapter.

Motor racing started again at Brooklands with the Easter Monday meeting

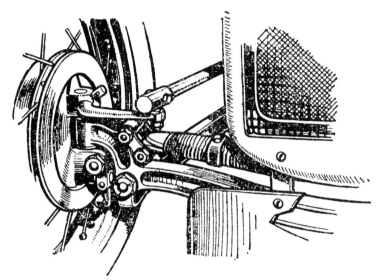

Fig. 19.   Dropped front axle—1929 Ulster.

at which Kaye Don broke the lap record in a Sunbeam at over 131 m.p.h. An Austin first appeared that year in the J.C.C. Double-Twelve hours race on 11th and 12th May, an occasion which was summed-up afterwards as the most successful track event that had ever been organised in this country. This was the first time that a twenty-four hours race had been staged in England and as it was not possible to race during the night owing to the fact that local residents around Brooklands would be disturbed, it was staged in two halves. The J.C.C. realised that the public would not be particularly interested in watching cars lapping the track for twelve hours a day so, for the first time, they converted Brooklands into a "Fun City" with a fair and amusement park and held a dance from nine p.m. until midnight; presumably this proved quieter than the car exhausts. Based on the annual Grand Prix d'Endurance race at Le Mans, drivers lined up on the far side of the track, ran to their vehicles, erected hoods and started the engines with electric starters. After ten laps the hoods had to be furled. No less than nineteen of the fifty-six entries were supercharged and of the fifty-two cars that actually started at eight a.m. on the Saturday only twenty-nine were to finish at eight p.m. on the Sunday. The Barnes brothers were the only competitors in class H and had to cover the 1,080 miles at an average speed of 45 m.p.h. which also had to be maintained in each of the four six-hour sections. Compared with the averages achieved by Ramponi's Alfa Romeo, 76 m.p.h., and Davis' Bentley, 81 m.p.h., the Austin's average speed of less than 49 may have seemed small. Its great success was in accomplishing the race without one involuntary stop.

Holbrook and Poppe took two of the Works' supercharged cars to compete for the *Daily Despatch* hundred guineas gold vase, presented to the winner of a 100-miles race at Ainsdale Beach, Southport on 18th May. Three other Sevens entered and Poppe was first in the 750 c.c. class.

Twelve cars lined up at the start of the 75 m.p.h. Short handicap at the B.A.R.C. Whitsun meeting amongst which were Austin Sevens driven by J. S. Wilson and Spero. Although Marsh's Riley overtook the little cars to win easily, it was disqualified later for having a silencer that did not conform to the regulations. This gave Wilson first place with an average speed of 73·92 m.p.h. and Spero was second. Wilson came second in a later Long handicap.

On 29th June the B.A.R.C. held another of its Six-hours Endurance races in which the Barnes brothers received a massive fifty-five lap start which proved almost too much for the winner – Barnato's Bentley, and throughout the race the Austin was his most serious rival and, in fact, it held the lead for the first four hours. For the first hour the Austin's average speed was 47·49, by half-time it had risen to 52·25 and remained in excess of 50 m.p.h. to win the class Trophy. Yet again, it was not necessary to make even one involuntary stop.

Southern Ireland staged its major international race in 1929, the Irish International Grand Prix, at the Phoenix Park course near Dublin in mid-July. Four Austins were to compete for the Saorstat Cup – Deering Jackson, W. Sullivan in a supercharged Gordon England model, and the Austin Works' entries, Gunnar Poppe in a supercharged car and Archie Frazer Nash in a similar car without the blower. During the official practice, Vic Cooper, the spare driver to Deering Jackson, turned the vehicle over whilst going around a right-angle bend. Fortunately, he was not seriously injured and the car was not damaged badly. Poppe, who had never entered a major race before, caused quite a stir at the same time by completing a lap at 66·70 m.p.h.; Frazer Nash's car could only manage 57·90. Supercharged 750 c.c. cars had to cover 258 miles on the day and the standard vehicles 240·8 miles. The only other light car was V. E. Horsman's Triumph which was out of the running after an hour. Frazer Nash completed sixty-one laps and Jackson sixty. Poppe was left to himself. His eleven-lap lead should have assured him of a place, but his inexperience led him to take the risk of attempting to finish without stopping to refuel – the inevitable happened and he ran out of petrol. Breathless and exhausted, Poppe and his mechanic pushed the car into the pits. After filling-up they rushed off, cast caution to the winds and dashed around the course skidding on every bend. The car spun round twice at one stage and crashed into the barriers. Without stopping, they hurried on and just managed to squeeze in the seventieth and final lap in time at an average speed of 61·70 m.p.h. Sullivan also finished in the other super-charged car at 60·50.

Sir Herbert was not particularly happy with the result of the Irish race which he regarded as a preview for the Ulster Tourist Trophy. If an Austin team was to win a race, then it would have to be managed by an experienced

team manager; Waite was not due to return from Australia until October so Austin approached Gordon England. England's business activities had been remarkably successful since he had ceased taking an active part in motor racing, and his standing in the motor industry had been acknowledged by his election to the Presidency of the Motor Agents' Association. In February, 1929 Gordon England (1929) Ltd. was incorporated as a public company with a capital of a quarter of a million pounds, and 648,000 five-shilling Ordinary shares were offered at par on the Stock Exchange. The company was formed to acquire the organisation and capital of the existing concern of George England Ltd. which had been operating for the past four years and had managed to progress rapidly from making only 26 bodies in 1925 to reach a total of 2,939 in 1928. At the time of the formation of the public company 100 bodies were being completed each week at Wembley and the intention was to increase this to 175 later on in the year. Profits in excess of £58,000 a year were anticipated and Gordon England obtained £88,000 in shares in the new company and £34,100 in cash to redeem outstanding debentures, together with more than £46,000 to settle all debts in full.

He was quite prepared, in spite of his commitments, to assist Sir Herbert with the racing team which was to represent the Company in Ulster, so as soon as he received the request he went up to Longbridge and asked to see the cars. After having inspected them, he spoke to the drivers and found that there was a certain lack of morale amongst the mechanics so he told Austin that he would take over the responsibility of getting the cars ready for the race and manage the team only on two conditions. First, that the cars, mechanics and drivers were all to be shipped to Belfast that week, and secondly, that Sir Herbert should provide him with a letter stating that he was to be solely in command, and that all Gordon England's decisions were to be taken as final without there being any appeal to Sir Herbert. Not unnaturally, Austin objected violently to Gordon England's demand that his services were available only upon his own terms. In Gordon England's own words:

> "He either gave me the letter as I had stipulated or he didn't, it was a matter of complete indifference to me which he did; but if he did I would play, if not I would forget the whole matter. I got the letter!"

Cars (registration numbers OF 1857, OF 3128, OF 3129 and OF 3130), drivers and mechanics were all put aboard the *Ulster Monarch* which arrived in Belfast on 8th August and Gordon England used Harry Ferguson's works as his base.

Initially, only two of the four official Works' cars were supercharged, but as it was soon apparent from the practice speeds that the blown cars could lap at 10 m.p.h. faster than the others, sufficient equipment was rushed over from Longbridge to supercharge all the engines. After constant trouble with the team and the mechanics, during which Gordon England blessed the fact that he had his letter of authority from Sir Herbert, eventually everything was running to his satisfaction. The race over the Ards circuit for the R.A.C. Tourist Trophy was held on 17th August before a huge crowd of more than fifty thousand. In addition to the Trophy, the *Daily Mail* presented prizes valued at £1,500. Thirty laps of the fourteen miles circuit had to be covered, some 410 miles altogether, and the 750 c.c. class obtained a five-lap start. Entrants were Frazer Nash, Coldicutt and Barnes, as the official Austin team, Holbrook and R. Heyn. The Barnes brothers had been lent a car by Austin as they had just put up for sale at £175 their own Double-Twelve and Six-hours Endurance racer, and R. Heyn withdrew before the day. His own driver-mechanic, W. Sullivan, was ill and was prevented from racing on his doctor's orders, but as he had prepared and tuned the car himself the owner preferred to cancel the entry rather than to seek outside or trade assistance and therefore spoil his amateur status. Two Triumphs started but never presented any real competition to the Austins. The Austins all began well; Holbrook was in the lead at the end of the first lap, closely followed by Frazer Nash; the crowd was very sympathetic towards the baby cars and cheered them loudly. Holbrook was still in the lead and Horsman's Triumph left

op – 36. Gunnar Poppe in July, 1929

bove – 37. H. C. Spero in Mrs. Jo Jo after winning the Brooklands' President's Gold
late on 5th August, 1929

Top – 38. Even children had them! A 1929 model ambulance
Above – 39. 1930–31 fabric saloon, introduced in July, 1930

the circuit with plug trouble; in spite of heavy rain, Holbrook and Barnes were keeping up lap averages in the middle fifties. More cheering when it was announced that Holbrook had lapped in 13 minutes 41 seconds, a speed of 59·97 m.p.h. At the end of ten laps the positions were:

(1) Holbrook 1 hour 10 min. 17 sec.
(2) Frazer Nash 1 hour 11 min. 13 sec.
(3) Coldicutt 1 hour 13 min. 35 sec.
(4) Barnes 1 hour 14 min. 8 sec.
(5) Grindley (Triumph) 1 hour 18 min. 38 sec.

Fig. 21. Swallow saloon.

The excitement increased when Frazer Nash broke the class record with a lap at 13 minutes 38 seconds (60·12 m.p.h.). Holbrook, whose wonderful driving was one of the features of the day, did better still to lap at 13 minutes 26 seconds – over 61 m.p.h. – and the Austins still headed the field at one p.m. Frazer Nash and Holbrook hummed round the course. Frazer Nash set up another record with a time of 13 minutes 4 seconds, an average of 62·73 m.p.h.; the Barnes brothers took it in turns to drive and their car gave them no trouble. Then came a report that Coldicutt's car had turned round twice at the Quarry, hit the bank and dented its tail but it was still in the race. By two p.m. the Austins still held the first four positions in the race, but Frazer Nash had taken the lead from Holbrook, Barnes being third and Coldicutt fourth. The duel between the Austins became most acute two-thirds of the way through the race. Holbrook lapped Frazer Nash, taking first place, but it was becoming obvious that Caracciola in his Mercedes was eating his way into the little Austin's margin. At two-thirty p.m. the Austins still held the first four places when Holbrook again made the crowd gasp by lapping in 12 minutes 52 seconds or at more than 63 m.p.h. At the end of twenty laps the times were:

(1) Holbrook   3 hours 28 min. 16 sec.
(2) Frazer Nash 3 hours 28 min. 17 sec.
(3) Barnes   3 hours 38 min. 18 sec.
(4) Coldicutt   3 hours 39 min. 15 sec.

At this, the most exciting point in the race, Holbrook had a lead of 17 minutes 43 seconds over the German and the question was whether he could keep his rival at bay. By the end of the twenty-fourth lap the Mercedes had made up a good deal of leeway when Holbrook and Frazer Nash were flagged in by Gordon England to refuel. There were to be no risks taken this time. The drama drew to a climax in the twenty-sixth lap when Campari's Alfa-Romeo shrieked past the Austins to take the lead for the first time. Caracciola overtook them all on the next lap to win the race at an average speed of 72·82 m.p.h., Campari was second at 67·55, Frazer Nash third at 59·60 and Holbrook fourth at 59·49 m.p.h. Barnes was sixteenth with an average of 56·65 m.p.h. and Coldicutt nineteenth at 55·77.

This fantastic effort had saved the day for England and in retrospect it seems almost unbelievable that the Austins were able to achieve such success against their larger rivals. In spite of the fact that an observer said afterwards that the refuelling of the Austins in the pits was so poorly carried out that much valuable time was lost, if Gordon England had not possessed his letter from Sir Herbert the Austin team would certainly not have done so well. Caracciola was as impressed as anyone and his first comments to the press were: "What a performance those little midget cars put up. They were wonderful. It was a great moment when I flashed past Campari, but I think it was a greater one when I got in front of those little Austins. I take my hat off to those little midgets, and to the brave drivers who were so splendid in this race." In a speech at a dinner given to the team later by Austin distributors, Sir Herbert said that to finish an entire team without a single adjustment being made, as Gordon England was able to confirm, and to do so well against so many world-famous drivers was good enough for one year. His remark that the Austin Company would not have had the kudos they had obtained even if they had won the race was well chosen, because had they done so no doubt the other contestants would have blamed the handicapping for their own failure to overtake the Austin Sevens.

At the Brooklands Bank Holiday meeting in August H. C. Spero, in "Mrs. Jo Jo", won the race for the President's Gold Plate by 300 yards from Clive Dunfee's Austro-Daimler at 80·70 m.p.h. To everyone's astonishment, at the closing B.A.R.C. meeting in September, Spero won the second race, a 75 m.p.h. Long handicap, at 78·81 m.p.h. driving "Mrs. Jo Jo", and came third in a similar race later in the day.

During the year the new M.G. Midgets began to appear and proved that they were going to be very serious rivals to the Austin Sevens. In the M.C.C. High Speed trial at Brooklands one averaged 61·52 m.p.h. against the best Austin speed of 59·74 put up by a "Cup" model. This was only a fraction better than a Morris Minor and was closely followed by a Triumph and a Singer.

The racing team was safe for the time being at least. Under the command of Gunnar Poppe the successful Ulster cars competed in the 1,100 c.c. class in the B.R.D.C. 500-miles race. This, the first event of its type organised by the club, was probably the fastest race of its kind the world had seen. The lack of obstacles and artificial turns allowed Jack Barclay's Bentley to win with an average of 107·32 m.p.h. Clive Dunfee's larger and more heavily handicapped

Fig. 22   Swallow tourer.

Bentley was even faster at 109·4. Seven of the thirty entrants were placed in the 1,100 c.c. class, Spero on "Mrs. Jo Jo" and the Austin supercharged Works' cars driven by Holbrook, Coldicutt, Poppe and Barnes, the others were an Amilcar and a Riley. After an hour Barnes pushed his car three-quarters of a mile to the pits and retired with a broken connecting rod. With a hundred miles covered the Amilcar was in the lead with an average of 94·06 m.p.h. followed by Coldicutt at over 84 m.p.h., Holbrook, Poppe and the Riley. Spero was sixth, having been delayed when his auxiliary oil tank worked loose. Coldicutt stayed closely behind the Amilcar for another hundred miles but by the half-way mark the larger cars began to dominate the race. Holbrook was now third and Coldicutt fifth when the latter discovered a cracked cylinder head. They took the one from Barnes' car but this suffered from the same fault so they decided to continue the race regardless. The Amilcar retired and towards the end Holbrook held sixth place after twelve contestants had fallen out. His average for the 500 miles was 80·25 m.p.h. and he won the 1,100 c.c. class and was sixth in the overall classification.

Coldicutt failed to complete the course in the prescribed time but was still running after 155 laps after setting up a new class H International 100 km. record at 82·69 m.p.h. Holbrook broke the 200 km. record at 83·80 m.p.h. All excellent and remarkable individual performances, but Austins still had not learnt the secret of team success which Gordon England had tried to teach them.

A 60 m.p.h. Austin Seven

From the *Light Car and Cyclecar*, 4th October, 1929

In view of the universal appeal of the popular Austin Seven chassis, and the increasing numbers of sporting and semi-sporting bodies which make their appearance on it, the following account of a successful attempt by a private owner to improve the power output of the engine and the general performance of the car should prove of interest to many readers.

The car in question is a 1928 Gordon England "Cup" model, and on delivery a very careful running-in was commenced, great care being taken not to allow the engine to labour in the least when under load. It was found that the initial stiffness – which was considerable – had to a great extent worn off after a couple of hundred miles' cautious driving. This process was continued until the 500-miles mark had been reached when the engine was quite free. A test for maximum speed was accordingly undertaken, which gave the figure of 45 m.p.h.

The first stage in "hotting up" was then started by the removal of the cylinder head, the combustion chambers of which were polished with meticulous care, which, together with similar attention to the induction passages, occupied no fewer than twenty hours' work. A thirty-second of an inch was then machined off the surface of the head in order to increase the compression ratio, and double valve springs, obtained from the Laystall concern, were fitted, it being necessary for the valve spring collars to be turned down slightly to register with the inner springs.

A slight modification was also made to the exhaust system concerning the matter of baffle plates, and the car was again tested, but it was soon found that these rudimentary attentions proved insufficient to increase the maximum speed to the required standard. The acceleration was considerably improved, and second gear was able to show a quite respectable 40 m.p.h., but the top gear maximum was no more than 47–48 m.p.h.

After a further 1,500 miles' running in this state, another attempt at improvement was made by removing the cylinder block and entrusting it to Laystalls, who bored out the valve ports $\frac{1}{16}$ in. oversize, and supplied a set of special valves, the inlets being of the tulip type.

This had an immediate and gratifying effect, as when the timing had been somewhat advanced, a maximum of 55 m.p.h. resulted together with 45–46 m.p.h. in second gear. At this stage of the proceedings the body was given a complete undershield, while the front and rear brakes were coupled to the foot pedal by means of a Bodelo attachment.

Having got this far, an irresistible craving for 60 m.p.h. began to make itself felt, and this led to the acquisition of an aluminium head of Ricardo type, a Solex MH 26 carburettor and a special induction pipe. After these alterations had been made 60 m.p.h. was obtained without difficulty.

It now began to be realised that the speed of the car was getting too great for its road-holding capabilities and to overcome this defect modifications were carried out by Boyd-Carpenter and Co. Ltd. By a flattening of the front and rear springs the chassis was lowered by two inches. An extra leaf was also added to each rear spring to stiffen up the suspension. The seats were also lowered as far as possible, and these modifications absolutely transformed the car from the driving point of view. It now holds the road in a simply amazing manner, whilst cornering is a sheer delight.

The final alteration was effected during a short stay in Algeria, where a pair of Marchal headlamps was fitted, and this has given one a lighting equipment which is worthy of the car's speed capabilities, as this to-all-appearances standard "Cup" model is now able to give a maximum of 63 m.p.h., with 50 m.p.h. available in second should it ever be required. The acceleration in this latter gear is naturally something quite out of the ordinary, as owners of considerably larger cars have at times found – as a rule very much to their surprise.

As a matter of interest the above mentioned performance is obtained with an average consumption of 35–40 m.p.g., under all conditions, with a choke tube of 22 mm. and main jet of 120 for the Solex carburettor. The oil consumption is in the neighbourhood of 1,500 m.p.g.

1930

The Baby Grows Up

Ramsay MacDonald's Labour administration could do nothing to forestall the depression of the early 'thirties. Vast sums were spent on improving the social services and in providing reasonable benefits for the unemployed, promises which had been made to the electorate, but the problem had deep roots which required much more drastic action. Instead of improving, the situation became more acute. The figure of a million unemployed had risen to two millions by September, 1930. Strangely enough, much of the motor industry remained in a remarkably healthy state, in spite of the fact that each week added a further 20,000 to those already out of work. Its market was amongst a section of the population upon which the effects of depression were delayed.

Some 178,800 cars had been built in the country in 1929, of which 166,500 were sold on the home market, and although there was a slight drop in the new car registrations for the first part of 1930 amounting to 5 per cent over the corresponding period in 1929, registrations in the 8 h.p. class increased by as much as 18·3 per cent. This continued prosperity was assisted by a reduction of 2d. a gallon in the price of petrol in September, a favourable Budget in April which increased income tax by 6d. in the pound but imposed no further burdens on the motorist and, most important of all, the Government's pointers on the future of the McKenna duties. Industry's continual campaign for a decision upon this question eventually resulted in extorting from the Chancellor a promise to retain the duties for at least another year. This assurance of continued safeguarding reduced imports still further and was an important factor in maintaining a strong demand on the home market. Profits which Austins had made in 1929 were distributed almost entirely to shareholders, and arrears in the Preference dividends were settled and, for the first time for nearly ten years, the Ordinary shareholders were given a handsome payment. 1930 was an equally successful year for the Company and they still continued to produce a good proportion of the total national output with a production of 43,000 vehicles, 6,000 more than in 1929, of which more than a half – 23,826 – were Austin Sevens.

Austin's Baby began to grow up in 1930 in preparation for the 1931 selling season which was to begin with the Olympia Motor Show in October. Sir Herbert had resisted previous attempts to develop the Seven into a true four-seater, but as the Morris Minor was able to carry four adults in reasonable comfort without becoming overloaded, the Austin had to follow suit. There was a perfectly good and justifiable reason for doing this but the changes in appearance, although some of them were undoubtedly necessary for technical reasons, ease of production and because the 1931 saloon body was given larger internal dimensions, supported the trend of the decade which was already established, whereby frequent changes became essential in order to "conform to all modern aesthetic requirements". Sir Herbert disliked making changes merely to alter the outward appearance of his products, but there was no alternative.

In retrospect, it would be more difficult to criticise alterations if the aesthetic requirements which the public of the day seemed to demand had resulted in cars which were more pleasing in appearance. Unfortunately they were not, and this is one of the reasons why enthusiasm grew, and has continued to increase, for the Vintage cars made during the 'twenties. Strictly speaking, the more recent products in a particular range should be more acceptable on the grounds that technical developments cause the breed to improve progressively. For this reason, a 1966 B.M.C. Mini is a better car than a similar model made five years before. A 1931 Austin Seven was a better car, if we accept the fact that there was more weight for the same engine to carry around, than a 1926 model, but this does not take into account the question of external appearance. Maybe this presents us with the old question of personal opinion, but it is as well to look at a 1926 "Top Hat" saloon alongside a 1936 Ruby and to decide whether or not the character of the former has more appeal than the "aesthetic qualities" of the latter. The question is, of course, would a 1926-style Seven have sold in 1936?

B- car number prefixes had started in 1929, with the introduction of the type E body. B1- began on 15th March, 1930, after which a number of mechanical alterations were made. A new dynamo and drive gear was used in April and first fitted to engine number 110,740. In conjunction with the new short scuttle body, the prototype of which was built in June and allocated car number B1-301, dial-type oil gauges, coupled brakes which allowed all four sets of shoes to operate simultaneously by either hand or foot pedal, rear springs and many of the rear axle components were modified to cope with the extra weight. A longitudinal centre strut was also added to the chassis and the starter button was moved back to a more convenient

position in front of the passenger seat on the central tunnel. In frontal
aspect, the appearance of the new saloons was altered by raising the top of
the radiator slightly and extending the bonnet back to within about four
inches of the windscreen, which was tilted back a few degrees to reduce glare
and dazzle. The moulded scuttle swept from the horizontal bonnet line to
the screen and this, together with the curved rear panels, provided more
rounded lines. There was also a slight tumble-in on the body from top to
bottom. A waist rail swept right along the side and was picked out in a
different colour to add to the impression of length. The deeper radiator
shell was chromium plated and was reduced in width at the edges; a five
gallon fuel tank, formerly let into the dash, was now mounted more rigidly
on a horizontal platform, and allowed for the extra gallon to be held in

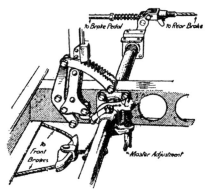

Fig. 23.   July, 1930—coupled brakes.

reserve by the use of a two-way tap. Beneath the central hinge of the long
bonnet a gutter was incorporated to catch the rain when the bonnet was
lifted and to prevent it from pouring on to the engine. A stronger thicker-
gauge under portion to the three-part metal of the floor of the fabric saloons
allowed for the recommended carrying capacity to be increased from thirty
to thirty-six stones. Domed rear quarters and other alterations increased
the body length by three inches and there was more leg-room in both front
and rear compartments. Both front seats tipped forward and pneumatic
upholstery was used. Door windows were now in one piece and were
lowered and raised by winder, and the thumb-screws used to clamp the
windscreen in its closed position were replaced by a new lever-operated
device. Door locks were flatter and made to operate by cords, there were
larger rear side windows, and a blind, controlled by the driver, was provided
for the rear window. The new metal and the fabric saloons were priced at
£140, with sunshine roofs available at £5 extra. Because the Startin-bodied
van was proving so popular a new metal van was also introduced, similar

in shape to the early fabric model, at £132 10s., finished in grey primer. Seven tourers at £130 were now the same price as the Morris Minor two-seater. Morris reduced his price to £125 in August, so Austin brought out his revised charges to take effect from 1st September: the chassis remained at £94 10s., the saloons were reduced by £10 to £130, and the tourers from £130 to £122 10s., and the new vans to £122 10s.

Austin Sevens continued to uphold their racing prestige. H. C. Spero produced a new tank-like white body for his old "Mrs. Jo Jo", a cowl covered the front wheels completely and tapered to a point between the rear wheels. His intention was to use it for record-breaking. It was known as the "clockwork mouse" and gained third place in a five-lap handicap at the B.A.R.C. invitation club races at the end of May. Later, Spero challenged any other unsupercharged 750 c.c. four-wheeler in the world to any race at Brooklands between five and twenty-five miles with a level start, for £50 a side. It appears that no one was prepared to accept his challenge.

That important preview to the Irish races, the J.C.C. Double-Twelve hours race was held at Brooklands on 9th and 10th May. Sir Herbert decided to watch the proceedings himself. Two orange Works' supercharged cars were entered and driven by Waite and the Earl of March and Frazer Nash and Poppe. The Barnes brothers also competed in an unsupercharged Seven. Unfortunately this popular event was marred by a fatal crash on the first day in which two Talbots collided; one jumped the track and crashed into spectators. Two people were killed and twenty injured. At the inquest shortly afterwards the jury brought in a verdict of accidental death but said that, in their opinion, the racing in these high-speed races should be under stricter supervision. Fifty-nine cars started of which only twenty-nine finished; in order to complete the course in time the Austins had to average 45 m.p.h. and the team of M.G. Midgets 49 m.p.h. Within an hour of the finish, Frazer Nash's car came into the pits misfiring badly, the plugs were changed and then the cylinder head was removed but nothing appeared to be at fault. In the end the magneto was replaced because the distributor had cracked. This delay probably caused the Austins to lose the team prize to the M.G.'s, which took fourteenth, eighteenth and nineteenth places at speeds between 57 and 60 m.p.h. Waite came seventh in the overall classification by covering 1,559·36 miles at an average of 64·97 m.p.h. and Barnes tenth with 1,372·96 at 57·20 m.p.h., being the only car in the race to complete the course without an involuntary stop.

Six Austins Sevens were entered for the second Irish Grand Prix held at the Phoenix Park course on 18th and 19th July. Austin's team, managed by D. Stewart Frazer, consisted of Frazer Nash and Poppe on supercharged cars, and Waite, who decided to obtain the additional handicap advantage by using a car with an unblown engine. In addition, the Barnes brothers, Lincoln and Nolan the Austin agents in Dublin, and Lookers, the

Manchester distributors, entered supercharged Austins driven by G. V. Cooke
and S. A. Crabtree. Cooke's car was the first to arrive on the course as early
as 29th May; his and the other supercharged Austins lapped at speeds just
less than 70 m.p.h. Waite managed a maximum speed of 61·60, and as he
was given an eighteen-lap handicap on the day, which based his average
speed at 59·90 he had an excellent chance of winning. So good were his
prospects that Earl Howe, Birkin and Malcolm Campbell all felt that the
handicappers were perhaps too generous towards the solitary unsupercharged class H contestant. The five blown Austins were given a twelve-lap
start and had to cover 250·4 miles against Waite's 228·6. Everyone seemed
quite confident that Waite would win.

Racing on the first day was confined to the slower cars with engines of up
to 1,500 c.c. Poppe retired with supercharger trouble after twenty-five laps,
and Waite skidded and hit a sandbank but regained control on the wet
surface after narrowly missing another car. Victor Gillow won the race
superbly on his Riley with an average speed of 72·20 m.p.h. Waite should
have been second but, much to his own and Sir Herbert's disgust, he was
given the finishing signal when he had still one more lap to complete. He lit
a cigarette and toured round the course slowly before pulling in to the pits.
The official announcement was made over the loud-speaker system and
Waite was conducted to the Viceregal box to be congratulated formally.
After more finishers had been flagged in, another statement came from the
timekeepers' box to the effect that Waite had been brought in a lap too soon
and was actually in fifth, and not second place with an average speed of
58·89 m.p.h. The time wasted in drifting round for his final lap caused him to
slip back; had he not received the signal he would have completed the final
section more quickly and would most certainly have been in third place
provided that his final lap had been completed at the same rate as those
preceding it. A strong protest was sent to the stewards afterwards, but whilst
they regretted the incident and agreed that a mistake had been made, there
was nothing that could be done to rectify matters. Sir Herbert asked them to
credit the final lap at Waite's average speed for the rest of the race, which
would have been fair to everyone, but they refused. This upset him to such
an extent that he decided that 1930 would be the Austin team's last racing
season. This was not to be, however, because the M.G.'s did so well in 1931
that the firm had to show that their removal from the scene was not caused by
their rivals' success. Waite announced his retirement from active motor
racing to concentrate upon the management of the firm's affairs in London.
Second place on the first day went to Eyston driving an Alfa-Romeo, Frazer
Nash was third, winning the *Irish Independent* cup with an average speed of
65·94 m.p.h. Crabtree was eighth at 65·01, Barnes fourteenth at 59·74 and
Cooke sixteenth with an average of 56·27 m.p.h. Although clouded by Waite's
misfortune, the results proved once again that the Sevens were still unbeatable

in their class and a force to be contended with by all cars in the under-1,500 c.c. category.

Although Waite had declared his intention to retire from competitive motoring he took his car to Brooklands in August and won the Mountain handicap race at an average speed of 60·98 m.p.h. and came second in the Cornwall Junior Long handicap.

Entries had already been put forward to the great Ulster T.T., which took place that year on 23rd August. Sir Herbert was not at all keen to attend and when Harry Ferguson made a special trip to Longbridge in order to persuade him, he pleaded that he was far too busy to leave Birmingham. Ferguson, however, was equally determined that Austin should be there and told him that arrangements had already been made by a well-known Ulster J.P. to reserve the best cabin on a vessel for the journeys to and from Ireland. Austin was nearly beaten, but still had one more excuse. What would happen if he were delayed at the last minute and missed the boat? Ferguson was ready for him – the steamship company agreed to delay sailing until Sir Herbert arrived. There was no alternative; a telegram was sent saying that Austin and his daughter, Waite's wife, would be there.

The team was to have consisted of Duller, Waite and Frazer Nash, but Duller was unable to take part so Poppe's name was substituted. They all drove supercharged cars and the only other Seven in the race was the Lookers entry driven by Crabtree. Class H was completed by two Triumphs driven by Barnes and Horsman. To provide a more accurate means of handicapping, the system was modified for the 1930 T.T. and cars were placed in five groups to start at intervals between eleven a.m. and ten minutes past; drivers and mechanics were seated and at the signal engines were started by electric starter. As soon as each group was away, each car was credited with its handicap laps; class H cars were allowed five laps and a two minute start. Caracciola, the previous year's winner, withdrew on the eve of the race because the stewards ruled that the supercharger on his car was larger than the types fitted to the other Mercedes. It would have been possible to change it, but Caracciola refused. Thirty-six cars lined up before nearly half a million spectators, each driver ready to dash around the wet, dangerous course and to beat all previous records. In a desperate attempt to keep ahead many of the cars were being driven recklessly; Campari's Alfa was flagged in just after noon and the stewards warned the Italian against cutting in at the corners. Kaye Don, on one of the other Alfas broke a rib when his car overturned and burst into flames, and Waite and Depper crashed on the sharp bend at Ballystockart Bridge. They came around the corner at terrific speed, but before Waite could negotiate the turn his front near side mudguard caught the hedge, the car screeched across the road, Depper was thrown over the hedge into a field and escaped with a severe shaking. The car turned over three times and Waite was pulled clear suffering from concussion. When the Austin hit the hedge and came to rest in the centre of the course, Waite was lying across the road. Just then another car came along and had it not been for the prompt action of Fred Quigley, one of the spectators, Waite would no doubt have been run over. Mr. Quigley jumped off the wall, lifted the car, and in pulling Waite across the road was just missed by two of the oncoming cars. A policeman helped to lift the injured man over the hedge to safety. Sir Herbert and Mrs. Waite dashed to the scene of the accident but Waite was still unconscious and had to be taken to hospital for treatment. Shortly afterwards, Frazer Nash was forced to retire with engine trouble and was soon followed by Crabtree whose car suffered from a similar fault.

Everything now depended upon the sole remaining Austin entry. Poppe could do nothing against the Alfas which came first, second and third; an Alvis took fourth place and he was fifth at an average speed of 61·46 m.p.h. Both the Triumphs failed to complete the course.

When Waite regained consciousness in the hospital it was discovered that his jaw was fractured. This prevented him from driving for the rest of the season and at the B.A.R.C. closing meeting on 20th September S. C. H. Davis drove the little car and managed to secure second place in one event, finishing 150 yards behind an Alfa-Romeo.

Entries were now coming in for the most fantastic race of the season, the B.R.D.C. 500-miles race which was to be run at Brooklands on Saturday, 4th October. The previous year's event had been the fastest and most thrilling race ever staged on the Weybridge course, so there were high hopes for another exciting spectacle. Only those cars which could lap the track in excess of 80 m.p.h. were permitted to compete. The new Maserati, a Mercedes and Malcolm Campbell's Bugatti scratched and thirty-five cars started. There were six Austin Sevens in class H; five of them were supercharged and the remaining standard car was entered by A. Wilkinson. The Works' team consisted of three entries, one driven by Sammy Davis and the Earl of March, another by Poppe and C. Goodacre and the last by S. A. Crabtree and J. D. Barnes. Boyd-Carpenter entered one of his B-C specials and the other car was driven by W. E. Harker. These six cars started at ten-thirty in the morning in heavy rain with poor visibility and Davis in car No. 1 took the lead. One of the first thrills for the spectators was when Wilkinson's car, which was being driven by Brewster, skidded and spun round completely two or three times, narrowly missing one of the marshals who was standing just outside the timing box and looking the other way. Brewster travelled broadside on for some distance in the middle of the track but gained control and was quickly off again. After half an hour Phillips brought in the B-C Austin with a dry universal joint, trouble which persisted and caused an early retirement. It was 12.09 p.m. when the six-litre Delage and the three Bentleys joined in, but Davis was still gaining on his handicap at each lap and the Austins held the first three places. They were soon broken up when Poppe retired with a seized piston which put Crabtree in second place with an average speed of 81·64 m.p.h. over fifty-four laps. At the half-way mark Davis was still in the lead at 83·07 m.p.h. and this was only reduced to 82·91 after the car had done 400 miles. The rest of the Austins in the race began to feel the strain. Crabtree fell out with an ignition fault and Wilkinson with piston trouble after covering 300 miles at 75·09 m.p.h. By four o'clock it was evident that Davis would be the winner and he brought the car in 7 minutes 21 seconds before Benjafield's Bentley with the remarkable average speed of 83·41 m.p.h.

Unlike the other two team cars, the winner was new and racing for the first time. Waite spent three weeks preparing it for the race and acted as team manager, his calculations allowed laps at 120 seconds in order to keep ahead of the theoretical speed of his most dangerous rivals, the Bentleys, the actual time for the 500 miles worked out at 119·6 seconds per lap. On 5th October the winning car was given a full rehearsal in order to prove Waite's calculations. His work, the tuning of the car and the superb driving by Davis all contributed to the greatest of all Austin Seven successes.

On 15th October Davis and Charles Goodacre, who worked for Austin, took the car which had been prepared by a young mechanic named Len Brockhas, to Brooklands and broke thirteen international class H records:

50 km. at	83·589 m.p.h.
100 km. at	84·566 m.p.h.
200 km. at	85·076 m.p.h.
500 km. at	83·82 m.p.h.
1000 km. at	82·80 m.p.h.
50 miles at	84·35 m.p.h.
100 miles at	84·94 m.p.h.
200 miles at	82·98 m.p.h.
500 miles at	83·72 m.p.h.
1 hour at	84·83 m.p.h.
3 hours at	83·45 m.p.h.
6 hours at	83·73 m.p.h.
12 hours at	81·71 m.p.h.

Later, Davis also broke the flying start kilometre record at 89 m.p.h. and the mile at 87·7 also; from a standing start, he covered the kilometre at 62·75 and the mile at 68·44 m.p.h. The standing start mile and the standing kilometre records were beaten again by Harker on a B-C special in November at 68·58 and 63·01 m.p.h. respectively. The only class H records not broken on these occasions were the 2,000 km. and the 24-hours, which were still held by Chase, Bland and Parker, and the flying start 5 miles and 5 km., and 10 miles and 10 km. which were held – in the middle 'nineties – by a Grazide car which had been driven by Venatier at Montlhéry. George Eyston finished the year by stealing three of the middle distance records in an unsupercharged M.G. Midget, which began the struggle which was to continue between the M.G.'s and the Austins for several years to come.

In May, the first production low-chassis sports model was built, and registered OG 1845; it was to sell for £185 in standard form and £225 with a Cozette supercharger. The engine developed 33 b.h.p. at 5,000 revs which gave a theoretical maximum road speed of a little over 76 m.p.h. in top gear when using the 4·9 to 1 final drive ratio; the unsupercharged engine produced 24 b.h.p. at 5,000 revs per minute. Springs were stiffer and cord bound and the chassis was three inches lower than on the standard car. Magneto ignition and a water pump were used on the blown cars, intermediate gear ratios were 7 to 1 and 12·5 to 1, against 9 and 16 to 1 on the tourers and saloons. The motoring press obtained the prototype car in June and the general impression was that it was "an intriguing little car", the chassis was virtually the same as on the normal cars and with the same dimensions and they were surprised at the difference that a few minor changes could make. Unlike the earlier sports models there was ample space and leg room for two full-sized adults, the body was 36 in. wide and there was plenty of support from the high seat squab which was 23 in. deep. On a long run over 150 miles the 8½ cwt. car averaged 30·5 m.p.g.; road holding "astonished" everyone who had driven the car, but with the 4·9 to 1 final drive they remarked at the comparatively low top speed, the maximum achieved being a mere 76·3 m.p.h. Most of the acceleration up to fifty was obtainable in second gear, and it took 38 seconds to get from 15 to 60 m.p.h. in top and 30 seconds from 30 to 60, but in second the car accelerated from 10 to 50 in 20 seconds. Using the gears, 0 to 40 took 14 seconds and 0 to 50, 23 seconds. Braking, under the most favourable conditions, from 40 m.p.h. took up 130 ft., but then Austin Seven brakes were never more than barely adequate.

Matchless Motorcycles (Colliers) Ltd., Plumstead, London, S.E.18, added another special body to the wide range already available. This old-established firm had concentrated on motorcycle and sidecar production but towards the middle of 1930 they decided to make the new Austin Seven Hawk bodies in their sidecar factory. The fabric-panelled body was designed for the sports chassis and allowed for a narrow radiator from which a long bonnet tapered back gently to the scuttle. A mascot depicting a hawk in flight was mounted on the radiator cap. The prototype was produced in September and the cars were to cost £150.

Abroad, the Rosengart, which now employed semi-elliptic rear springs from a chassis which was extended back and over the rear axle and was supported by a cross-member, bore very little resemblance to the original Austin Seven. It was very popular and successful in France and by the middle of 1930, 11,000 had been sold. A clever advertising campaign had heralded its arrival on the scene in 1928 but initial reaction, in spite of Rosengart's personal standing in France, was of amusement rather than respect. Its failure to create an immediate interest sprang from the inherent difference between the French and British attitudes towards cars, which was summed up by an observer of the period:

"The Frenchman making a casual visit to England will tell you that the average English light car looks like a hideous square box on wheels, whilst the Englishman making a casual visit to France will tell you that the average French light car looks like a cross between a submarine and a bicycle garnished with gimp."

Before long the public began to take the newcomer seriously and within less than a year it was firmly established. The first hundred Rosengarts had been assembled from imported parts, but after that everything was made in Rosengart's Bellanger factory at Neuilly.

In Germany, Dixis were being turned out at the rate of 350 to 400 a month and nearly 14,000 had been sold altogether; the three/four-seater and the two-seater sports cost £110 and the newly introduced saloons and coupés were £125 each. The company, in an attempt to encourage buyers, began a two-year hire purchase scheme which, with monthly insurance premiums, made it possible for open cars to be bought for £4 13s. a month and closed cars for £5 7s. Unfortunately, the situation in America was not so satisfactory. Light cars were by no means new to the States; as early as 1912 no less than two dozen American firms undertook the manufacture of cycle-cars. Great things were predicted for them, and money was invested in the enterprise, but by 1915 the last cycle-car factory had failed with the loss of millions of dollars to the investors. Snobbishness, ridicule and lack of finance all added to the problems which the American Austin Car Co. had to face and, although it should have been a success in theory, the Bantam project failed miserably. As an American public relations exercise it was superb; fantastic enthusiasm grew but the only people to benefit from the project were cartoonists and just about every second-rate comedian in the business, who lived on the "baby" throughout the whole of 1930. Sir Herbert had estimated that the Butler factory would turn out 100,000 Bantams during its first year and he boarded the *Berengaria* again, to arrive in New York in time for the 1930 National Automobile Show to see the prototypes which were exhibited there.

In Britain, the press was quiet for several months until someone got hold of a rumour that 167,000 Bantams had been sold. This was disturbing news because the figure was greater than the total annual output of the entire British motor industry. It was even more disturbing to Sir Herbert, because he had to tell the annual general meeting of Austin shareholders in October that up to that time neither he nor the Company had received so much as a penny piece in royalty payments from America. Sir Herbert was still hopeful and his own words on the subject should have inspired confidence:

40. Arthur Waite,
Austin and Alf Depper
at the 1930 Double
Twelve

41. A beautifully
restored 1930 Dixi
sports model

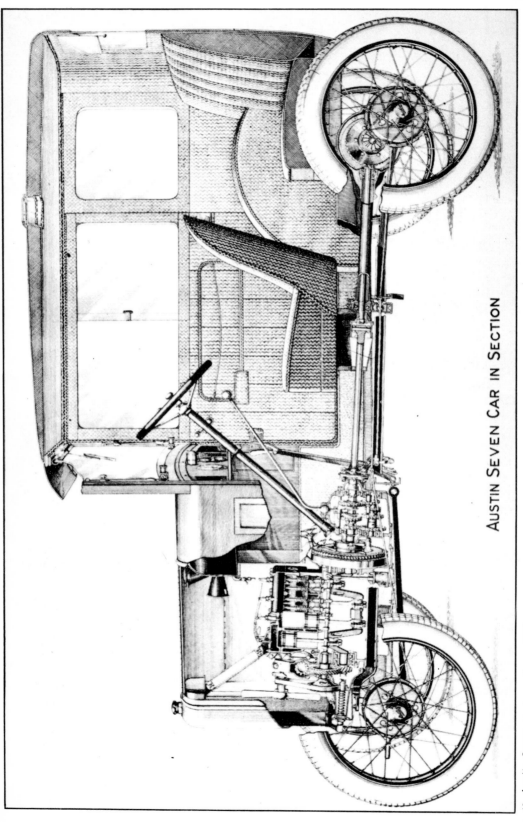

AUSTIN SEVEN CAR IN SECTION

42. Austin Seven car in section – 1930

"The factory has been turning out two hundred cars a day. Fresh capital has now been found and plans are in hand to increase the output to a figure of five hundred cars a day. Production started only in May this year, but by December over 50,000 Austin Bantams will have been sold in America."

To clarify matters he obtained a definite statement from the American company to the effect that they had orders on hand for 184,117 cars as at 30th June. Results speak better than promises, and the promise of 50,000 resulted in a mere 8,558 cars. Imaginations were fired by the supposed demand that was promised for the little car, and it was rumoured that another English car, the Riley, was also to be built in America. In September, Durant, a prominent man over there in the motor industry, formed the American Mathis Inc. to manufacture the small French Mathis car. His prospectus stated that the company required $m3 for its immediate needs and that 50,000 cars – the magical figure again – a year would be produced and that sales would commence at the end of the year. With the exception of M. Mathis, the board of directors was made up almost entirely of wealthy American industrialists. This project failed as dismally as did the American Austin Car Co.

Another project of passing interest, in which there was very little reward, concerns the Military Sevens. When the War Department decided to investigate the possibility of extending the mechanisation of the Army in 1927 the Experimental Armoured Force was formed, to gain experience with the vehicles which had been developed since the war. Two or three Austin Sevens were bought and fitted with two-seater bodies by Gordon England. These trials proved highly successful so the Experimental Force was disbanded in 1929 and two new formations, converted from infantry brigades, were assembled, one in Southern Command and the other in Aldershot District. The two-seater Scouts were particularly well suited for cavalry scouting, so it was decided to equip each cavalry regiment of the 1st and 2nd Cavalry Brigades with troops of eleven Austin Sevens. Motor-cycles and sidecars had been used previously in reconnaissance work. Tests were carried out on a number of cars but the Austin was chosen after trials over open country around Aldershot, the last of which hurtled the car over an embankment and on to rough ground twelve feet below. Unfortunately, it came to rest upside-down but the engine was still running. In March, 1929 the Army asked Austin's to supply a hundred chassis as soon as possible, the original intention being to build two-seater bodies for them in Army workshops. This presented too many problems, so the work was carried out by Mulliner of Birmingham. Altogether, they produced 118 in 1929 and 40 more during the following year. As the cars were expected to cover all types of country, the rear axle ratios were lowered slightly and stronger springs were fitted. To

8

extricate the cars should they become bogged down, towing hooks were provided for the front axles and, later, bobbins on each wheel hub for attaching tow ropes. On the first cars the tool kits included clips for clamping on to the hubs so that the cars could be lifted bodily on to firm ground if the terrain became too soft. Subsequently, military saloons and two-seaters were built completely at Longbridge between 1932 and 1937.

1931

The £100 Car at Last

Just prior to the 1930 Motor Show a rumour appeared in one of the daily newspapers that Austin was to produce the long-awaited car that would sell for £100. This was hotly denied by Sir Herbert who wrote immediately to the press declaring that publicity of this nature was damaging to the industry which was busy enough trying to sell its cars at the current prices, without people being encouraged to hope for decreases. This caused potential customers to delay their purchases in the hope that something cheaper would be available later on. Morris kept silent for a while, then just before Christmas and much to everyone's surprise, he disclosed that he would soon be producing an economy two-seater Morris Minor with a side-valve engine which would cost £100 – £22 10s. less than the equivalent Austin. In spite of his earlier denial, Sir Herbert had been working on a cheap two-seater but he could not produce it for less than about £110, and then it was to have been given a fabric body. There was no hope of this being able to compete with the new Morris and the day of the "rag" body, as Sir Herbert had foreseen, was drawing to a close. Demand for the Mulliner and the standard fabric saloons had declined rapidly during the latter part of 1930 and only some 1,200 were sold during 1931 against nearly 11,000 in the year of peak fabric popularity in 1929. Sir Herbert, very wisely, decided not to attempt to attack Morris by introducing a new and cheaper model, but to reduce Austin Seven prices and to give the car the same appeal as those in the 10 h.p. range, a group which was becoming increasingly popular. In fact, Morris was taking a risk. Tourers were almost as unpopular as fabric bodies; saloons were accounting for an increasingly large share of the market and even though the long-awaited £100 car was now a reality, how many people would be prepared to accept it in open two-seater form? Sir Herbert had a more logical answer with his de luxe saloon.

Under Ramsay MacDonald the country continued to decline. Unemployment rose to the horrifying level of 2,700,000, exports had decreased, public expenditure rose, £m130 had to be borrowed from abroad and in October, 1931 the Prime Minister obtained the King's assent to dissolve parliament. The Socialists lost 213 of the 265 seats which they held at the dissolution, but the state of the country was beyond party politics and a National Coalition strove to solve the financial problems before reverting to the party system again. In spite of all this, Austin sold 21,282 Austin Sevens, the firm's total output increased and the Ordinary shareholders were given a 100 per cent dividend. More than half the new registrations in the 8 h.p. taxation class throughout the year were accounted for by new Austin Sevens. The £100 Minor had not made its mark, in spite of the fact that it was, in many ways, a better car than the Austin.

Encouraged by the defeat of the government, by President Hoover's decision to waive War Loan debts until we could afford to pay them, and by the continued demand for cars, the Company decreased prices with effect from 2nd September. The chassis remained at £94 10s. and the tourer, two-seater and saloon were all reduced to £118; the two-seater did not, of course, have much chance of success against the Morris or against its own self-made rivals and only 559 were made during the year. The saloons proved the most popular and sold in the greatest quantity. Sir Herbert saw that he would have to make the Seven into a real four-seater to give it wider appeal and the new 1932 de luxe saloon was introduced in October, 1931 at £128. The chassis was six inches longer than on the standard cars, giving a wheel base of 6 ft. 9 in. against the normal 6 ft. 3 in. This made it possible to use a new body which was made both wider and longer, overall dimensions being 9 ft. 8 in. × 4 ft. 5 in.; the chassis frame was extended and splayed out over the rear axle to take the extra weight and the rear axle was lengthened to increase the rear track from 3 ft. 4 in. to 3 ft. 7 in. In fact, the body was only two inches wider. The size and location of the front seats were not altered but the rear seat was improved; the wells on each side of the propeller shaft were extended under the front seats and there was more knee room than before. Doors were 53 in. across and the back edges were not curved and no longer overlapped the wheel arches which provided easier access to the rear compartment. Total weight was increased to 10¾ cwt. so the rear axle was lowered to give gear ratios of 5·25, 9·65 and 17·1 to 1 and it took 37 seconds to accelerate from a standstill to 40 m.p.h. The car was upholstered in leather; new wings, a sunshine roof, louvres in the bonnet sides and Magna wheels with chromium-plated centres were standard equipment. A 5 cwt. van body was also introduced using the new chassis. The first four de luxe cars, known as RN saloons, were completed on 7th October and given car numbers B4-5441, 5127, 5281 and 5378. (About 13,000 of them were made from October, 1931 to September, 1932.) A number of other minor alterations were introduced during the year, the most noticeable being the Lucas-

Graves double filament dipping lamps controlled by a switch mounted on the steering column just below the wheel; this was first applied to car number B4-4206 in September.

Sports models were still available but were sold only in very small numbers, which seems surprising; the only serious competitor was the M.G. Montlhéry, but this was twice the price of the Austin. At £185 for the standard and £225 for the supercharged car the Ulster, a name which it had earned with every justification and which was first given to the model in August, 1931, represented outstanding value for money. During the year

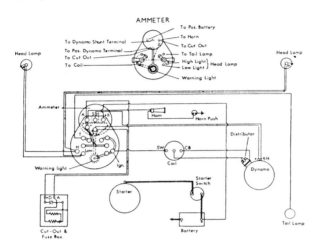

Fig. 24. 1931 wiring diagram.

one or two minor alterations were made: cast-iron clutch linings were fitted and a new close ratio gearbox which gave 5·2, 7·5 and 13·5 to 1 ratios.

Abroad, the Dixi was still popular – 5,501 had been sold in 1930 and B.M.W. state that total pre-war Dixi and B.M.W. Ausin Seven production totalled 25,356 – the Bantam had failed and the Rosengart company were making a six-cylinder engine based on the Austin Seven design. At home there was one interesting development when Brough, the motor-cycle manufacturer, asked Sir Herbert to design an Austin engine for him to use in his new Brough Superior machine. This was an Austin Seven water-cooled engine and gearbox unit with twin radiators and an aluminium cylinder head, shaft driven to a crown wheel and pinion between two rear wheels. It was not intended for solo use and, had it been successful, would have proved an excellent machine, but unfortunately it was far too expensive. The first left Brough's Works on 24th February 1932 and the last on 30th July 1934, probably no more than ten having been built.

Only 752 chassis went to special body builders in 1931. There was another attempt to introduce a Seven taxi, this time by Voss Motors of Liverpool; a body was built but after inspecting the vehicle the Hackney Carriage Subcommittee of the Liverpool Watch Committee found that it was not suitable for hiring in the streets of the city. Another new body made its first appearance in February in the form of an ugly two-seater coupé with a sliding roof made by T. & D. Motors Ltd., 29 Fairfax Place, N.W.6, with large deep doors trailing down to hang well below the chassis. The effect of depth on the severe, squarely cut body was accentuated even more by the lack of running boards and the use of very narrow wings. It was priced at £193 10s. Production of the Matchless Hawk continued at £150 and Compton's of Hanwell offered a pleasant two-seater known as the Spear at £160 with aluminium decking behind the seats on an attractive pointed tail. This same firm still listed the Arrow two-seater at £145 and the Arrow coupé at £155. Normand Garages listed the highly tuned and modified B.C. Special which sold for £192 10s. and a new semi-sports B.C. Junior at £125. There was also the Hawk fabric two-seater with cycle-type wings made by Herwin, Canny and Co., of Woolwich at £150, the Hoyal two-seater from Weybridge at £140, three models by Mulliner of Birmingham, the sports two-seater at £140, fabric coupé at £155 and a fabric saloon priced at £150. Coventry-built Swallows on the sports chassis included a two-seater at £165, a two-seater coupé at £175 and the saloon at £187 10s. 1931 saloons had an improved rear compartment and a new Vee-type radiator cowl.

When Campbell sailed for Daytona early in January, not only did he take the Napier Bluebird, but also Brockhas and the supercharged Austin Seven. The car had been completed as a single-seater racer in April, 1930 and had broken the mile and kilometre records on 22nd October. Waite hoped that this would be the first 750 c.c. car to reach 100 m.p.h. Campbell, who had never driven an Austin Seven before, was very keen to see what it could do on a track like Daytona Beach and also to be the first man to exceed the magic figure in a light car over the two shorter distances. If he were successful in this and in breaking the world's speed record he would be proving that British cars led the world, whether they were giants or midgets. In its first trial the Austin achieved a maximum of 88 m.p.h., but on 5th February immediately after taking the world record on Bluebird at more than 245 m.p.h., he had a disappointing run on the Austin with an average speed of only 81·09 for the mile. On the following day, however, Campbell averaged 94·061, clocking 94·069 on his first run and 93·994 on the second. For the kilometre the speed was 93·962 m.p.h. The battle to be the first to do a hundred in a 750 c.c. car was on. On 10th February, Eyston captured the five kilometres with J. M. Palmes' M.G. Midget at Montlhéry at 97·07 m.p.h. and although he was faster for the shorter distances his effort did not constitute a record because it was necessary for a run to be made in each direction to capture the class H records. Eyston raced the M.G. again three days later and took the four, five and ten miles and the equivalent kilometre class H records at between 101 and 103·13 m.p.h., gaining the honour of being the first man to cover a measured distance at more than a hundred miles an hour in a 750 c.c. car. Eyston went all out to beat Campbell's remaining records and managed to do so in March with 97·09 m.p.h. for the kilometre and 96·93 m.p.h. for the mile.

Just after the introduction of the new "Montlhéry" M.G. Midget, Waite and Cecil Kimber, the man behind the M.G. concern, met in an hotel in Oxfordshire. Kimber agreed that the Austin Seven had not been opposed in the past but that now the fight was on. "We are now at war," he said. "We hope it will be a friendly war, but it will certainly be war." Waite replied: "I accept the challenge. My firm will fight. We will meet you on the racing track and in road races, and may the best man win." When he announced the new streamlined single-seater which he had been designing with Sir Herbert, he added: "We are not going to let our sporting challengers rest on their laurels." Models of a number of special prototypes were taken to be tested in the Vickers' wind tunnel during development. The engine was substantially the same as the Sports unit, but fitted with an Austin-built supercharger which increased the b.h.p. to 56 at 6,000 revs per minute. In the previous year it had been decided that the orange racing cars would be faster if they could be made lower with the resultant reduction in the frontal resistance and side area. Firstly, the driving seat had to be lowered which meant setting the engine, gearbox and propeller shaft at an angle across the chassis. The rear-axle differential casing was placed right over on the near side and the rear axle bevels had to be machined to compensate for this so that the universal joints on the drive shaft would not have to work at a peculiar angle; it was then possible to sink the seat down so that its rear end rested upon the rear chassis cross member. The body was made of sufficient width to accommodate the driver, with a section of streamlining down the tail directly behind the driver's head. Two separate streamlined casings were used, one to cover the front axle and the other for the rear part of the chassis. Wind tunnel tests resulted in long fairings being placed from wheel to wheel on each side of the car with a small tail behind each rear wheel. These modifications allowed the bottom of the driver's seat to be within 3½ in. of the ground. With regard to the remainder of the car, the old principle of retaining as much of the original specification as possible applied. The engine was the standard sports unit but with a mechanical fuel pump working from the camshaft. More noticeable was the new position for the supercharger which was mounted vertically on the offside and at the front of the engine driven by bevels from the water pump drive shaft.

Originally it was hoped that Sir Malcolm Campbell, who had just been knighted, would drive the car at Brooklands on Easter Monday, but he was not particularly keen to do so and it was finally decided that Sammy Davis would become Austin's number one driver. Unfortunately, the Invicta which he drove at Brooklands at the Easter meeting on 6th April overturned during the Mountain handicap; he was pinned under the car and broke his leg. The race was won easily by Elves' Austin Seven with an M.G. in second place. Davis' unfortunate accident caused the plans to be changed again and when Waite was interviewed by the press shortly afterwards he said:

"Davis – who will not be able to drive for some time – is as keen as I am that we should find somebody to take his place, and already I am considering two or three likely people. Plans for our attack on class H records are definitely going ahead and it is possible that the car will go all out in the course of the next few weeks. I am, of course, optimistic but I prefer not to say anything else at the moment. We are quite satisfied with the behaviour of the vehicle – although it stalled on the line in the Easter meeting.

As a matter of fact, rather than disappoint the public – many of whom were largely looking forward to seeing the potential record-breaker – I instructed Gunnar Poppe to take it over. Poppe had previously never even sat in the car and it is probable that before he was accustomed to the controls he incautiously let the revs drop and sooted-up a plug. That was the only trouble.

Davis had, of course, made a number of trial runs in the new Baby at Brooklands prior to the Easter meeting, and without giving anything away I think I can say that its performance exceeded his expectations."

Poppe had only managed to tour around the track in the vivid yellow car, which gained for itself the nickname "Yellow Canary" from the crowd. Leon Cushman, who owned the Invicta in which Davis crashed, was one of the drivers on Waite's list, but Campbell offered to drive the car in any record-breaking attempts whilst Davis was still unable to take the wheel himself. Other Austins did well at the Easter meeting. A B-C special driven by E. Philips won the Junior handicap at 78·96 m.p.h., but the main consolation came in the last race of the day, the Second Mountain handicap, in which Austin Sevens driven by Vernon Balls, Randell and Searle took the first three places.

Before any more time could be spent on record-breaking something had to be done about the J.C.C. Double-Twelve which was to be run at Brooklands on 8th and 9th May. No less than nine Austins and fourteen M.G. Midgets had entered, the Austin Works' team consisting of Frazer Nash and L. P. Drisoll, Poppe and J. D. Barnes, and F. S. Barnes and W. H. Green. Another team of three Austins was led by Miss V. Worsley in competition with another lady, the Hon. Mrs. A. Chetwynd who was to drive an M.G. The race, the first in which the M.G.'s had been out in force against the Austins, developed into a struggle between the two makes. The supercharged Austins were at a

Views of a saloon made in mid–1930

44. 1930–31 two-seater

45. Leon Cushman
and L. P. Driscoll
with one of the 1931
500 miles racing cars
at Brooklands after
having taken six
class H Inter-
national records in
October, 1931

46. The stern look
of defeat. Gunnar
Poppe and J. D.
Barnes after losing
the 1931 Double-
Twelve hours race
to the M.G. s. How-
ever, the car covered
1,637 miles at an
average speed of
68·24 m.p.h.

47. Rear view of a 1931 Ulster

48. A sporting front axle

49. Malcolm Campbell breaking records in an Austin Seven at Daytona Beach in January, 1931

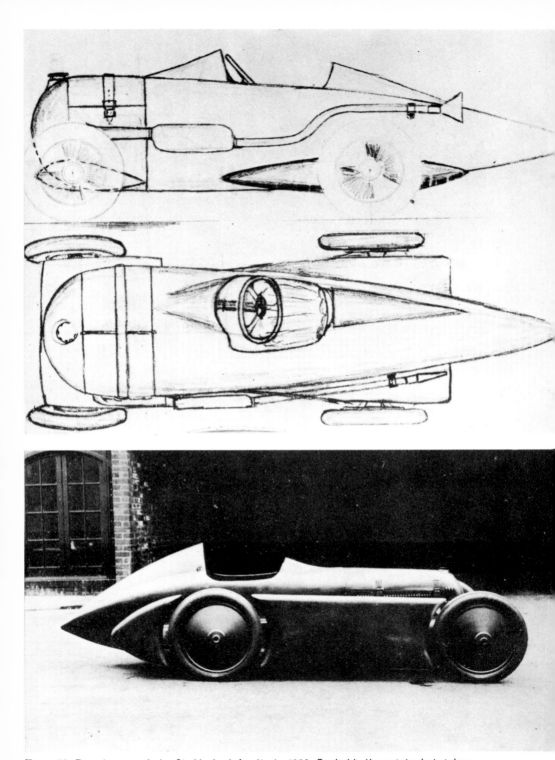

Top – 50. Drawings made by Sir Herbert Austin in 1930. Probably the original sketches which he made for the 1931 supercharged Works' racer

Above – 51. The 1931 supercharged car

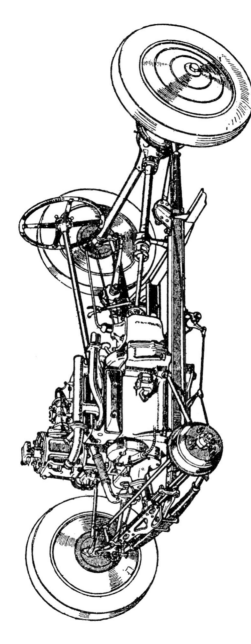

Fig. 25.   Layout of the Works' racer.

disadvantage to their unblown rivals on handicap, but Kimber's car proved too much for them. The ultimate result was as encouraging for the new marque as it was disastrous for the Austins, for they managed to take the first five places with average speeds which varied from the Earl of March's 65·62 m.p.h. to 62·46. Miss Worsley brought the first Austin in to tie with another Austin in seventh place at an average speed of 59·92, so on equal terms the M.G.'s won the day. The supercharged Works' team all finished, Poppe in ninth place at 68·24 having completed the fastest lap in the class at 72·44, Barnes eleventh at 65·59 and Frazer Nash twenty-first at 58·33 m.p.h. As far as reliability was concerned only one of the ten Austins was forced to retire but only seven of the M.G.'s were still running after twenty-four hours; six of the failures were due to engine trouble. Speedy teamwork got Frazer Nash out of trouble. Late on the first night the Austin cracked a cylinder head; Waite telephoned to Sir Herbert at home and he went down to the factory to supervise personally the dispatch by road of a new cylinder block and head. It arrived at Weybridge at seven the next morning and was fitted in time for the car to continue on the second day. This very important race had proved that the unsupercharged Austins had more than met their match and that the heavily penalised supercharged cars were unable to beat their new rivals.

Even stiffer opposition was planned for the Irish Grand Prix on 5th and 6th June. Six Austins, three of which were private entries and the others the Works' team, consisting of Frazer Nash, Leon Cushman and J. D. Barnes, competed against no less than ten unsupercharged Midgets. During practice one of the M.G.'s lapped at 65·5 m.p.h. against the best Austin speed of 65·80, which was certainly not going to be good enough to overcome the handicap which made it necessary for the Austins to cover fifty-seven against the M.G.'s fifty-one laps. Could the Austins gain a lap lead in each eight and a half laps – this was what was necessary to beat the M.G.'s. Everything was against them, and they failed; the M.G.'s swept all competition aside winning at 64·76 m.p.h. and also taking second, third, sixth, seventh, tenth, twelfth and thirteenth places which proved that they were consistent and reliable. Frazer Nash brought the first Austin home in eighth place at 69·61 and Cushman was fourteenth at 66·03 m.p.h. Although the Austins were slightly faster they were far too slow in comparison with the unsupercharged Midgets.

After these outstanding successes Kimber decided to fit superchargers; in theory supercharged M.G.'s on equal terms with the Austins would gain even greater supremacy. No less than twenty-two teams drove in the Light Car Club's Ninety-lap Relay race for which a special trophy was awarded by the confident M.G. Company. Each team consisted of three cars and those entered by the Austin Company were driven by Cushman, J. D. Barnes and Goodacre. There were three other all-Austin groups and four M.G. Midget teams. Over this 250-odd miles race the Austins had their revenge and came into their own; the Works' cars won with an average speed of 81·77 m.p.h. and won the M.G. trophy, and third place was taken by one of the un-supercharged Austin teams. The best team of supercharged Midgets completed the course at only 75·18 m.p.h. although the fastest M.G. lap was 92·23 against Cushman's best Austin round of 89·74.

Cushman took the streamlined special to Brooklands again in May. He participated in the second and third races but the car failed with a broken valve spring. Randall's Double-Twelve car, incidentally, won the Mountain Speed race at 53·6 m.p.h. with Vernon Ball's supercharged car third. Cushman was now established as the Austin record-breaking driver and tested the car again at Brooklands during the August Bank Holiday; he finished second in two of the races, lapping at 99 m.p.h.

Austin's great day came on 8th August, a wet and windy day at Brooklands, when Cushman became the first man in the world to exceed a hundred miles an hour in a class H record in this country and the first to better the magic figure over the shorter distances. The speeds were 102·28 m.p.h. for the flying kilometre, 100·67 for the flying mile, 65·01 for the standing kilometre and 74·12 for the standing mile. Shortly afterwards, Viscount Ridley turned up at Brooklands with his own little car, which he had designed and built himself, and a spare sparking plug to beat Cushman's records by a few miles an hour.

Within twenty-four hours, George Eyston decided to build a new single-seater M.G. In the meantime he busied himself breaking 1,100 c.c. records with a Riley, so Mrs. Gwenda Stewart took the record-breaking Austin, which now had a modified radiator in an attempt to cure the overheating which had been experienced earlier, to Montlhéry where on 8th September she took four of the International class H records: the five kilometres at 109·128 m.p.h. the five miles at 109·06, the ten kilometres at 109·05 and the ten miles at 108·95 m.p.h. A week later she went to Montlhéry again, primarily to gain data for the building of three similar cars for the 500-miles race, and although the car had trouble with its crankshaft she managed to cover 50 kilometres at 98·09 m.p.h. and 50 miles at 98·43 m.p.h. The information which she brought back led to the fuel tanks being moved under the scuttles and a foot or more being taken off the pointed tails to give more stability in high winds. Now it was Eyston's turn again. His new M.G. took the speeds even higher but, unfortunately, a connecting rod broke and the car caught fire and crashed. Eyston was severely burned and also broke his shoulder blade after having covered a hundred miles in less than sixty minutes. E. A. Eldridge took another M.G. to Montlhéry and his fastest run was made over the five kilometres distance at 110·28 m.p.h.

Austin's supremacy over the M.G. supercharged team was shortlived. They met again at the Ulster T.T. on 22nd August, thirteen M.G.'s against five Austins, in which it was established that the overhead camshaft cars were faster than the best side-valve Sevens. M.G.'s were first, at 67·9 m.p.h., third and seventh, and Cushman could do no better than gain ninth place at an average speed of 65·99 m.p.h. Light cars had been doing so well in racing events that the B.R.D.C. decided to penalise the supercharged 750 c.c. cars heavily for their famous 500-miles race. To have equal chances of winning these cars would have had to average 93·97 m.p.h. supercharged and 87·38 in standard form. Against this, the best Austin was only able to average 83·42 in 1930. The three new orange single-seater racers* driven by L. P. Driscoll, J. D. Barnes and Goodacre joined Cushman's record-breaking car for the Works' entry and they were to struggle with no less than twelve Midgets. As might have been expected, a light car could do no better than gain third place; this was by Hall's M.G. at the phenomenal average speed of 92·17 m.p.h. Another M.G. came third, but of the seventeen baby cars competing only three finished. Austins were not amongst them; every one of the Works' racers broke down with radiator trouble. These cooling problems were soon overcome and in October, Cushman and Driscoll took six more International class H records at Brooklands: the 200 kilometres at 90·73 m.p.h., 200 miles at 90·78, three hours at 90·38, 500 kilometres at 89·61, 500 miles at 90·11 and the six hours at an average speed of 90·12 m.p.h. On this same day Lord Ridley, the other contender for class H laurels, crashed his car at Brooklands. He was seriously injured and the car was very badly damaged.

* Four or five racers are said to have taken part in the event.

1932

Four-speed Gearbox, No Speed Racing

"Although the past few years have been a period of unparalleled difficulties for British trade and have called for tremendous efforts and sacrifices from all sections of the public, there have been definite signs that the corner is turned, and we can look forward to the future with renewed hope and determination."

Sir Herbert Austin, 18th April, 1932.

At last the Ford Company were convinced that Europe's demand for a light economy car was a reality, and early in 1932 they introduced their new 950 c.c., 8 h.p. saloon built at the newly completed Dagenham factory. Prototypes were shown at a special exhibition at the Albert Hall on 19th February and were surprisingly similar in outside appearance to the new de luxe Austin Seven. This was still the lowest-priced saloon at £118, and it was evident that something of outstanding quality and appeal was needed to attract people away from the excellent products already available in the 7 and 8 h.p. range. Nothing more was heard of the new Ford for some months and it was not until August that the Ford 8 Tudor saloon, scarcely resembling the prototypes at all, was offered for sale. It was given more sweeping lines and used a synchro-mesh gearbox, something entirely new for a small car, and transverse front and rear springs. The four-door saloon was to cost £135 and the two-door version £120. Ford's entry into the light-car war was delayed partly due to the need for a new factory and partly because the Americans still failed to believe in the cheap, economy car. In the States, the American Austin Car Company produced 8,558 cars in 1930 and only 1,279 in 1931, and although the figure rose to 3,846 in 1932 there was certainly nothing to show that people in America wanted to buy small cars. There was much talk at the time of orders being placed for thousands more Bantams but even if the American company had been able to make them it is unlikely that they would have been bought.

125

In England it had been proved conclusively year after year that the bulk of sales were in the 8 h.p. category; in the first nine months of 1932 there were 31,702 registrations in the group, of which more than half came from Longbridge. Final figures for the previous year, however, showed a marked tendency towards an increase in demand for 10 h.p. cars, and for the first time the new registrations of 10's were higher than for the 7's. Austin saw this and was ready with the four-door Austin Ten saloon which was announced in April at £168. During the year, 20,121 Sevens were made, less than in the previous year in spite of the fact that there was a 30 per cent increase in total Austin production. Demand for the Austin Seven remained

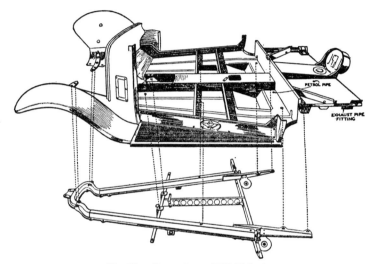

Fig. 26.   Removing a 1932-33 body.

at this level for the next five years in spite of the increasing demand for the larger four-door saloons and the high rate of production of the Ford 8 at Dagenham. Austin total production continued to rise rapidly until the ruinous period just before the outbreak of the war.

Three-quarters of the Sevens produced in 1932 were saloons, special body builders took only 620 chassis, there were a few hundred two-seaters, some vans, but only 1,062 tourers. The greatest demand was for the new de luxe saloon which represented better value for money than almost any other British car. There were seven Austin models ranging from 7 to 20 h.p., yet in 1932 one in every four Austins made was a Seven de luxe saloon. Part of the added competition presented by the new Ford was offset by the increase in demand for the Austin Ten but, even so, the Seven had to be modified to keep up to date and it had to be reduced in price. After October the chassis cost £85, the two-seater was £105, the tourer £110, the standard saloon £115 and the de luxe £125. 1933 models were first built in September and the first car with new features was B6-2938, chassis number 159,534. Most important of the changes was the new four-speed twin-top gearbox giving drive ration of 5·25, 9·05, 14·4 and 23·3 to 1, which incorporated double helical teeth for the constant mesh and third gear clusters. Another transmission alteration, for ease of maintenance, consisted of an improved clutch withdrawal mechanism which could be lubricated with less difficulty. There was also a new "thermal-flow" combined inlet and exhaust manifold casting with a

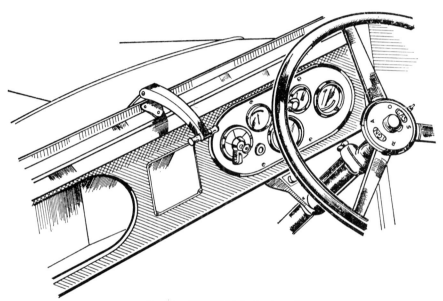

Fig. 27.   The 1932 interior layout.

more effective hot-spot, a horizontal Zenith carburettor was used in place of the vertical type, and a rear mounted five gallon petrol tank from which fuel was pumped to the carburettor bowl by an A.C. mechanical pump driven from the camshaft. An electric petrol gauge was mounted on the dash. The electric starter motor was transferred to a new position on the offside of the engine, instead of on the clutch housing where it used to protrude into the inside of the body – where it gave rather a mechanical look to the interior; the starter switch was mounted on the motor itself with a remote control knob on the steering column bracket. In order to accommodate the four-speed box the engine was moved forward in the chassis frame approximately one inch, the fan spindle was lengthened, the exhaust pipe altered and the starting handle bracket modified; the radiator was moved and a new plated quick release spring-type cap employed. There were wide brake drums front and rear with improved controls. The new instrument panel had a moving figure speedometer, ignition lock and warning light and dash lamp, there were also new controls on the top of the steering column. Standard coachwork colours for the tourer and the two-seater were Royal Blue, Opal Blue and Maroon, the saloons light Royal Blue and light Maroon with light Auto Brown, and Opal Blue or Fawn with black tops for the de luxe saloons. Tests on the new model saloon which weighed 10 cwt., 2 qr. showed that it pulled up from 30 m.p.h. in 42 ft., could cover a quarter-mile

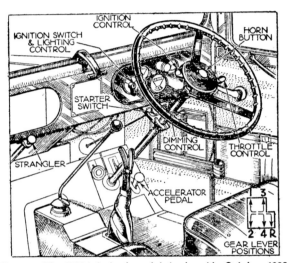

Fig. 28.   The 1933 interior layout, introduced in October, 1932.

at 48·91 m.p.h., and took 10⅘ seconds to accelerate from 10 to 30 m.p.h. in third gear, 19 seconds in top, and 28 seconds from 20 to 40 m.p.h. in top gear.

1932 was not a particularly exciting or successful year for Austin in either racing or record-breaking. As soon as Eyston had recovered from the injuries sustained in his crash, he went to Montlhéry with the single-seater supercharged Midget in an attempt to beat the records which Mrs. Gwenda Stewart had set up in 1931. He managed to cover the five miles at an average speed of 114·74 m.p.h. Determined not to be burned again, he clothed himself in an asbestos suit and even went to the extent of wearing hand-knitted asbestos socks, and took the M.G. to Pendine Sands in February in an attempt to exceed 120 m.p.h. He covered the flying mile at 118·38. At the Brooklands opening B.A.R.C. meeting on 28th March Driscoll, driving one of the Works' cars, won the first race at an average of 95·97 and set up a new 750 c.c. lap record at 102·48 m.p.h. He increased it again in the seventh

Top – 54. The long wheelbase saloon, a 1932–33 saloon de-luxe which was first
introduced in October, 1931 with black lamps and no trafficators
Above – 55. 1933–34 Sports 65 – the Nippy

race to 103·11, but the M.G.'s had the last word at Whitsun when Eyston lapped at 112 m.p.h. The 750 c.c. class for the B.R.D.C. British Empire Trophy race on 30th April consisted of two supercharged Midgets and one of the supercharged Austins, driven by the Earl of March. He was the fastest of the three, completing the course at over 92 m.p.h. Barnes and Goodacre used the other two racers in the German International race for cars of up to 1,500 c.c. in which Barnes drove over the course of 121 miles at 87·31 m.p.h. to finish second. Goodacre finished in fourth position.

On 16th July there was a repeat of the popular L.C.C. Relay race which Waite's team had won in 1931 with an average speed of 81·77 m.p.h. For this event, however, they were up against the new Morgans for the first time and also more severely handicapped than usual, and in spite of the fact that the three Austins averaged 91·13 m.p.h. over the 248 miles, they only managed to gain fourth place. The three-wheeler Morgans were lapping at just under a hundred but failed to stay the course and the Eustace Watkins' Wolseley Hornet specials won at 77·51 m.p.h. J. D. Barnes, Driscoll and George Duller drove the three supercharged Austins in the B.R.D.C. 500-miles race on 24th September and finished at speeds in the upper eighties, but a privately entered M.G. won.

Everyone was surprised at Austin's decision not to enter a team for the Ulster T.T.; the official reason for not taking part was based solely on the fact that they were too busy because of "the demands of the various Departments". Sir Herbert said:

"We are very busy with our different cars for various markets, and we find that we cannot this year devote the time which is necessary to carrying out research and other work to provide the cars for the T.T. race. We have, as you know, established a high standard for our baby cars in the Ulster race, and it is either a case of improving on that standard or not competing at all. It is simply stress of work that has prevented us from preparing for the race."

This statement and the decision which followed it, not to enter the 1,000-miles race which had been organised by the J.C.C. to replace the Double-Twelve, was really an admission of the inability to increase the performance of the side-valve engines to compete against the Midgets. This was overcome, as we shall see, with the help of T. Murray Jamieson who worked with the Company from 1933 until shortly before his tragic death in 1938.

1933

No Changes—Prices Up

The motor industry continued to be successful, and was to go on increasing in prosperity throughout the 1930's until the next major set-backi n 1937. Austin produced over 60,000 of the combined output of the industry which amounted to some 180,000 in 1933, and although the 10 h.p. range provided the greatest proportion of the total new registrations, 20,475 Austin Sevens were made. More than half this total – 11,837 – were the popular de luxe saloons.

In June a new model, the "65" sports, was introduced at £148; this new sports car proved quite popular and no less than 234 were sold in the first six months of production. The car was a low-slung two-seater, the driver's seat being only about fourteen inches from the ground; the radiator was lower and squarer than on the standard cars and was protected by a chromium-plated stone guard. Apart from the engine, the chief chassis modification was made to the suspension in order to lower the centre of gravity. At the front, the axle beam was bowed and the cord-bound transverse front spring was curved very slightly; this lowered the axle considerably. At the back, the quarter elliptic rear springs were anchored below the axle instead of above. With regard to the engine, which developed 23 b.h.p. at 4,800 revs per minute against the standard 12 at 2,600, the most obvious change was in the use of a down-draught Zenith carburettor in conjunction with a new inlet manifold. A new material, chromidium, which gave a longer life than ordinary cast iron was employed for the cylinder block and head casting, and in the head the combustion chambers were smaller and concentrated over the valves. In addition, the sparking plugs were placed over the valves instead of above the cylinder bores. There was a high lift camshaft and double valve springs and the valve heads were given a square hole in place of the normal screwdriver slot. Crankshafts were machined all over with modified lubrication passages and the big end bearings had a diameter of $1\frac{1}{2}$ in. instead of the normal

$1\frac{5}{16}$ in.; the shaft was both statically and dynamically balanced. Connecting rods were machined and there were fully floating gudgeon pins with aluminium end pads; the sump was much larger, its capacity being one gallon, and ribs were cast in the base to assist in cooling the oil. Final drive ratio was 5·6 to 1 and a close ratio gearbox gave intermediate gears of 8·6, 13·7 and 19·6 to 1. There was a Bluemel spring-spoked steering wheel and a Burgess silencer.

Very few alterations were introduced during 1933. In January and from engine number 168,230 the outside diameter of the camshaft rear bearing was increased, and from chassis number 167,588 the petrol pipe unions and joints were changed to prevent leaking. To provide greater strength, the lower end of the gear lever was increased in diameter from chassis number 175,450 in May, and a Hardy Spicer rear universal joint was fitted first to chassis number 176,687 in the following month, but the fabric coupling at the front end of the shaft remained unaltered. Only one major introduction was made for the 1934 season. Gearboxes had changed very little since the earliest days of motoring and it was still very difficult to master gear changing; the only way to accomplish it silently was by the double declutching method, an art which most people never mastered. Other manufacturers were using either the Wilson pre-selector box or the new synchro-mesh system which employed friction cones to slow down the speed of the gear wheels relative to each other prior to selection. The latter was foolproof and cheap to produce, and although Sir Herbert was experimenting at great cost with the novel Hayes infinitely variable transmission, it was only developed for the Austin Sixteen and Eighteen, and all the other models in 1933 were fitted with synchro-mesh on third and top gears. On the Seven, this took place in August from chassis number 179,368, and the majority of the components were designed to fit both the Seven and the Ten gearboxes. At the same time improved dip and switch lamps, a stop-tail lamp and direction indicators also appeared and later, at chassis number 180,000, an aluminium steering box replaced the steel type and was fixed to the frame by bolts instead of set screws. De luxe saloons had a sun visor and a fabric cover over the spare wheel. At first glance, the outward appearance of the de luxe saloon remained scracely distinguishable from that of the first long-wheel-base car which first appeared in October, 1931.

Sir Herbert had been hinting that he would probably have to raise prices to meet the increased costs of raw materials which had risen between 5 and 15 per cent over the preceding twelve months. Ford's cheapest Tudor saloon was priced at £120, Singers put their prices up, and even Morris no longer had a hundred pound car – the cheapest in his range was the two-seater Minor at £110. In mid-August, Sir Herbert decided to keep the two-seater at a hundred guineas but to add between £2 and £4 to the other models. The de luxe saloon was now £128, the saloon £118, the tourer £112 10s., the "65" sports £152, the 5 cwt. van £112 10s. and the chassis £87 10s.

Special body builders were never again as active as they had been in the late 'twenties, but one or two were still producing special coachwork in very small quantities in 1933. A. E. Wright Ltd. of Bedford Road, London, N.22 produced the A.E.W. sports two-seater which was the first use made outside the factory of the long-wheel-base chassis. It was introduced in January at £135 and shortly afterwards a four-seater version was offered at £145.

Austin was determined to win back some of the International class H records held by the Magic Midget and he did not care how it was done or who

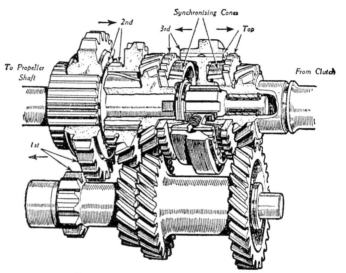

Fig. 29. The 1933—34 synchro gearbox.

did it. Some time during 1932 the late Stan Yeal was at the Brooklands track with one of the Works' cars and was impressed with the performance of a white Ulster being driven by a very serious young man wearing glasses. Yeal introduced himself to the driver, T. Murray Jamieson, who told him that he was engaged in testing a new Amherst Villiers supercharger which he had just designed himself. Following a run in the car, Yeal was so impressed and convinced that Jamieson's car would very soon be faster than the Works' racers, that he told Waite about his experience. Waite contacted Amherst Villiers, by whom Jamieson was employed, and the result was that Austin's bought the car, all spare parts and the tools which had been made to construct the blower, and Jamieson was offered a job with the Company with a free hand and instructions to build a 750 c.c. racer that could beat the M.G. records.

On 8th August, Driscoll took the old single-seater to Brooklands and beat the M.G. 50 km. record at 100·24 m.p.h. and on the 14th of the same month, in an unsuccessful attempt on the hour record, he increased the speed over the same distance to 101·52 and took the 50 miles at 102·23 and the 100 km. at 102·26 m.p.h. His success was short-lived, however, because exactly a month later the Magic Midget took them all up another 4 m.p.h. Now it was Jamieson's turn; the new car, about which rumours had been current as early as January, 1933, was ready in September. It resembled the previous record-breaker in that the propeller shaft was taken across at an angle to one side of the rear axle in order that the driving position could be kept as low as possible. There was a three speed gearbox and the engine, which developed nearly 70 b.h.p., had an extra stiff crankshaft running on one ball and one roller bearing, oil being fed through from the front of the shaft, along channels cut in the webs, to the big ends. No oil was retained in the crankcase, but was held in a separate tank on the dashboard. One pump took the oil through a cooler to the engine where it was pressure fed to the crankshaft, and each cam had its own oil pipe. The crankcase was cleared by a scavenging pump which passed the oil through another cooler before returning it to the tank. Dozens of extra bolts secured the cylinder block to the crankcase and the aluminium cylinder head was covered with additional nuts. One side of the head was cut away to take a flange for the cooling system which used a pump to force the water around the jackets and in to a small radiator which, because of its position low down in the frame, was provided with a header tank on the dashboard next to the oil tank. Air passing over the radiator was ducted through channels built into either side of the aluminium body which passed the warm air out close to the ground just in front of the driver's cockpit. At the front of the engine and driven direct from the crankshaft, was a two-bladed supercharger which fed the inlet ports via a safety valve. Beside this unit there was a two cylinder air pump· to provide air pressure for the fuel tank which was mounted in the tail; it had another pressure system which could be operated by a hand pump on the instrument board. Ignition was by Lucas magneto to two sets of plugs for each cylinder.

Jamieson took this new Austin hope to Montlhéry on 14th October, and although he was unable to reach his goal of 120 m.p.h. he took three of Eyston's records: the 5 miles at 119·38, the 10 km. at 119·39 and the 10 miles at 119·19 m.p.h. The streamlined body of the Magic Midget was modified and restreamlined for another attempt five days later; in fact, it was altered to such an extent that Eyston would not fit in the cockpit so the wheel was taken by A. Denly, who took six short records at between 125 and 128 m.p.h. What could a side-valve Austin Seven do against that? Murray Jamieson knew the answer – nothing! However, a week later he went to Montlhéry again and took the old M.G. 50 km. record, which stood at 105·76, up to

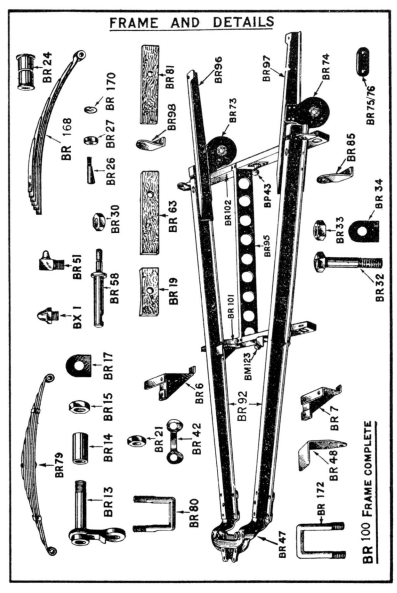

FRAME AND DETAILS

BR 24
BR 168
BR 26 BR 27 BR 170
BR 81
BR 98
BR 96
BR 97
BR 74
BR 75/76
BR 73
BR 85
BP 43
BR 30
BR 63
BR 34
BR 33
BR102
BR 51
BR 95
BR 58
BX I
BR 19
BR 101
BR 32
BR 17
BR 15
BR 6
BM123
BR 7
BR 14
BR 21
BR 42
BR 92
BR 79
BR 48
BR 172
BR 13
BR 80
BR 47
BR 100 FRAME COMPLETE

Fig. 30. A page from the spare parts list showing the high frame chassis in its final form.

113.47 m.p.h. Even this only stood for eleven days and the year finished with the M.G.'s holding every International class H record.

On 6th May the single-seaters driven by Driscoll, Barnes and Goodacre, were entered for the J.C.C. International Trophy race at Brooklands. For this race the Club tried an experiment to provide the spectators with all the thrills of a scratch race, and at the same time handicapping the cars according to their speeds. Competitors were divided into appropriate classes and on one part of the track three sand banked "channels" were arranged; the one for the fast cars contained a difficult bend which made it necessary to brake and slow down from over 100 m.p.h. to about 30 m.p.h., and the hazards became less for the slower cars. This novel form of handicapping meant that the first past the post at the end of the 250 miles course was the winner and would receive £500 and a trophy presented by Sir William Morris. Unfortunately, two of the cups were stolen in a smash and grab raid from a London showroom in which they were being exhibited, so the presentation after the race had to be postponed. Of the twenty-eight starters only eight finished; an M.G. Midget crashed on the initial lap, a wheel came adrift from Eyston's car and struck a pit marshal and, although no Midgets finished, three of the 1,086 c.c. Magnettes were highly successful, coming second, third and fourth behind an Alfa-Romeo. The Austins won the team award with average speeds of 78·03, 74·09 and 72·64 m.p.h.

Shortly afterwards, Barnes and Goodacre raced in the Avus Grand Prix and came second and fourth respectively in the smallest class. The Works' trio entered for the L.C.C. Relay race on 22nd July, but as supercharged cars they were severely handicapped and the M.G. Car Club team won and the Morgans were second; the Austins only managed to gain fourth place with a remarkable average speed of 91·60 m.p.h. over the 250-miles course. No Austins were entered for the Ulster T.T. at which the 750 c.c. class consisted of no less than eight Midgets and two Morris Minor specials. The Works' team appeared only once more in 1933 when Driscoll, with C. B. Bickell as his mechanic, Barnes and B. P. Twist, and George Duller, the jockey, making his appearance in motor racing again after a long absence, partnered by Charlie Goodacre, were entered for the B.R.D.C. 500-miles race at Brooklands on 16th September. Eyston, fresh from his record-breaking successes, was also amongst the twenty-eight starters with the Magic Midget. All the Austins suffered from minor mechanical defects; Driscoll was in trouble first with a broken oil pipe which was repaired, but a few minutes later he was out again with fuel trouble. Next, Duller pushed his car into the pits for a new set of plugs and made regular visits thereafter. Barnes gave up with a seized clutch and Driscoll burnt out a valve shortly afterwards, and finally Duller, who had never managed to find the cause of his engine's misfiring, gave up for good. There was some little consolation in the fact that the Magic Midget was also forced to retire.

Finally, on 30th September, Sir Herbert entered two of the racing cars to be driven at the Shelsley Walsh hill climb by Driscoll and Barnes. Although the cars did quite well in the 850 c.c. class it was rather disappointing for them to be beaten by a supercharged Morris Minor which climbed the hill faster than the Austins in $46\frac{2}{5}$ seconds.

1934

Cheap Jewelry and the First £100 Austin

"It is an unfortunate fact that the public demand for change does not always allow us to derive the full benefit of settled design. Whilst I appreciate the advances these new models represent, it is not without a tinge of regret that I see the passing of our familiar radiator shell which has been associated with the name of Austin since the founding of the firm."

Sir Herbert Austin at the introduction of the new models at Longbridge on 13th August, 1934

All motor manufacturers agreed to abide by a ruling made by the Society of Motor Manufacturers and Traders in 1934, not to announce or describe any new models for the coming year until 13th August. Sir Herbert had one very important modification to put forward for the 1935 season, so he invited the press to lunch at Longbridge at the first opportunity – on the day that the restriction was lifted. He wished to introduce his new jewels – the Ruby, the Pearl and the Opal – without any delay, and after he had said how sorry he was to see the last of the old familiar radiator shell, he went on to say:

"The most notable changes which have taken place are the fitting of a newly designed radiator shell, the introduction of sweeping lines, lengthened bonnets, the absence of projecting fittings and the fact that equipment is now unified and becomes a definite part of the vehicle construction. . . . I recollect that when we met in Paris during last year's Motor Show the principal speakers gave me to understand that our old radiator shell was the one obstacle in the way of unlimited sales."

As this statement shows, Sir Herbert was most reluctant to introduce the new designs but, although the press and his own salesmen were right in saying that these changes in appearance were being demanded by the public and were needed to keep ahead in the competitive markets all over the world, they were a little ambitious when they told Sir Herbert that this was the sole obstacle in the way of unlimited sales. Austin's did extremely well in the 1934–35 season in selling more than 77,000 cars, 20 per cent more than they had ever made before and about a quarter of the total output of the industry for that period. During 1934, Austin Seven production rose to 22,542 and, again, the vast majority were de luxe saloons, with a total of 13,638.

There was also a one hundred pound car for the first time in Austin history, the Opal two-seater, which was to remain the only model with the old flat-fronted radiator shell. Following current practice, in order to provide a more streamlined appearance, the radiators on the other models were shielded behind a cowling of deeper and more rounded design which was cellulosed in the same colour as the body, and had vertical slats. The base of this cowling merged into the front wings and the radiator filler cap was beneath the bonnet. At the rear, a larger petrol tank was mounted on rubber insulated brackets, and the frame was lowered so that footwells were no longer needed in the rear compartment; this brought the floor five inches nearer to the ground. Larger, 4·00 × 17 in. tyres on smaller wheels were used on the new saloons but the other models retained the old 3·50 × 19's. There were narrower door pillars which gave more window space, and a sloping tail section comprised a concealed luggage grid and space for the spare wheel. The battery and tool box were placed under the scuttle, and on the saloons the ventilation was improved by adjustable louvres in the scuttle sides, supplemented by opening rear quarter windows which hinged outwards from the front, in the same manner as on current B.M.C. Minis. Other alterations included single bar bumpers and flush fitting direction indicators with an automatic return switch on the steering column head, and a hinged interior visor for the closed models; separate side lamps mounted on the wings, new chromium plated head lamps (black with plated rims on the fixed head saloons), an illuminated instrument panel, foot-operated dip switch and a new gearbox with synchro-mesh on second gear, were common to all cars. (A full list of alterations is given at the end of this chapter.)

Revised prices for the season were:

Ruby saloon	£120
Ruby fixed head saloon	£112
Pearl cabriolet	£128
Open Road tourer	£108
Opal two-seater	£100
Five cwt. van	£108
Nippy sports	£142
Speedy sports	£172

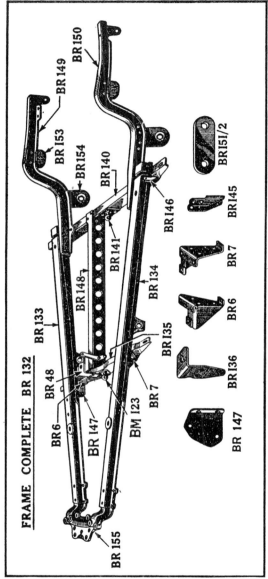

Fig. 31.   The dropped chassis, August, 1934.

Standard colours for the new range were as follows:
Ruby: Royal blue, maroon, Westminster green, Dove grey and black.
Ruby (fixed head): Royal blue, maroon and black.
Pearl: As for Ruby but Cherry red in place of maroon.
Open Road: Royal blue, maroon and Auto brown.
Opal: Royal blue and Dove grey.
Other colours available: Turquoise blue and Pueblo brown.

Ruby and Pearl models were upholstered in hide or rep, fixed head Ruby in mohair or leather, and the others in leather cloth. Nippy and Speedy standard colours were primrose, Turquoise blue, Cherry red and black.

The Nippy was, in fact, a new name for the 1933 "65" sports model and the only difference in the outward appearance in the 1934 Nippy was a different hood and cover, and side lights on the front wings. Gearboxes were the same with ratios of 22·91, 13·28, 8·38 and 5·6 to 1 and the engine was still rated at 21 b.h.p. at 4,400 revs per minute. This was the cheapest sports four-wheeler on the market and could cover a flying quarter mile at 55 m.p.h. with a maximum speed of a little over 65 m.p.h., it took 27 seconds to cover the standing quarter-mile and averaged between 40 and 45 miles on a gallon of petrol. To begin with, the Speedy was known as the "75" sports model and the first car, chassis number 193,974 was produced in April, 1934. A longer bonnet was fitted in August, and during the year 228 sports models were produced, the vast majority of which must have been Nippys.

A quotation from the Austin catalogue provides some details of the rarer model.

"The Speedy is a fast two-seater sports car, suitable for both road and track events. It is designed to conform to racing regulations, and is quickly stripped of lamps, hood, mudwings and its Vee-type Triplex windscreen. The streamlined body is low, the scuttle and doors are flared to protect the occupant when the car is in racing trim, and the bonnet sides are secured by a.strap. The radiator embodies a stone-guard. There is a spring steering wheel, pneumatic seats, and the battery and tools are easily accessible under the bonnet. Immediately behind the driver is the snap-lever quick filler cap for the twelve gallon capacity rear petrol tank, and the instrument board, which includes a combined speedometer and revolution counter with a five-inch dial, is directly in front of the driver. The Speedy develops 23 b.h.p. at 4,800 revs per minute, the special cylinder head gives a high compression ratio, there is a high lift camshaft, a down-draught carburettor and a special silencer, also a deep sump with cooling fins and a full pressure oiling system. There are also bound road springs."

Gear ratios on the early Speedy were 22·9, 13·85, 8·73 and 5·25 to 1, but later they were changed to 20·48, 12·39, 7·82 and 5·25 to 1.

Early in the year, Arrow Coachworks Ltd., of Boston Road, Hanwell, W.7, produced the first of their attractive two-seaters on the sports "65" chassis.   In addition to the two bucket seats there was plenty of luggage room under a neat tonneau cover, the front wings swept back into the steeply sloping running boards which, with the low doors, gave the car very handsome lines.   At the rear there was an imposing competition-type seven gallon tank, with a quick-release filler cap.   The spare wheel was mounted outside the body on the flat rear tail and guarded by a chromium-plated triangular strap; the strapped bonnet was lengthened and louvred in two rows on top as well as at the sides.   Other details included a front cowl, radiator and lamp stone guards, spiral radiator overflow pipe, tandem electric screen wipers, a special instrument panel set in a mottled aluminium fascia, a spring steering wheel and dummy hub caps.   Known as the Competition "65", the car cost £187 10s., and the firm also made a sports foursome at £160 and a coupé at £184.

A. E. Wright offered a Speed "65" two-seater at £179 10s. in addition to their sports two-seater at £139 10s. and a sports four-seater for £149 10s.

Most serious competition to the Austin Seven still came from Ford and Morris; the Minor was replaced by the new Morris 8 tourer which was priced at £118.   There was also a saloon version for £120.   The two-door Ford Popular was offered at the same price but £4 was added for a sliding roof; similarly, the sliding roof Morris 8 was also more expensive than the standard version.   At £120 the Ruby remained the cheapest car of its type and it only failed to compete against the others amongst customers requiring four doors. Both the Morris and the Ford were available in this form at £142 and £145 respectively, but the cheapest four-door Austin was the Ten saloon at £172.

Jamieson persisted with the side-valve racer during the winter of 1933–34 and in March the battle for the baby car speed honours was resumed.   The Austin was provided with some additional streamlining to extend the length of the tail, and the blower was modified in preparation for a series of events on Southport Sands which was organised by the Southport Motor Club. High speeds were expected on the sand and in addition to Driscoll in the Austin, the Silver Bullet, a car owned by Jack Field, was to make an attempt on the British Empire records.   During one of his practice runs, before making a final bid for the class H records, Driscoll was struck in the face by a timing thread as he flashed past and was badly cut on the nose.   On 23rd March, after minor attention to the clutch and exhaust system, Driscoll broke the flying kilometre record at 122·74 m.p.h. and the same accident occurred as in the preliminary trials; this time he received a slightly more severe cut less than an inch from his previous injury.   On 25th March, Driscoll made another attempt to beat Denly's World's small car record of 128·62 m.p.h., but only managed a speed of 114·33.

Brooklands Mountain lap records, standing start mile and kilometre class

H records were seldom held by one person for more than a few weeks at a time during 1934. Driscoll started when he took the record-breaker to Brooklands on 2nd April; he drove it in a short and a long handicap without much success, but on Whit Monday he broke the Mountain class record in the Merrow handicap race at 69·74 m.p.h. On the same day, Everitt's Q-type M.G. exceeded Driscoll's speed by a fraction. Driscoll finished up in October with a speed of 73·64 m.p.h. at the closing Brooklands event, but Everitt was not content to let matters rest until the following year, so a special run was organised at which he flew around the course with an average speed of 74·58 m.p.h.

On 1st August, Everitt raised E. R. Hall's standing start mile and kilometre records to 79·88 and 69·75 respectively, other M.G.'s raised these figures slightly, but the Austin reply came from a German driver, E. C. Burgaller, who had been driving a car very similar to Driscoll's on the Continent. On 10th October, Burgaller went to Prague for the Hungarian International meeting and beat the M.G. figures at 83·59 and 73·34 m.p.h. Two weeks later, Everitt drove another M.G. at Montlhéry but as he was unaware of Burgaller's effort he did not quite obtain the necessary speeds. However, he went to Brooklands a few days later just to make sure that 1934 ended with all the International class H records down to M.G.'s.

Shortly after the Southport Sands record it was decided that the side-valve record-breaker had achieved as much as it ever would against the overhead valve M.G.'s, so Jamieson converted it into a track racing sprint car to uphold the firm's racing prestige until such time as the o.h.v. racer was ready. The engine and transmission were put into a new frame with a tubular front axle and a very light body shell with a bulbous nose cowling was fitted; the cowlings between the wheels at the sides were removed and the body sides were cut away to reduce weight as much as possible. The car was now beginning to take the well-known form of the later o.h.v. racers. This beautiful little car first appeared at the Whit Monday meeting at Brooklands and was driven by Driscoll. In this form the last side-valve car was so successful that two or three others were built in 1934 and 1935.

Goodacre and Driscoll were unsuccessful in both the J.C.C. International Trophy and the British Empire Trophy races and the only major Austin success of the year, in the L.C.C. Relay race in July, was not obtained by the official Works' team. The weather was absolutely foul; the track was completely under water to a depth of about two inches and at the side of the circuit it was ankle deep. Owing to the withdrawal of Eyston's M.G. team, the official Austin supercharged entries were the nominal scratch cars with only a four-minute start, but they were not able to live up to their handicap, although they started well with average lap speeds of 103 and 104 m.p.h. Driscoll was going well when, after fourteen laps, the Austin's fuel pipe fractured and the car came to a halt. Under the rules, he had to complete the circuit on foot so that he could hand his sash over to C. D. Parish, the second driver in the team. He did this in a very short time and Parish dashed off to try to make up the time which had been lost. Shortly afterwards, however, the organisers discovered that Driscoll had broken the regulations by coming across country instead of keeping to the circuit, and the team was automatically disqualified after having covered only thirty-six laps. It was now up to W. L. Thompson's privately entered team to save the day for Austin. They were given a 23-minute start which was fairly generous when it is considered that Thompson was driving one of the old Works' cars and Selby, the second member of the team, was using Thompson's very fast racing car in which he had been doing so well over the past twelve months. The Austins won after completing the 250-mile course at an average speed of 84·65 m.p.h. without so much as an involuntary stop.

Thompson joined Driscoll and Goodacre in the "duck" racers for the B.R.D.C. 500-miles race on 22nd September, in which the 750 c.c. class handicap speed was raised this year by 4.61 m.p.h. This meant that the M.G.'s and Austins had to average 109·46 m.p.h. and received 24 minutes 8 seconds start from the high-powered cars over the 181-lap course. All the cars had to complete one lap at 100 m.p.h. within the first hour in order to qualify. Goodacre was the first in trouble and retired with a lack of oil pressure after 29 laps; Driscoll lasted longer but his engine stopped in the 98th, and Thompson, who had been plagued with plug trouble, stopped after having changed them on numerous occasions and retired in the 142nd lap.

Driscoll and three other supercharged Sevens were entered in the 850 c.c. class at Shelsley Walsh on 9th June. One was to have been driven by A. Issigonis – the designer of the Morris 1,000 and the B.M.C. transverse cars – who had entered cars before but had not appeared; Goodacre was to have driven another in place of Burgaller but as he did not appear either, Issigonis was down to drive in his place. Driscoll managed a climb in 46 seconds but was beaten by an M.G. and, in fact, only bettered the time of Miss Barbara Skinner's Morris Minor special by a mere two seconds. It was on this day that Whitney Straight set up a new Shelsley record in a Maserati of $41\frac{1}{2}$ seconds.

All the cars entered again for the climb on 29th September. Driscoll was fastest in the class with a time of $46\frac{3}{4}$ seconds, Goodacre was 48 seconds and Issigonis' car failed half-way up.

Not a particularly exciting or successful year but the side-valve racer was now more or less reliable, as Driscoll was to prove in the coming year.

Modifications embodied in the 1934–35 Ruby and Pearl models on the low frame chassis:

Modified engine mounting.
Sloping radiator cowl with filler under bonnet.
Petrol tank, silencer and tail pipe to suit new body.
Carburettor with air strangler and throttle control interconnected.
Modified accelerator control.
Dynamo and distributor for automatic ignition advance.
Concealed lighting for instrument panel.
Automatic return for direction indicators combined with the horn switch on steering wheel.
Five-lamp lighting set with modified head lamps.
Foot-operated headlamp dip switch.
Magnetic speedometer.
Gearbox with synchro-mesh on second, third and top gears.
Modified hand brake and foot controls to suit lowered frame.
Hardy-Spicer needle bearing propeller shaft.

The first low frame was manufactured on 7th July, chassis number 198,596, which included no less than 242 separate modifications.

56. 1934–35 Speedy

57. Military tourer,
1934

58. August, 1934. The
first of the Ruby
saloons

59. 1936–37 Ruby

*60. January, 1937.
The new cabriolet*

*61. C. D. Buckley
driving a Grass-
hopper in the 1936
Colmore Trophy
competition*

1935

Peak Production

There was some doubt as to how the Seven h.p. cars would fare in 1935. As early as April of the previous year, the Chancellor of the Exchequer announced that motor taxation would be reduced from £1 to 15s. per h.p. from 1st January, 1935. In theory this should have increased the requirement for larger cars and there certainly was a tendency towards those in the 10 h.p. range. Austin catered for this section with the excellent Austin Ten, but as there was an increased demand for cars anyway, the Seven still sold extremely well, the total output for the year being the greatest ever achieved for the model at 27,280. The total output of the motor industry was 20 per cent greater than in the previous year, but Austin's share fell slightly whereas Morris nearly doubled his during the same period.

Earlier trends continued more or less along the same lines. More than half the production consisted of the Ruby de luxe saloons, tourers were even less popular, and the two-seater, still in its old form with a plated radiator shell for most of the year, only managed to attract a total of 735 customers. The Pearl cabriolet was only a little more successful, and the sports models remained at the same level which had been established in 1933, with a production of 220. Special body builders began to take an interest in the sports chassis and the number of chassis sold was almost double that of the previous year with a total of 1,392. The Arrow "75" Competition two-seater was introduced at £207, and there was also a "65" sports two-seater for £189; these cars were almost identical in outward appearance but the performance of the "75" was considerably better than that of the cheaper model. A.E.W.'s were still being sold for £185, but the body was completely redesigned in August and the price increased to £205.

During the year the Seven's most serious competitor, the Ford 8, was reduced to £115 for the cheapest model, but Austin still produced the cheapest saloon on the market – the fixed head Ruby at £112. It was decided to increase the Austin prices by a few pounds in August and the cheap saloon was to be £118, the Ruby de luxe £125, the Pearl remained at £128, the tourer was £112 and the two-seater £102 10s. This last model was redesigned with a new cowled radiator on the low chassis and brought into line with the other models in the range. The Nippy was still sold for £142, and the Speedy was withdrawn from the catalogues in August although it is possible that they could still have been obtainable to special order. Ford brought out their new Ford 8 at the Motor Show, the first saloon ever to be offered for £100, and this proved to be one of the main reasons for the demise of the Austin Seven. To begin with, however, the Ford simply took the increase in demand and it took two years before it made serious inroads into the Seven sales.

From July, all Sevens were fitted with Moseley "Float-on-Air" pneumatic upholstery, and the braking system was improved by modified shoes and linkages, first employed on chassis number 226,847. Little else of importance was changed in 1935, but the radiator filler position was reversed to place it on the same side of the car as the oil filler.

Taking advantage of the long slump in America, the comparatively low level of production there and the falling off in their export trade, the British motor industry went all out to satisfy the demand from overseas. In 1935, Austin's doubled their export figures of the previous year and the principle of allowing foreign manufacturers to use British ideas under licence was no longer feasible because they could all make perfectly satisfactory cars of their own designs themselves.

Japan had been an exception in every respect. Trade with that country was far from brisk; the first Austin sent out there was an Austin Twenty chassis imported in the early 'twenties (by a lucky coincidence this very car is still in existence and restoration was being carried out by the late Viscount Tokiyoshi Hiramatsu). A few more Austins followed during the next ten or twelve years, but most of the cars imported into the country came from the United States. Strangely enough, the motor industry in Japan had its beginnings as early as 1922 when, as a means of building up a programme for defence, the army assisted in the initial organisation. Private commercial manufacture did not begin until 1927, again with financial aid from outside, this time provided by government subsidies, and these still existed as late as 1935. The main reason for this support was in order to build up vehicle and aircraft factories with a potential which could soon be adapted to produce military vehicles and aeroplanes, and much of the output of the motor concerns was already devoted to heavier commercial vehicles to satisfy the military requirements. But there was a limited demand for small cars and motor-cycles, and light three-wheel delivery vans.

Car taxation in Japan was extremely high and was based upon engine capacity. In order to combat this, the Japanese Datsun Company started to manufacture prototypes of a very small car in 1932, with a 495 c.c. four-cylinder water-cooled engine of 54 mm. bore and stroke. To reduce the effects as taxation even further, one model available had a single-seater body and of such it was considered as a motor-cycle for taxation purposes and, perhaps even more important, no driving licence was required. This was a most important advantage as it could take anything up to six months to obtain a licence in Japan at that time, and it was only issued after a particularly severe test. In 1933, Japan doubled her output of motor vehicles and there was concern in Europe that cheap labour would create severe competition. Competition from countries where labour costs were low was always regarded as "unfair" opposition by the West and their products were generally thought to be inferior. This was not the case with the Japanese motor industry, however, and a recent report that they had been turning out thousands of bicycles which were being sold for 30s. each was something which made Britain think. J. P. Black, the managing director of the Standard company, stated:

"I rather anticipated that they would come into the motor market before long, but I feel sure they have a great deal to learn about the business yet. The Japanese are fine copyists, but it remains to be seen what sort of motor cars they turn out."

The 7 h.p. Datsun was first brought to the notice of the readers of the motoring press in this country in April, 1934, and a sample car arrived in Sydney in July.

There was nothing wrong with the car and there was no doubt that it resembled the Austin, but it was both shorter and narrower with a chassis which swept up over the rear axle and it used half elliptic rear springs. The cars were made by Jidosha Seizo, K.K. of Tokyo, an organisation which had factories in Yokahama and Osaka. Rumours existed that the car was to cost only £50 so Austin sent out Crane-Williams, the Company's chief representative in the Far East, and in his report he said that he felt sure that the rumours of a £50 product from Japan were nonsense. In fact, the open model sold for £105 and the saloon £114. It has been said in recent years that the Datsun was nothing less than an exact copy of the Austin Seven and an infringement of the Austin patents. It certainly resembled it closely and Sir Herbert arranged for one to be brought over to England in 1935 but did not seem to be particularly worried about the situation.

Driscoll established two class H records at Brooklands early in the season by covering the standing start mile at 85·98 and the standing start kilometre at 77·43 m.p.h. These were only to last for a month, when the Magic Midget increased them by another ten miles an hour. At the same time the flying start kilometre record was broken at 130·89 m.p.h. Driscoll did not waste any more time on record-breaking in 1935. Reports were already circulating about the new o.h.v. racing cars and although Jamieson was working on them throughout 1935 it was not possible to prepare them in time for any events that year. Two side-valve racers took part in the J.C.C. International

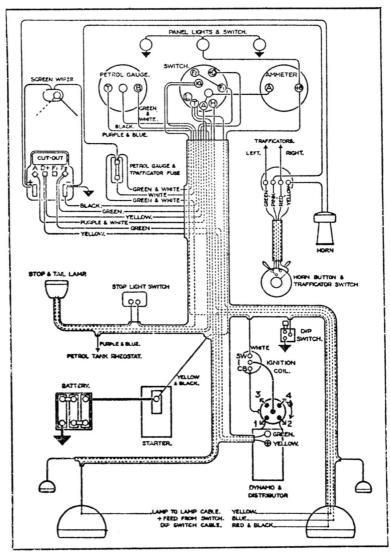

Fig. 32.   1935 wiring diagram.

Trophy race on 6th May, in which Driscoll was joined by C. J. P. Dodson new to Austin driving but with a great deal of experience in competition work both on cars and motor-cycles. In practice Driscoll covered a lap at 92 m.p.h, but on the day suffered from constant ignition trouble which led to his retirement after forty-six laps. Dodson had to make several visits to the pits which culminated in his withdrawal with a blown gasket after thirty-one laps.

An Austin team of three cars was entered for the Mannin Beg "Round the Houses" race for cars of up to 1,500 c.c. in the Isle of Man on 29th May, at which an interesting duel was expected between the Sevens and the M.G. Midgets, but the entry was withdrawn at the last minute because the new o.h.v. cars could not be prepared in time and the others were destined to go to Le Mans. For the Le Mans event Driscoll, Dodson and Goodacre entered, but Dodson's was the only Austin to complete the course; he came twenty-eighth of the twenty-eight finishers. Dodson and Driscoll were joined by a newcomer, Stanley Woods, and these three were destined to become the official Works' drivers for 1936. In 1932 and 1933, Woods achieved the unparalleled feat of winning both the Junior and Senior T.T. motor-cycle races and his record of success as a motor-cyclist went back as far as 1923, when he first won the Junior race. His first attempt with the Austin was disappointing, however; Driscoll had a car in Ireland for the Co. Down Trophy race and had to retire after nineteen laps, in spite of completing one at 78 m.p.h., so he lent the car to Woods in order to compete in a "Round the Houses" race in Limerick. It let Woods down with a blown head gasket in the first lap. The Works' team appeared in a few more events that summer. In the 150 miles Nuffield Trophy race at Donington on 13th July, Driscoll retired after twenty laps, but came second in a 25 miles junior handicap on the same day with an average speed of 61·07 m.p.h. Parish, Goodacre and Driscoll, all lapping in the 90's were twelfth in the L.C.C. Relay race with a speed of 86·15, and Driscoll won the Siam Challenge Trophy race at Brooklands in August. He also achieved some good hill climbing. He was second in the open class (up to 1,100 c.c.), second in the unlimited capacity class and third in the all-comers' handicap at the Ulster A.C.'s annual hill climb at Craigantlet. Sir Herbert went to Shelsley on 18th May to see Driscoll, Goodacre, R. F. Turner and Walter Baumer perform in the side-valve cars. Baumer was in England to collect a car to enter in events in Germany and used the record-breaker but could only climb the hill in $45\frac{4}{5}$ seconds. Goodacre's time was $44\frac{1}{5}$ seconds, and Driscoll won the £100 prize for the fastest climb in the 750 c.c. racing class which was also the third fastest of the day at $43\frac{2}{5}$ seconds.

The solitary racer shown in the 1934 production figures in the table was sold to G. H. Smith of New Zealand. It was similar to the Works' racers and had the separated radiator and a single-seater body, and Smith took it to the opening of the new Gloucester Park Speedway, near Auckland, in January, 1935. He started from scratch in the first race, a handicap for cars of up to 1,500 c.c., and came second. In the five-lap Championship event he was first, taking the lead from the start and winning by a margin of 30 yards, much to the delight of the spectators. Then, in the four-lap handicap, he won again by a comfortable margin. During the year this car became one of the most successful racers in New Zealand.

Three new trials-type sports models made their debut in the London–Land's End trial and were driven by R. J. Richardson, J. Orford and W. Milton. Orford secured a Gold Medal and Milton a Second Class award. These trial cars, later known as "Grasshoppers", bore the registration numbers AOX 4, AOX 3 and AOV 343.

These cars were registered in March or April, 1935. Four more cars were built for Le Mans and registered in May as BOA 57, 58, 59 and 60. They were not particularly successful: two came in at the end of the event, the others failed to complete the course. Three were later fitted with doors and the engines supercharged for use as Works' team cars as "Grasshoppers" to be driven by Bill Scriven, Alf Langley and Dennis Buckley. BOA 59 was to have been Driscoll's car for the 1935 Le Mans and was later converted to a Works' trial car to be used by Goodacre; this car and COA 121 which was built for the cancelled 1936 Le Mans – the spare car to the three which ran but retired in 1937 – still exist today (1982). In all twelve of these cars were built between 1935 and 1937.

1936

Three Main Bearings and the O.H.C. Racers

1936 was the British motor industry's most successful year so far. Statistically, all calculations were made to cover the period which ended on 30th September, and at this period and for the first time, car production exceeded 350,000, as against 311,544 during 1934–35. This represented an increase of 13·5 per cent and compared with an increase in American production for the same period of 14·1 per cent. Sales on the home market rose from 271,704 to 302,057, an increase of 11·1 per cent, which indicated that there was a substantial fall in the rate of increase compared with the preceding three years (24·6 per cent in 1932–33, 25·8 per cent in 1933–34 and 23·7 per cent in 1934–35), and it is difficult to establish a reason for this failure to maintain the rate of growth. Such a large difference could hardly be ascribed to a sudden jump towards saturation point, as one would have expected a more gradual fall in the rate of increased sales over a relatively long period as the demand at home was slowly being met.

The sudden fall may have been the result of the big increase in sales during each of the three preceding years, which was a result of the reaction from deferred buying during the period of depression between 1930 and 1932. In effect, those people who did not buy new cars during the worst years of depression, but who would have done so under normal circumstances, acquired them between 1933 and 1935, and so the relatively low growth in the rate of sales in 1936 was a natural reaction.

Home sales increases were chiefly in the 7–10 h.p. and 11–15 h.p. ranges, with increases of approximately 14,000 and 12,000 fulfilling 84·9 per cent of the home demand, almost exactly the same proportion as in the two preceding years. The question of home sales in horse power groups is one of importance, because it was directly related to the prospect of the export trade in cars. One of the main objects of the reduction in car taxation from £1 to 15s. per h.p. made two years before had been to encourage the sale at home of cars of sizes most in favour overseas, so that increased production with its tendency to reduce manufacturing costs would enable British manufacturers

151

to compete more successfully in overseas markets against American competition. Unfortunately, statistics show that the tax concession did little in inducing the home buyers to buy more powerful cars. The proportion of British production to be exported only rose from 16·2 to 16·8 per cent in 1936 over the previous year, but it is interesting to observe that the Americans were only able to export 4·5 per cent of their total output during the nine months up to 30th September, 1936.

Of the 353,838 cars produced in 1935–36, 70,956 were made by Austin, which represented about one in five of the British output. The figure for Austin Sevens, with a total for the year of some 23,500 (unfortunately, precise figures for this period are not available), was much better, and the Seven remained one of the most popular cars with an engine rated at 8 h.p. Throughout the year prices remained at £128 for the Pearl cabriolet, the Ruby was £125 (£118 for the fixed head model), the Open Road tourer £112, the two-seater £102 10s., the Nippy £142 and the van £108.

Towards the end of 1935, at chassis number 236,210, the positive pole of the battery was earthed instead of the negative in order to prevent corrosion. In February, 1936 from engine number 241,541, the Nippy embodied the type of engine formerly fitted to the faster Speedy Model, which had the full pressure lubrication system. It was found that there remained a small demand for a sports model without such good performance so, in October, the Nippy was produced with a standard engine and sold for £130. The barrel-type speedometer was replaced by the older needle model on all products except the van in January at chassis number 239,165. Cast-iron brake drums and steel brake shoes were introduced in May. The major changes were made shortly afterwards and in preparation for the 1936–37 selling season, and to coincide as nearly as possible with the Motor Show. Most noticeable of the modifications in the saloon body was the fully panelled doors; in other words, in place of a very light frame around the window, the door panel was itself extended upwards. The rear quarter windows were provided with winding mechanisms instead of being hinged at the front, and there was a slightly more pronounced slope to the windscreen. On the saloons, the new R.R. body (the first of which was built in July – chassis number 249,701) had a new waistline moulding. Instead of following round the rear of the body with a slight upwards sweep, the moulding finished at the rear quarter, where it widened out and sloped downwards. Cabriolet, tourer, two-seater and Nippy bodies were not altered at this stage.

Mechanical alterations related to the clutch, the engine and the braking system; the new clutch was of the Borg and Beck type with a flexible driven plate carrying the friction lining which provided springiness for the disc, giving progressive engagement and smoother operation. Most important of the changes related to the engine; in fact the only significant one which had been made since the model was introduced in 1922. The first car with the three main bearing crankshaft was produced on 16th June and allocated car number ARQ 35724, chassis number 247,765, engine number 249,052. In addition to the end ball and roller bearings, a centre main bearing of plain white metal of 1¾ in. diameter was added. It was lubricated under pressure from the main oil system and the extra rigidity provided smoother running and enabled the power output of the engine to be increased to 16½ b.h.p. at 3,400 revs per minute which, with a higher compression ratio of 6·1 to 1, gave livelier performance. 14 mm. plugs were used which enabled the design of the cylinder head water passages to be improved, there was a new cylinder head gasket and the water outlet branch was of the type used previously on Sports models, with transverse flanges secured by two of the cylinder head studs which were of extra length for this purpose. Semi-Girling brakes were used on the Seven; owing to the transverse front springing it was not possible to employ the normal cone operation of the brake shoe plungers, so cam operation was used. The same method of adjustment was applied to the pivot ends of the shoes, but at the other tips there were normal Girling plungers.

At last, the o.h.c. racer was in operation. A full report appeared in *Motor Sport* in April and this excellent technical description is reproduced as an Appendix to this chapter. Lord Austin (he had been created a Baron in 1936) had given Jamieson a free hand to do his best with the new design towards the end of 1934; a year passed before the first of the new racers was tested over 6,000 miles at Donington and Austin was becoming impatient. There were differences of opinion with Jamieson, the press were anxious to have details of the cars, the Company were spending a great deal of money on their development, and there were still some technical problems yet to be overcome. I do not propose to dwell on the subject in this book, because all these difficulties are explained in great detail in Roland Harrison's *Austin Racing History*, published in 1949, in which there is first-hand information from the team who worked with Jamieson.

On 18th March, a reception was held at the Grand Hotel in Birmingham where a single-seater car and a polished chassis were shown. In his speech introducing the new cars, Austin said that since the Seven first appeared on the racing track at Easter, 1923 it had won over 3,000 events all over the world. Two cars had been built at that time and one more was in the course of manufacture and although he hoped that the new vehicles would win many races and add much to Britain's motoring prestige, his main objective was to beat the M.G. flying mile record which stood at 130·51 m.p.h. The cars were due to appear for the first time at the Brooklands Easter meeting on 13th April, but the meeting was abandoned because of rain and had to be postponed until the following Saturday. Things did not go well for the Austins; Dodson was blinded by the sun and collided, then Driscoll, in the second o.h.c. car skidded round and simultaneously Bert Hadley, driving the side-valve racer, oiled up a plug while trying to avoid him and finished on three cylinders.

Driscoll, Goodacre and Dodson entered o.h.c. cars in the J.C.C. International Trophy race on 2nd May. The event was run over ninety laps and covered 250 miles; on the twenty-third circuit, Driscoll's car struck a piece of metal dropped from Earl Howe's E.R.A. and the fragment damaged the Austin's oil cooler. Worse was to follow; Goodacre's magneto gave out after twenty-seven laps, and Dodson gave up in the seventy-ninth because the supercharger valve would not stay in position and the resultant drop in pressure caused the sparking plugs to oil up. Austin entered the three 744 c.c. cars in the Isle of Man R.A.C. International car race on 28th May, but later it was decided only to send Dodson over so that the other two racers, together with a side-valve car, could compete at Shelsley. Dodson did a practice lap on the island at 69·23 m.p.h., but in the actual race had to retire after forty-four laps after having held sixth place at the end of ten laps only 50 seconds behind the leader. With only six laps left to complete the course, he had to stop in order to examine his air pressure pump; later he hit the bank at Willaston Corner, and then a stone flew through the radiator guard and smashed a sparking plug.

At Shelsley Walsh on 6th June the three o.h.c. cars, this time fitted with twin rear wheels, were joined by two of the older side-valve models driven by S. C. H. Davis and Walter Baumer. This was a notable event because, for the first time in this country, one of the new German Auto-Unions appeared, in the hands of the European hill-climbing champion Hans Von Stuck, but a dangerously wet course prevented him from breaking any records on the day. The fastest time, $41\frac{3}{5}$ seconds was achieved by Raymond Mays driving a 1·5 litre E.R.A. The o.h.c. Austin engines were still not working satisfactorily; Goodacre managed an ascent in $43\frac{1}{5}$ seconds, Dodson at $44\frac{3}{5}$ and Driscoll could do no better than $47\frac{3}{5}$ seconds. Walter Baumer swept the board in the 750 c.c. class in a side-valve car and tied with Fane's Frazer Nash for second fastest time of the day with a magnificent climb in $42\frac{3}{5}$ seconds. The new Baron Austin was not amused! Immediately after his success, Baumer went back to Germany with the car to take fifth place in a 1,500 c.c. race at Nürburgring.

Goodacre, Dodson and Driscoll took the three cars to Ireland for the County Down Trophy race in June. After only two or three laps Goodacre had to retire with throttle trouble, Driscoll followed shortly afterwards with a broken oil pipe, and all hopes rested on Dodson who was doing very well and even managed to break the lap record for the course at 84·51 m.p.h. He was well ahead of his handicap time, but unfortunately the car broke down. The Nuffield Trophy race, one of the major races of the year for small cars, was run over sixty laps at Donington on 4th July. In the 750 c.c. class the o.h.c. trio failed again with the ever present problem of burned piston crowns, but Bira, driving a side-valve racer, managed to finish fifth at an average speed of 62·29 m.p.h.

It was not until 16th July, at the Madresfield Speed trials, that the new cars found their form. Cars were clocked from a standing start for a kilometre over a series of undulations, the surface was poor and it was another wet day. Dodson and Driscoll drove o.h.c. cars with twin rear wheels and Hadley the one with the side-valve engine; they took first, second and third places in their class. Dodson's fastest run was made after he replaced the twin rears with single wheels; he was only beaten by two other cars and was as fast as an E.R.A. and an Alta.

Towards the end of July near Bristol, in an attempt on the Blackwell Hill House record, the Works' team had the misfortune to lose both a car and a driver. The road was just drying out after a rainstorm and in a very treacherous condition when Driscoll, going very fast, came into the spectators' view at high speed at the top of the hill. Suddenly, the car appeared to skid broadside, dashed off into the woods at the side of the road, hit a tree and overturned. Driscoll was thrown into the road and fractured his skull, and the car was damaged almost beyond repair. The crashed car was taken back to Longbridge, and it was decided not to carry out repairs but to run only the two remaining o.h.c. cars. These two, driven by Goodacre and George Duller and Dodson and Hadley, both ran in the 500-miles race at Brooklands. Dodson retired with engine trouble after seventy-three laps, but Goodacre did well to finish tenth with 163 laps to his credit when the race finished; one was covered at 117·19 m.p.h.

In hill-climbing events the side-valve car was, up to now, still proving to be consistently faster than the remaining two o.h.c. racers. At the Craigantlet hill climb in August, one of the high spots was Bert Hadley's record-breaking run in the side-valve car in which he beat E. R. Hall's previous fastest climb in a 1,087 supercharged M.G. by a fifth of a second, against competition from a similar M.G. and a Bugatti. His first run was made in 1 minute 27 seconds, the second two seconds better and, finally, he knocked off another $\frac{4}{5}$ after some speedy repairs to a broken fuel pipe. He might have been even faster, had it not been for a tendency to skid on the road, the surface of which had been melted by the strong sun. On a rainy day at Shelsley, Goodacre did a little better with a time of 45·48 seconds, only just beating both Baumer and Hadley. Goodacre and Dodson raced on other occasions during 1936, but their cars always let them down.

Record breaking proved more successful for the o.h.c. cars than competitive motor racing. Directly after the Motor Show, Dodson went to Brooklands and took a number of records, amongst which was the Brooklands outer circuit class record at 121·14 m.p.h. and the Mountain lap record at 77·02 m.p.h. The major series of three record-breaking runs began on Wednesday, 21st October when he took no less than nine records from five to a hundred miles, three of these were accepted as International class H times: 100 km. at 114·57 m.p.h., 100 miles at 115·06 m.p.h. and the 1 hour at 113·99 m.p.h. On the following Saturday, 24th October he succeeded in raising the figures for four of the records made on his previous run, in addition to which he also increased the speeds for the 50 km. and the 50 miles. On neither of these occasions was Dodson able to beat any short-distance figures which were held by Kohlrausch's M.G. at over 140 m.p.h., but he managed to take his own outer circuit record to 121·22 m.p.h. and produced the following results:

International class H
1 hour at 113·99 m.p.h.
50 km. at 118·15 m.p.h.
100 km. at 114·57 m.p.h.
100 miles at 115·06 m.p.h.

British class H
1 mile at 121·21 m.p.h.
5 km. at 120·99 m.p.h.
5 miles at 121·10 m.p.h.
10 km. at 120·25 m.p.h.
10 miles at 120·26 m.p.h.
20 miles at 114·22 m.p.h.

The most outstanding achievement during this attempt was a first-lap standing start speed of no less than 103·97 m.p.h.

Again, on 28th October, Dodson took the International class H 100 km. up to 116·38 m.p.h. and managed a new International record for the 50 miles at 116·54 m.p.h., more than two miles an hour faster than Denly's previous time. After a final run on 5th November, the following records in class H stood to the credit of Austin Seven cars:

International class H
1 km. (standing start) 83·60 m.p.h.
50 km. 118·51 m.p.h.
50 miles 116·54 m.p.h.
100 km. 116·38 m.p.h.
100 miles 115·06 m.p.h.
1 hour 113·99 m.p.h.

British class H In addition to the above International records:

Flying km. 122·74 m.p.h.
(In 1933 by Driscoll at Southport)
1 mile (standing start) 85·98 m.p.h.
(In 1935 by Driscoll at Brooklands)
1 mile (flying start) 121·21 m.p.h.
5 km. 120·99 m.p.h.
5 miles 121·10 m.p.h.
10 km. 120·25 m.p.h.
10 miles 120·26 m.p.h.

All other class H records were held by M.G.'s.

The Double-Camshaft Austin Seven Arrives

Reprinted from *Motor Sport*, April, 1936

A perfect little road-racing car which achieved 121 m.p.h. on its first outing.
Engine gives 116 h.p. and designed for 12,000 r.p.m. Complete car weighs
9¾ cwt.

After a long period of waiting the new 750 c.c. Austin racing car has at last
been pronounced completed, and this new aspirant for small-car honours,
which was shown to members of the press last month, certainly fulfils, both
in looks and design, the high expectations which it had aroused. A 750 c.c.
engine developing close on 120 h.p., itself a magnificent achievement, is
fitted on to a chassis with a wheelbase of only 6 ft. 10 in. – and track 3 ft.
11 in. The side-members and the driver's seat are not more than 6 in. from
the ground, and the body and the tail, with its stabilising fin, are very little
larger than those of the car which Driscoll drove so successfully last year.
The latter car, of course, had offset transmission. All credit, therefore, to
Mr. T. Murray Jamieson, who was responsible for the design of both cars,
and to the enterprise of Sir Herbert Austin, who made possible the development of these amazing little "seven fifties".
    Attention focuses first of all on the engine. The cylinder head and the huge
crankcase casing form one unit and the cylinder block and the crankshaft
another, both being cast in R.R. 50 light alloy, while pipes and other parts
not subject to stress are made in elektron.
    Starting from the top of the engine, the first things which impress one are
the massive camshafts, running in three bearings, with cams 2 in. wide.
These bear directly on the valves, and when it is considered that the triple
springs required if the engine is to run up to 12,000 r.p.m. will have a
combined tension of 550 lb. per valve, the need for a robust valve-operating
mechanism is readily understood. The cams and the valve-buttons are
chromium-plated to resist wear. The valves are inclined at 90 degrees to one
another in the hemispherical combustion chambers, and centrally disposed
14 mm. sparking plugs are used.
    The camshafts and auxiliaries are driven from the rear of the engine by a
train of no less than eleven gears. A Murray Jamieson Rootes-type supercharger, also driven by gears is neatly built in at the back of the engine, with
an enormous single S.U. carburettor, which has a rectangular float in order
to pack neatly into the space available. The blower runs at one-and-a-half
times engine speed, giving a boost of 20 lb.
    Wet liners of nitrided steel are used for the cylinders, the liners projecting
above the block into the head where they make metal-to-metal joints. These
upper portions, which are finned, are surrounded by detachable water jackets.

The crankshaft is machined from the solid and has a plain bearing in the centre and a roller bearing at each end. The connecting rods are H-section steel and have white metal big-ends centrifugally cast. The pistons are of the slipper type, with three piston rings. The bore and stroke are respectively 60·32 × 65·09 mm. or $2\frac{3}{8}$ × $2\frac{9}{16}$ in., giving a capacity of 744 c.c.

The auxiliary drive is from the rear end of the engine. A small pinion on the crankshaft meshes with a much bigger one above it, and on either side are other pinions which drive respectively the water pump and the Scintilla magneto. The starting handle connects with the near-side pinion through skew gears, as the engine is carried so low in the chassis that one would be unable to swing a handle applied directly to the crankshaft. The triple oil-pump for the dry-sump oiling system is driven by skew gears from the off-side pinion, which has high-pressure, low-pressure and scavenge sections. A beautiful little oil cooler made of steel tubes six-thousandths of an inch thick is carried behind the radiator cowling, while the oil tanks, which have a capacity of three gallons, are disposed on either side of the propeller shaft.

Returning to the camshaft drives, there are three pinions on the shaft, one meshing with "A" and a second with the trains of gears driving the camshafts at "C" and "D". By compounding the drive in this way, the necessary gearing down and up is effected without using large pinions which would be difficult to accommodate. The blower is driven from a third pinion on shaft "C" and the ratio can be changed without disturbing the timing gears.

The engine has so far only been run up to 8,500 r.p.m. giving the formidable figure of 116 h.p., with which the car reached a speed of 121 m.p.h. on the Donington test-track early in March. In order to attain the intended engine speed of 12,000 r.p.m., lead-bronze big-ends will be required, but the engine has been designed to accommodate this and other alterations such as stouter connecting rods or crankshaft.

Now as to the transmission. A single-plate clutch is used, but no ordinary one, as it has no less than five toggles and fifteen springs. The gearbox is in unit with the engine, and has either straight pinions or synchromesh gears according to the type of race for which the car is entered. The synchro-mesh mechanism, which is fitted to the top three gears, is used in hill climbs or road races, as it gives a distinctly quicker change than the "clash-type" gears. A remote control from the gearbox brings the lever under the driver's left hand.

An open propeller shaft with two Hardy Spicer joints takes the drive back to a cross-member under the seat. Here is situated a steady bearing, and the rear half of the transmission line passes through a torque tube to the back axle. Although the shaft is only 2 ft. long there is a danger of whipping, which might be unpleasant for the driver at 12,000 r.p.m., so in the centre of the torque tube a second steady bearing is utilised.

Mr. Jamieson considers that the heeling-over which always accompanies

"Schwingachsen" off-sets the advantage of better wheel-adhesion, and has therefore avoided making use of independent suspension for the rear wheels. The crux of the matter, he considers, is low unsprung weight and this he secures with quarter-elliptic springing. The rear springs are splayed out from the side-members, which pass under the rear axle, and above each spring is mounted a radius rod. A double reduction is used for the final drive to avoid having a crown wheel of excessive size. The bevels give a reduction of 1·8 to 1 and a pair of straight pinions mounted above them bring the over-all ratio to about 5·5 to 1.

The chassis is built on light but straightforward lines. The side-members are of channel section and almost straight from front to rear. There is a tubular cross-member in front of the engine which is rigidly mounted and acts as an "anti-lozenging" tie, a banjo-forging built in at the rear spring mountings which serves to support the front end of the torque tube, a light pressing which supports the driving seat and resists the twisting of the rear shock-absorbers, and a tubular member at the extreme rear. This and the pressing in front of it support the fuel tank, which holds 25 gallons. The fuel consumption should work out at $7\frac{1}{2}$ m.p.g. for long distance events and $3\frac{1}{2}$ to 4 using sprint fuel. Pressure from a hand-pump forces the fuel to the carburettor.

The layout of the front axle is practically the same as that used on last year's racing cars. The front axle is tubular and straight and made in two parts, a joint with an internal roller bearing allowing either of the parts, with its steering pivot, to rotate independently of the other. The suspension is by means of a flat transverse half-elliptic spring carried under the axle tube, and braking and springing torques are resisted by means of radius rods running to the top and bottom of each steering head. The steering wheel is mounted centrally in the chassis on a short steering column. The steering box is up in the scuttle, and a fore-and-aft rod runs to a bell-crank lever mounted near the front of the chassis; from here a second connecting link joins up to the steering arm.

12-in. brakes are used on the front wheels and 10-in. on the rear, the shoes being expanded by miniature crankshafts and links. The brakes are operated by enclosed cables, and are fully compensated with swinging links. The front brakes exert nearly three times as much pressure as the rear ones, and in order to prevent the front pull-off springs applying the rear brakes, one of the minor problems of the fully compensated system, stops limiting the movement of the rear brake arms have had to be fitted.

The cars are fitted with trim little single-seater bodies, similar except for slightly higher tails to those used on Driscoll's car last year. Complete with fuel, oil, water and tyres the weight in $9\frac{3}{4}$ cwt. The tyres, incidentally, are low-pressure racing Dunlops 5·25 × 16 in., mounted on triple-spoked wheels with alloy rims.

The new cars were to have made their debut at the Empire Trophy, at Donington, but the handicap allowances (7 minutes for a 250-mile race against 3-litre Alfa-Romeos) was considered too unfavourable. Instead one or more will appear at the Brooklands Easter meeting, and a team will be competing in the International Trophy on 2nd May and in the Isle of Man race at the end of that month.

Three cars have been made, and will be allotted to Driscoll, Charlie Dodson and Goodacre. The side-valve cars will remain at the factory and will be used to give less experienced drivers a chance of taking the wheel. In particular, an effort will be made to encourage racing mechanics from the Austin factory, a very sensible and praiseworthy scheme, and a new driver, by name, Bert Hadley, is already shaping well.

1937

The Big Seven and Success with the Racers

Yet another peak was reached in 1936–37, a year which was successful both for the industry as a whole with a 10 per cent increase in sales on the home market, and for Austin's in particular because their production reached almost 100,000 vehicles. This proved to be the last year of growing prosperity for the firm and it was not until 1948–49, after a pause for re-armament, a world war and its aftermath, that the total annual output was to exceed 100,000. High working costs loomed largest in the minds of motor manufacturers in 1937. The industry, like all metal users, was striving to increase its output, and like them was hampered by the shortage of steel owing to the demand created by increased armament production, and in having to meet the increasing charges for raw materials and labour. Reduced overhead costs partly offset this tendency, but a small rise in retail prices was nevertheless found to be necessary. An increase of £10 to £15 per vehicle did not greatly increase the total price, but it meant much to the manufacturer, who normally worked on a small margin. Estimates made at the time put the trading profit per vehicle produced in 1936 at £10 for an Austin, £15 for a Morris and as little as £8 for a Standard. Ford's managed £9 with, at the other extreme, £24 for Vauxhall.

It was felt that under the favourable conditions that existed, the market would not be unduly disturbed by a moderate increase in prices, following a series of reductions which had continued right up until the previous year. The fundamental economics of the motor industry led to inevitable wide fluctuations in the profits of individual companies between one season and another. The reason for this was that a successful change in one firm's models produced increased sales which more than compensated the company for the increased expenditure which the change involved. Against this, retaining the same models for a second or subsequent year, without appreciable alteration, often checked home sales which would more than compensate the company for increased attention to the export trade.

In the 1920's it was usual for one particular model to catch the public's fancy and enjoy enormous sales. By the mid-1930's, however, it was more usual for a range of models from one particular maker to enjoy a spell of popularity and most of the manufacturers deliberately increased the number of their models in an attempt to cater for all the different sections of the market. The vast increase in the number of vehicles sold at home was not reflected in the sales of Austin Sevens, which remained at between 20,000 and 27,000 a year between 1927 and 1937. In fact, some 23,000 were produced in the last twelve months of this ten-year period. Admittedly, the increase in 8 h.p. sales as a proportion of the total was getting less each year and Ford's were progressively capturing more of the market. There was quite a large gap between the Seven saloon and the Austin Ten and Lord Austin felt that something between the two with a four-door body was needed. He realised also by this time that the Seven must be nearing the end of its extremely long production run and that something would have to be done very soon to educate the public into accepting another, slightly larger, cheap car in the Austin range.

To begin with, a new Seven cabriolet was announced in January to sell at £128. In this model, unlike the earlier type, the space between the cant rails was entirely free of cross bars when the car was open. The outline of the cabriolet was now exactly like that of the saloon; the windows were the same size and shape, the internal space and seating was identical and, in fact, the sides of the cabriolet and the saloon were made from the same pressing. Instead of a rigid roof, however, hood material was used from waist level at the back to the top of the screen. At the front there was a stretcher bar by which the fabric could be pulled tight. Farther back were two cross bars, one in front of the door pillar and one behind it, which were attached to the fabric and fitted into sockets in the cant rails. Still farther back a link mechanism was clipped to the body at the top of each rear quarter. There was also a rear window at the back. Between the open and closed positions it was possible for the top to be arranged to act as a sunshine roof, and after releasing the material at the front it could be rolled back, with the cross bars, until the top was fully open. The fabric was then strapped in place along the top of the rear section. To complete the operation, the clips at the rear were released and the back section of the fabric, together with the rolled portion, would then be folded down. The top cant rails remained in position all the time and the windows could be raised and lowered.

Nippy sports models were continued with the two-bearing engine until the first three-bearing crank was fitted to chassis number 257,842 in December, 1936. The Nippy at £130 and the Nippy with sports engine at £142 10s. last appeared in the catalogues in February of the following year. A £4 increase in the price of the Ruby fixed head saloon to £122 in March heralded the all-round rises made when the 1938 programme was announced in July. No changes were made in the Seven's specification, and the Pearl cabriolets now cost £135, Rubys £131, fixed head Rubys £128, Open Road tourers £120, two-seaters £112 and the new vans £115. Lord Austin invited the trade and the press to Longbridge on 13th July to tell them about the new models. In his speech he said:

> "Today is an auspicious one for the company in so much as we are introducing for the first time since 1922 another small car, the Big Seven. My thoughts naturally go back to a day fifteen years ago when I introduced to a somewhat sceptical meeting of pressmen the first Baby Austin. Conditions at that time were somewhat less favourable than they are today. The Company, along with the entire country, were suffering from the economic aftermath of the war. Many of those who should have been in a position to judge did not view the advent of the Baby with any degree of confidence. How wrong they were is, of course, a matter of history.
>
> The Big Seven, which I am introducing today, is built on the unique experience we have gained in building over 300,000 Sevens, an experience that I think you will agree counts for a lot. When I tell you we are very satisfied with the performance of the Big Seven and its market possibilities, I think that will count for something too. I should like to emphasise that the Big Seven is an addition to the Austin family and does not in any way supersede the famous Baby. It is our opinion that the time is opportune to introduce a car which in size, running costs, accommodation and price comes between the Seven and the Ten."

This was partly true, but it would have been unwise to put the whole plan before the public. The Big Seven four-door saloons were an addition to the Austin family, they were not superseding the "famous Baby" – not in 1937, but the reason for introducing the new car in this way was to give the Seven-buying motorists a chance to get used to the idea that by 1938 the Austin Seven would be no more. As far as the new model itself was concerned, it was based on the Seven, but had a wheelbase 6½ in. longer, a larger four-door body and an engine with bore and stroke of 56·77 mm. × 88·9 mm. which gave a capacity of 900 c.c. The triangular chassis frame was still used with a transverse front and quarter elliptic rear springs, and the two models were priced at £155 for the fixed head and £165 for the saloon with the sliding roof. In November these prices were reduced to £145 and £149 10s. respectively and only 6,671 cars were produced during 1937.

At the very beginning of the year, both Austin's and Riley's were reported as having decided not to participate in racing. An official of Austin's actually told Thomas Wisdom, who was at that time correspondent to the paper *Sporting Life:*

"We have no racing programme for this season. Demands of the production side and the new aero factory on the experimental department, which dealt with the racing cars, will not permit it. We shall be competing, however, with three sports cars in the French 24-hours race at Le Mans, and the German ace – Walter Baumer – will drive one of the special racers in Germany. Official participation by the Works' team in British events, however, has had to be shelved for this season."

In conjunction with this, Jamieson decided to sever his connections with the Company and to join E.R.A. Each of the o.h.c. racers had cost £3,000 to build, and to put them to one side at this stage, just as they looked like being successful, seemed rather wasteful, so Lord Austin was prevailed upon by the experimental department until he agreed that they should take part in a limited number of events during 1937 as an official Works' team.

On 10th April, the B.R.D.C. held its British Empire Trophy race at Donington, where the event was run over a shorter distance than before to enable spectators to reach the course in time for the start, which was to take place at 2 p.m. Grouping and handicapping also underwent alteration and the first section was for cars up to 1,100 c.c. unsupercharged and up to 750 c.c. with supercharged engines; they were given a sixteen-minute start and a speed of 64·24 m.p.h. was assumed for the 750 c.c. entrants. Dodson's lap record for the course was 67·84 whilst the best average speed over ten laps for a similar car was 65·06 m.p.h. If all went well, Dodson and Hadley in the o.h.c. cars and Kay Petre in the side-valve model, should do well. Heavy rain overnight, during the morning and for the first forty-five minutes of the race, made conditions very bad and kept speeds down, and the winner, Raymond Mays in his E.R.A., only managed an average speed of 62·96 m.p.h. Mrs. Petre, the only woman to start, was lost at one stage of the race but was eventually traced to Coppice Wood, from where she had to walk back to the pits, an early retirer from the race after having completed only seven laps. Dodson pulled in to refuel at the end of his sixteenth lap, and the engine was kept running to enable two mechanics to locate a fault which had been causing the engine to misfire, while petrol was being poured into the tank at the same time. As might have been expected, the petrol spilled on to the hot exhaust pipe and the car burst into flames. The driver's clothes caught fire and he was burned about the face and neck; fortunately, he was not seriously injured but was unable to continue. Hadley's car just kept running and at the end he had seventy-four laps to his credit.

Many people thought that the Coronation day meeting held at Donington in May would be a failure, but it established two records. A record crowd of 14,000 spectators attended in spite of the fact that the day was overcast and wet, and one driver won all four events. Goodacre, now recovered from his accident, and Hadley drove the two supercharged o.h.c. racers using a hand-

operated fuel pump in place of the mechanical system which had given so
much trouble before, with Kay Petre at the wheel of the Works' side-valve
car. The first race was over five laps for cars of up to 850 c.c., and included
five supercharged models on scratch. In the initial lap, Goodacre showed the
Austin's speed by appearing on the Starkey Straight way ahead of the other
scratch drivers; timings showed that the gap between the first two cars was
closing at almost exactly the amount of the handicap, and the result was in
some doubt until the last lap. Goodacre beat his closest rival by some four
seconds with an average speed over the twelve miles of 64·95 m.p.h. The
second event was a handicap including cars of up to 1,500 c.c. over the same
distance; other contestants included an M.G., E.R.A., Riley, Bugatti and a
Maserati. The M.G. got away first, but Goodacre was again soon ahead down
Starkey Straight, closely followed by the Riley. Goodacre won, this time
with an average speed of 64·75 m.p.h. He repeated his success yet again in the
third race; then came the most important event of the day – the race for the
J.C.C. Coronation Trophy, a handicap over 100 miles for cars up to 5 litres.
Goodacre was joined by Hadley and Mrs. Petre; Hadley started very well,
but was soon passed by the two other Austins, and seven laps from the end he
was forced to retire when a stone fractured his oil pipe. Mrs. Petre finished
in sixth place, being the only other car to finish in the small-car class.
Goodacre won on handicap with an average speed of 61·66 m.p.h., ahead of
two Alfa-Romeos, an E.R.A. and a Riley.

There was an excellent entry of ten teams each of three cars for the L.C.C.
Relay race at Brooklands on 26th June. Each car in a team had to complete
thirty laps and then pull into the pits for the sash to be handed over to the
next driver, who had to run to the paddock, start his car and complete his
section of the course. Substitution by another car in the team was allowed
should there be any failures before thirty laps were finished, but the replacement still had to complete his own quota in addition to the balance not
completed by his team mate. Hadley was away first at a high speed in order
to reduce the large handicap; he kept the car well up on the banking and
rushed down on to the Railway Straight at well over 130 m.p.h. After forty-
three minutes he pulled in to his pit to hand over to Goodacre. With sixty
laps to their credit, Goodacre was in fifth place when Mrs. Petre took over
in the slower side-valve car. After ten laps she crept into second position,
two laps later she gained the lead, and crossed the finishing line nearly five
minutes ahead of her nearest rival. The Austin team won the 250 km. race
at the extraordinary average speed of 105·63 m.p.h. and their fine performance
is seen in an even better light when it is realised that they were conceding over
forty minutes' start to the limit man (who finished fifth). Both o.h.c. cars were
consistently averaging 118 m.p.h. per lap, and when they finished their section
their combined speed was 115·28 with a highest lap speed of 121·68 m.p.h. Mrs.
Petre did superbly with an average of 95 m.p.h. for her section of the course.

The cars and drivers performed equally well in hill climbs at Shelsley Walsh. Unusually fine weather helped to make the Midland Automobile Club's June meeting particularly successful; there was also a new paddock with covered pits to which only drivers, mechanics and officials were admitted and a new timing device was responsible for reduced waiting time between runs. On his second run Raymond Mays lowered the record once again in his E.R.A. with a remarkable time of 39·09 seconds. But perhaps the most outstanding performance of the meeting was that of Bert Hadley, on one of the o.h.v. cars. On his two runs he clocked 40·83 seconds in each instance, breaking the 750 c.c. record held by Walter Baumer by 1·57 seconds and only 1·74 seconds outside Mays' new record for the hill in a car with twice the engine capacity. Baumer returned splendid figures with 43·30 seconds on his first run, and 42·31 for his second, just beating his own previous record and securing for him the award for the fastest time by a foreign competitor. Charlie Goodacre drove the car with the side-valve engine, which was in splendid form, being faster than Baumer on the first run with 42·62 seconds, his time being 42·86 on the second. Mrs. Petre, whose best time was 46·79 seconds, also put up an excellent performance with the side-valve Seven.

At the second Shelsley meeting, in September, a Frazer Nash lowered the record yet again, and Goodacre set up a new 750 c.c. class record at 40·70 seconds, with Hadley only a little way behind with climbs in 40·83 and 40·74 seconds. Mrs. Petre broke the ladies' record by nearly two seconds in 43·78 seconds.

There were many other successes during the year: both the racing team and the trials cars BOA 57, 58 and 60, driven by C. D. Buckley, Hadley and W. H. Scriven, competed in many trials held during 1936 and 1937 and obtained awards in most of them. A new type of sports model, developed from these, made its first appearance at Le Mans in June. A number were built, based on the Nippy production chassis with unsupercharged engines, Jamieson-designed camshafts and cylinder heads and two-seater bodies without doors. Later, doors were fitted and Centric superchargers added to the engines.

The final race of the year to be described is the B.R.D.C. 500 which was held on 18th September and in which, for the first time, the distance to be covered was reduced from 500 miles to 500 km. The two o.h.c. cars and the side-valve machine in the Austin team were given a handicap speed of 114·49 m.p.h. and the system of handicapping by credit laps made a massed start possible; the Austins were given an eleven-lap credit on starting. Whilst training on a wet track on the day before the race, Mrs. Petre was being overtaken by Parnell's M.G. and, as he was about to pass, the cars touched. The M.G. shot down the banking, but kept the right way up and crashed into the iron railings on the inner edge of the track and Parnell, although suffering from shock, escaped injury. Mrs. Petre was not so fortunate: the Austin immediately went into a series of somersaults and she was eventually thrown out on to the track where she was found lying unconscious. This left only Hadley and Goodacre to take part in the race. Hadley soon had to retire with engine trouble, in spite of a fast lap at 111·92 m.p.h., but Goodacre continued in fine form. At 3.45 he was lying third, having covered sixty-two laps at an average speed of 109·90 m.p.h. At the end of eighty-three laps he still occupied the same position with his average speed now up to 111, his fastest circuit being at 120·01 m.p.h., but he had the bad luck to break a track rod and had to retire ten laps from the end.

1938-39

The End of the Austin Seven?

Dodson and Hadley continued to race the two o.h.c. racers, which had been modified slightly during the winter by fitting new front cowlings which enclosed the radiator filler caps. Both the drivers appeared at the British Empire Trophy race at Donington in April, with Hadley in an unsupercharged car. But for a crash whilst practising, Bira, the Siamese racing prince, might have won the event; his 1937 ex-works' E.R.A. was damaged so he had to use a 1935 vehicle and he failed to win by a mere 98 seconds at the end of nearly 200 miles. Raymond Mays and Earl Howe, in the two works' E.R.A.'s both failed to complete the course and this gave Dodson his big chance. His green car ran into first place after about twenty laps on handicap, and he quickly increased his lead to about one and a half minutes; he stopped to refuel, took to the grass once but other than that met with no more problems, and held on to his lead until the end to win with an average speed of 69·62 m.p.h. Hadley held fifth, fourth and third positions successively in the early stages, but a slipping clutch held him up and he finished sixth at an average of 64·03 m.p.h.

Murray Jamieson, the man responsible for Austin's racing success, who was at that time the chief designer at the E.R.A. factory at Bourne in Lincolnshire, died in hospital on 10th May from injuries received in a crash at Brooklands on the previous Saturday. The tragedy occurred whilst he was acting as an official on the track at the spot where Joseph Paul's Delage left the course and ploughed into the spectators. His period with the Austin Company was short and although he was ably assisted by Appleby and Brown and other members of Austin's experimental staff, and backed up by some first-class racing drivers, he was a quiet, diffident man, often unwilling to take the credit that was due to him, and without his o.h.c. Austin – the most successful 750 c.c. racer the world has ever known – the Company would not have made its mark in competitive motor racing in the late 1930's.

168

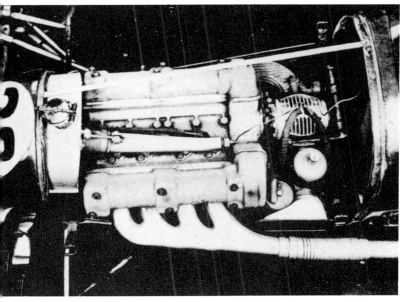

62. Jamieson's twin o.h.c. engine

63. The first appearance of the new side-valve racer at Shelsley Walsh on 18th May, 1935

64. L. P. Driscoll with the side-valve racer in 1935

65. The Nuffield Trophy race at Donington on 4th July 1936. Bira (4) s.v., Goodacre (2) o.h.c., Dodson (6) o.h.c., and Driscoll (5) o.h.c. at Red Gate Corner

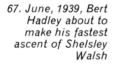

66. Dodson at the start of his record-breaking runs – October, 1936

67. June, 1939, Bert Hadley about to make his fastest ascent of Shelsley Walsh

Top – 68. A Ruby 5 cwt. van

Above – 69. The prototype 1938 Reliant three-wheeler van, which used an Austin Seven power unit

70. The first Big
Seven "Forlite"
saloon

71. 1938 Big Seven
"Forlite" saloon

72. The Austin
Seven's replace-
ment – the 1939
Eight

Hadley beat the Shelsley record for 750 c.c. cars again on 28th May with a climb in 40·09 seconds, and was even quicker at a similar event in September – 40·05 seconds, only about two seconds behind the unlimited records set up by the E.R.A.'s. Charlie Goodacre joined the Ethyl Export Company in February, 1938, Dodson was going off to Germany to race with the Auto Union team and finished up driving a Maserati, but Hadley continued racing the Austins until just before the war started. On 1st April, 1939 Hadley took his Austin to Donington for the final British Empire Trophy race; both driver and car performed magnificently and took second place with an average speed of 69·57 m.p.h.

One of the most interesting improvements to the Seven for the 1939 season, announced on 27th July, 1938, was the provision of a sturdier rear axle with full Girling brakes having cone instead of cam expanders for the brake shoes. A water trap was placed in the radiator to eliminate the loss of water and the bonnet was fitted with concealed hinges. On both the Seven and the Big Seven de luxe models a low mounted sliding roof panel was employed; although not a flush fitting with the roof it did not protrude and was neat in appearance. 1939 Big Sevens were also to have running boards with rubber tops. Undoubted evidence showed that there was a recession in the industry. As early as May, 1937 sales began to fall off slightly, but this was not really significant and there was no reason to believe that this would not be followed by a year of full prosperity. In fact, June and July of that year showed a happier state of affairs, but in September sales were down by 5¾ per cent on the previous September, October sales by 12½ per cent, November by 13¼ and in January, 1938 they were 13½ per cent lower than during the same period in the previous year. These falls were steep in a trade accustomed to such healthy expansion, and were as great as had been experienced at the beginning of the last depression in 1930 when the average fall in that year against 1929 sales was in the region of 10 per cent.

Austin suffered badly; there was a 30 per cent fall in sales during 1937-38 which improved slightly in the following year, and in 1938 only about 8,500 Austin Sevens were built. One way of trying to offset this decline in demand, which was much greater than the national average, was to reduce prices. The cheapest was £126; the Ford was increased to £120 in April so the Sevens were brought down in price slightly to £129 for the Pearl, £125 for the Ruby, £122 for the fixed head saloon, £115 for the four-seater, £108 for the two-seater tourer and £110 for the van.

In March, 1938, with the Big Seven Sixlite saloons at £149 10s. and £145, a new two-door Forlite was introduced at £139 as the direct replacement for the Seven, with a cheaper fixed head model at £137. However, this was not to be, because only about 8,000 Big Sevens were made in 1938 and six more in 1939. As far as the Austin Seven itself was concerned, about 800 were produced in the first three months of 1939 and 152 between 11th March and

29th July, most of which were vans. The replacement for the Sevens was to be the new Austin 8, which was accepted by the Army as a staff car, and the Company supplied over 46,000 during the war. This car was introduced in February, 1939 at the following prices:

Two-door fixed head saloon £128, sliding head £139.
Four-door fixed head saloon £139, sliding head £149.
Four-seater tourer £135.
Two-seater tourer £132 10s.

Only the engine and the gearbox followed previous Austin light-car practice, and even then there were certain differences. For instance, although side-valves were still used, they were operated by large-diameter barrel-type tappets, and the base of each tappet was flat with altered cams to suit the new design which provided quiet operation and a longer life. Compression ratio was raised to $6\frac{1}{2}$ to 1 and to cope with the extra power there was a stouter crankshaft. Otherwise it was a completely different car from the Seven with a welded, braced pressed steel platform chassis with semi-elliptic suspension all round. A "mousetrap" bonnet lifted from the front and there was a new frontal design which altered the appearance of Austin cars more than any previous modification.

All was not quite at an end as far as Austin Seven production was concerned; in March, 1938 Austin entered into a contract to supply 500 Austin Seven power units to the Reliant Engineering Co. (Tamworth) Limited, for their new three-wheeler 8 cwt. van and truck which had the merit of costing only £4 a year to tax. Fully equipped, in grey primer, it cost £106 10s. ex-works – rather costly in comparison with the 5 cwt. Seven van at £110, but nevertheless to prove very successful both before and after the war. It employed the standard Austin Seven power unit, rubber mounted on two channel section cross-members. Transmission was through the Austin clutch, four-speed gearbox and propeller shaft to a spiral bevel rear axle made by Reliant themselves. The chassis consisted of downswept channel section side members with a tubular cross-member giving support for the steering head and the top fastening for the radiator. Lower down, a light angle cross-member supported the lower end of the radiator, then there were the two channel section members carrying the engine. Girling brakes were fitted to all three wheels and the bodywork was steel panelled with a streamlined back giving a carrying capacity of 74 cu. ft.

So passed into history one of the most remarkable motor-cars the world has ever seen. For most of its sixteen years the Austin Seven had defied any and every form of serious competition in its own field. Regarded as a freak, a phenomenon, and by many as doomed to failure, it went on from the perambulator joke stage through all the storms of public ridicule and expert scepticism, not only to confound the scoffers, but also to establish the name of its inventor throughout the world and to prove the turning point in the development of the concern which he founded. It also brought to more than half a million people, who had purchased Sevens either new or second hand, their first taste of motoring. For that alone it deserves to be remembered with gratitude.

Organisations for Austin Seven owners started almost as soon as it ceased to be available as a new car. In January, 1939, "W. B." wrote in a motoring magazine that in order to provide trials and similar events for enthusiastic owners of Austin Sevens, and in view of the fact that there was a movement towards increasing the lowest division to include all cars with engines up to 1,100 c.c., there should be a "750" club. There seemed to be others who felt the same and the first rally was held at Virginia Water on 16th April, 1939 when the twenty-seven cars which appeared were led on a run by W.B. – Bill Boddy, the motor-racing historian and present editor of *Motor Sport*. The club flourished during the period after the war when most of the original Austin Sevens not still in regular use, and many of them were until quite recently, were converted into sporting specials. There is now a section devoted to preserving Austin Sevens in their original form, and a number of other organisations, representing some thousands of Seven-owners all over the world between them sprang up, amongst which the Vintage Austin Register caters for the owners of Sevens made between 1922 and 1930. As long as Austin Sevens remain in existence there will be those to care for them and to ensure that they, and the man who made them, are remembered.

Appendix 1
AUSTIN SEVEN
Wings and Running Boards 1923-32

Date	Commencing Car Numbers	Front Wings		Running Boards		Rear Wings	
1923 January	A1-1	Tourer	Fig. A	None fitted		Tourer	Fig. A
1923 March	A1-101	Tourer	Fig. B	Tourer	Fig. A	Tourer	Fig. A
1923 July	A1-961	Tourer	Fig. C	Tourer	Fig. B	Tourer	Fig. A
1924 June	A1-4771	Tourer	Fig. D	Tourer	Fig. B	Tourer	Fig. A
1926 February	A2-7074 Also Series A3, A4, A5 and A6 (partly)	All Models	Fig. D	Tourer Saloon	Fig. B Fig. C	Other than Fabric Saloon Fabric Saloon only	Fig. B Fig. C
1928 August	A6-9388 Also Series A7, A8 and A9 (partly)	As above		Other than Coupé Coupé only	Fig. C Fig. D	Other than Coupé Coupé only	Fig. D Fig. E
1929 September	A9-9265 Also Series B (partly)	All Models: (short wing) (long wing)	Fig. E Fig. F	All Models: (short wing) (long wing)	Fig. E Fig. F	Other than Coupé Coupé only	Fig. F Fig. G
1930 January	B6230 Also Series B1, B2, B3 and B4 (partly)	All Models	Fig. G	Other than Short Scuttle Saloon Short Scuttle Saloon only	Fig. F Fig. G	Tourer Two-Seater Coupé Long Scuttle Saloon Short Scuttle Saloon Van	Fig. H Fig. H Fig. J Fig. H Fig. K Fig. L

Date / Chassis		
September	Van — Fig. G Two-Seater — Fig. H Saloon — Fig. H	Two-Seater 6′ 3″ wheelbase — Fig. H Saloon 6′ 3″ wheelbase — Fig. J Saloon 6′ 9″ wheelbase — Fig. K Van 6′ 3″ wheelbase — Fig. L	Two-Seater 6′ 3″ wheelbase — Fig. H Saloon 6′ 3″ wheelbase — Fig. K Van 6′ 3″ wheelbase — Fig. L
1931 November B4-6850	Van 6′ 3″ wheelbase — Fig. G Tourer — Fig. J Two-Seater — Fig. J Saloon — Fig. J	As above	As above
B4-8296 Also Series B5 and B6 (partly)	Van, 6′ 9″ wheelbase (Others as above) — Fig. K	Van 6′ 9″ wheelbase (Others as above) — Fig. M	Van 6′ 9″ wheelbase (Others as above) — Fig. M
1932 July B6-800	As above	Tourer 6′ 9″ wheelbase (Others as above) — Fig. K	Tourer 6′ 9″ wheelbase (Others as above) — Fig. N
B6-1000	All Models including Van — Fig. J	As above	As above
6-2938	As above	All Models 6′ 9″ wheelbase — Fig. K	Saloon — Fig. M Van — Fig. M Two-Seater — Fig. O Tourer — Fig. P
1932 October B6-6000 also Series B7 and B8	As above	As above	Two-Seater — Fig. O Other Models — Fig. P

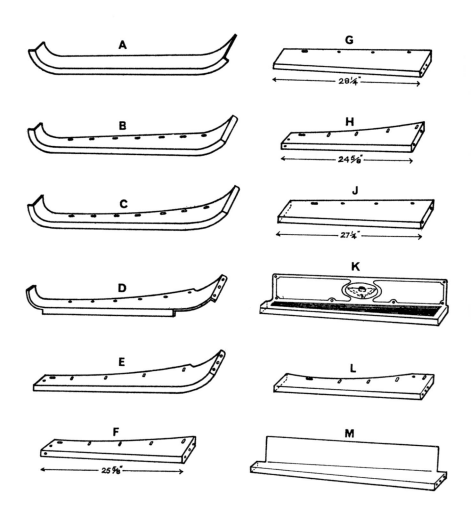

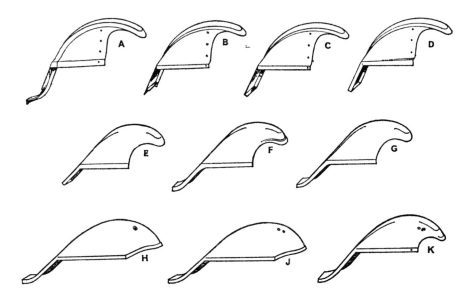

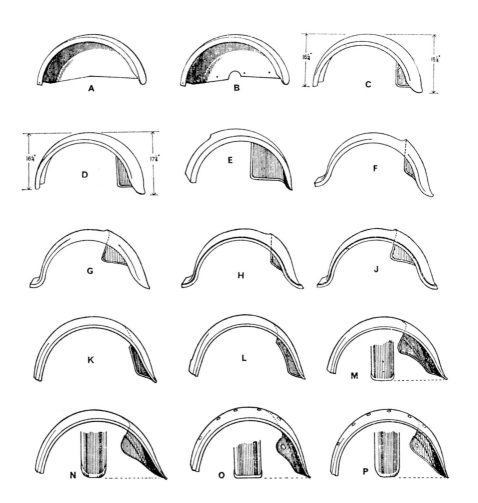

Appendix 2
Austin Seven Production Figures 1922-39

	1923	1924	1925	1926	1927	1928	1929	1930	1931	1932	1933	1934	1935	1936	1937	1938	1939
Chassis	2					2719	4430	1528	752	620	789	713	1392				
Tourers	1934					8233	5304	3187	1647	1062	1484	1449	1362				
Saloons						2142	3607	11101	12758	2998	2765	2901	4343				
De luxe Saloons									2970	12434	11837	13638	15864				
Fabric Saloons						4331	8309	5120	782								
Cabriolets												76	1052				
Two-Seaters							107	425	559	476	865	1015	735				
Coupés						51	347	128	7								
Vans							1	115	1144	2364	2497	2380	1916				
Startin Vans						316	391	631	50								
Sports							1	48	97	22	234	228	220				
Super Sports							2										
Racers												1					
W.O. Two-Seaters											4	141	396				
W.O. Saloons										127							
W.O. Mulliners										18							
Mulliner Fabric Saloons						2868	2549	1269	424								
Mulliner Vans							118	40	92								
Mulliner Sports						2											
Mulliner Two-Seaters						4											
Mulliner Coupés						7											
G.E. Saloons						1024	683	178									
G.E. Cups						908	494										
G.E. Milk Vans								56									
G.E. Vans						101	104										
Others						3											
TOTAL	1936	4700	7043	14000*	22500*	22709	26447	23826	21282	20121	20475	22542	27280	23500*	23000*	8500*	1000*
Export (included in TOTAL)						4871	7669	4619	3656	3966	3372	3740	6536				

Years run from January to December except:: 1923 – up to October only; 1924 – from November, 1923 to December, 1924; 1939 – up to March only.
* Approximate totals only; breakdown by types available only between 1928 and 1935.

177

Appendix 3
A List of Modifications showing Car, Chassis and Engine Numbers

Year		Car No.	Chassis No.	Engine No.
1923				
March	Piston	A1-101		
	Wings	A1-101		
July	Wings and running boards	A1-961		
October	Fan	A1-2145		
November	Mechanical starter	A1-2140 (except A1-2440)		
December	Electric starter	about A1-2570		
1924				
February	Fabric joint	A1-2995		
February-May	Speedometer first fitted			
February-March	Tappets, mixed between	A1-2939 and A1-3501		
March-May	Shock-absorber, mixed between	A1-3145 and A1-4052		
March	First Sports	A1-3126		
June	Type "C" touring body – Body No. 4602			
July	Rear axle nut	A1-5047		
September	B.B. plate support	A1-6352		
December	Autoram greasers	A1-7722		
1925				
February	Wheels and balloon tyres and speedometer	A1-8250		
April	Piston less skirt		8900 (mixed)	9187
	Screen type F		10653-10697 (mixed)	
June-July	Austin shock-absorbers		10700	
August	Magneto and control	A2-700	12025	
	Petrol tank and pipe		1322?	

178

Month	Change	Serial No.	Serial No.
February	Torque tube socket	A2-7074 – A2-7340 (mixed)	16666
	Type "D" touring body	A2-7300	17074
March	Universal joint socket		17330
May	Balloon tyres, second-type wheel		20032
	First Saloon	A3-137	19000
July	Gearbox and change fork		
August	Deeper frame side-members and speedometer, all Saloons with heavier rear springs	A3-3400 A3-3727	23501
September	Large brake drums	(All after except A3-3747 3763 3764 3800 3801 3826 3839)	
	Lamps moved to front position, from: to:	A3-4572 A3-6753	
	Four-piece bonnet – mixed between	A3-4725 and -4572	
October	Screen-wipers	A3-5345	
	Lucas switchboard	A3-5700	25140 (mixed)
November	Parallel wheel bearings	A3-5935	26513
1927			
February	Gear teeth shape altered	A3-9000	31511
	Tank filler cap – spring fitting	A3-9936	41031
July	Change speed lever		44401
September	Gearbox and change fork		45016
September-October	Gearbox and gear-driven speedometer	A5-1675	46920
	New speedometer drive		37780
	Front axle and shock absorber link bolt, mixed from: standard from:		49922
December	Radiator drain tap		50456
	Frame extension to side-members		50901 (mixed)

Year		Car No.	Chassis No.	Engine No.
1928				
January	Grease gun and adaptor			
	Shock-absorber arms, mixed from:		52286	
	standard from:		52600	
February	Hub clamping screw		53000	
March	Rubber shock-absorber bushes		55201	
April	Starting handle extended for radiator muff		56890	
June	Clutch disc centre, longer spline, 1st motion shaft, mixed from:		59275	
	standard from:		61344	
21 June	8g wheel spokes, mixed from:		62324	
	Diff. case in two equal halves and crown wheel	A6-6570	63806	
	Brake shoe pivot pin		64801	
July	Steering wheel and column		64943	
	Torque tube ball seating		65442	
August	Raised radiator nickel cowl, new wings – mixed:	A6-9330	67024	
September	Jubilee clip for u/j cover		67847	
	Coil ignition, mixed from:	A7-1280	68814	69000
	to:	A7-1569	69104	69117
	standard from:	A7-1600		
October	First R.K. wide door Saloon, oil pressure indicator, facia glove boxes			
	Gearbox front cover, mixed between:		68326	
	and:		68904	
December	R.K. Saloon standardised	A7-6400		
1929				
January	Pistons and rings	A8-367	77801	77780
	Petrol pipe and die cast F.Z.B. carburettor			
May	Rear axle and torque tube	A8-6567	84001	
	Austin radiator – very mixed, long transition from	A8-6850		
	Silencer and tail pipe	A8-7257	84691	
23 May	Steering jaws		85348	
	Frame and comp. levers		86511	
30 May	Torque tube socket	A8-9322	86766	
June	Front spring, mixed from:	A8-9700		
	standard from:			
June	(First week) Oil in rear axle		90030	

Date	Modification	No.	No.	No.
24 June	Handbrake trigger	A9-2168	89501	
	Steering column inner bush	A9-2437	89770	
August	Front rubber bush for shock-absorber link	A9-8208	95541	
	Pistons and rings revert to 1A.77			96201
September	Frame front spring, silencer, wings	A9-9265	96598	
	B. base plate etc., E. body		96867	
	Rubber bushes for rear shock absorber link			97600
2 October	Enlarged engine bearings	B-257	97489	
29 October	Ball change speed and starter switch	B-1769	99001	
November	Tank filler position			
	Clutch thrust bearing housing		99900	
December	Distributor and ignition lever			
1930				
10 January	Wings with moulding	B-6230	103458	
3 February	Grease gun			
15 March	Carburettor F2A with air cleaner (export)		107228	
April	B1 – series commences			108175
May	Dynamo and gear	B1-3500	110700	110740
	Dial-type oil indicator – mixed from:	B1-3700	110900	
	to:			112479
June	Cylinder valve cover and jointing	B1-301		
	First short scuttle body	B1-4314		
	Second short scuttle body	B1-5000		
	Then mixed to:			
July	Coupled brakes	B1-5941	113068	
2 July	Change speed positions as on gate type		114871	
17 July	1st motion shaft and clutch disc centre		115239	
August	Rear spring and starting nut on all K.G. and R.L. Saloons		116000	
	Bevel pinion shaft and altered crown wheel angles			116600
26 August	Reverse fork rod		116799	
5 September	Rear axle case and torque tube, experimental from:	B1-9670	116881	
	to:	B1-9699		
	early numbers:			
26 September	Rear axle bearings and case	B2-1475	118501	

Year		Car No.	Chassis No.	Engine No.
1930				
3 November	Axle case oil filler hole (axle No. 3310)	B2-4735	121761	
	Crown wheel		122030	
	Dash plate with altered air strangler bracket		122800	
	Amal carburettors	B2-6158 B2-6315 B2-6366 etc.		
25 November	P.L. Fabric two-seater			
	Axle hub nut instead of flange			
1931				
2 January	Diff. shaft and larger bush (not 126467 to 126470)		126386	
February	Bearing retaining nut			
February-March	Longer short scuttle			
March	Steering column socket and bush	B3-3000	130860	
31 March	Starting handle and nut (peg type)	B3-6253	133178	
1 April	Bevel pinion and nut (L.H. thread)		133313	
17 April	Torque tube and distance pieces			
20 April	Lockwasher for bearing retaining nut			
April	Brake cross tube lever	3-7800		
	Rubber grease bag for joint			
24 May	Brake catch and rod with B.A. thread		137700	
May-June	Cylinder and valve guide, mixed from:			137000
	to:			138000
	approx.:			139000
Mid-June	Road wheel 7g spokes (Rubery-Owen)	B4-1550	138350	
8 June	Cam spindle bearings		140300	
16 July	Conversion to show details. Front wings, lamp brackets, dippers, wheels etc.			
September	All standard (except Vans) from:	B4-4209		
	(Vans have old wings and wheels and special dipper lamps)			
September	Camshaft front bearing		141868	
	Rear cam and spindle bearing without brass housing	B4-5441 B4-5127 B4-5281		
7 October	First R.N. Saloons			

Date	Description			
October	Steering box in cast steel (Export)		142643	
	(Home-Saloon and Touring only)		143183	
	Four-blade fan on Export, first from:	B4-6195	142996	
	Brake cross-tube housing, after 1st October			
	25 long chassis and short chassis from 3rd week in October			
	Lamp and front wing to suit with separate cable lead in	B4-6850	144300	
	Cut-out on dynamo			
14 November	24941 coil introduced, interchangeable with 2H767 except for W.O.			
1932				
21 January	Starter switch		145200	
26 January	Radiator seating			
6 April	Tail lamp and rear number plate	B5-6000		
11 April	Steering column and worm, altered splining			
September	Engine and 4-speed gearbox for 1933. Petrol pump, wide drums, starting motor and switch on offside of engine, intake and exhaust combined manifold, new carburettor, rear tank, electric gauge, speedo-moving pattern, switchbox with key and warning light, dash lamp in instrument panel, quick-release radiator cap, rear axle case	B6-2938	159534	
			159844	
	Brake cam levers – reverted to earlier type			
	Experimental pistons on 101 engines mixed between:			159463 & 161385
October	Steering wheel with blank top		161387	
	R.P. Saloon (1 in. narrower at back)	B6-5934		
	Standard from:	B6-6000		
20 December	First van with 4-speed gearbox		166315	
1933				
5 January	Rear camshaft bearing		167588	168230
7 March	Petrol pump with Austin connections		170810	
April	Torque tube ball seating			
	Piston with bottom scraper above gudgeon pin			174921
14 June	Change speed lever		175450	
22 August	Hardy-Spicer joint		176687	
	Synchromesh gearbox, modified head, stop and tail lamps, rubber engine mountings			
28 August	First Sports with synchro and 1933 crankcase (i.e. not rubber mountings)		179368	
4 September	Dynamo and wiring		179403	
18 September	Aluminium steering box (except some 7 vans)		179525	
21 September	1934 unit with carburettor as on Vans		180000	
			180260	

183

Year	Car No.	Chassis No.	Engine No.	
1933				
6 November		183354	184729	Sports Hardy-Spicer prop-shaft
6 November		183595		Carburettor 10979
6 November				Engine rubber mounting set screw replaced by stud
1934				
23 January				Crankshaft, double purpose front bearing (previous engines 188331-189499) on 21st December, 1933
5 February		190001	190766	Rear springs, off-side and near-side different (Over 80 Vans using up L.H. parts – 1933 types – were made)
		190743		Rubber mountings for Van engines
		191728		Vans have Twin-Top up to:
				Vans have synchromesh and petrol pump (standard chassis except tank piping and springs)
13 April		191742		L.H. Vans on standard chassis
18 April		193662		Export carburettor with air cleaner
19 April	B9-7590	193882		Export shock-absorbers (larger)
		193954		1st 75 m.p.h. Sports
		193974		Silencer front end joint
1 May		195100		Frame with washers welded on to engine seating
1 June		196080		"C" series of car numbers commenced
June		196274		A.C. "T" type fuel pump with priming lever
3 June		198348	198747	Chekko brake linings used from:
		198397		to:
7 July		198596		First low frame Saloon, needle type propeller shaft, 4·00 × 19 in. tyres and wheels
30 July		198678		2nd speed synchro on high frame, including Sports, but not Van, also automatic controls and trafficator switch
August		198778		Sports, longer bonnet and petrol tap
October		201289		Torque tube socket on low frame only – not on Sports, with 19 exceptions up to:
		201514		
12 November		204656		Sports torque tube socket
19 November		205849		Rear axle roller bearing for pinion end
November	ARQ-5585			Piston 1A.77 (commenced North Works on 29th November)
30 November		206001	207700	High frame, exhaust pipe and silencer
1 December		207167	207444	Sports engine mounting with larger sleeves and washers

184

Date	Description	Part No.	No.	Alt. No.
18 February	Vans have 5 lamp sets	AVH-5014		
March	E.L.P. tyres and wheels first fitted to Sports chassis	AVH-5327	216701	
March	Needle propeller shaft, front and rear joint on high chassis frame		216890	
	Stop light switch			
7 March	Van headlamp with cable harness and traffic switch	AVH-5323	218948	
30 March	Radiator filler position reversed	ARQ-16223	219428	
8 April	Headlamp with cable harness	ARQ-16836	220395	
24 April	65 Sports propeller shaft		221834	
1 May	Tank filler tube and connection		222023	
29 May	Gearbox with zinc bush for clutch pedal spindle			
3 June	Engine mounting stud and bushes (Saloon only, low frame)		224721	
	Stronger front springs for Export chassis		224864	
26 June	Crankcase front bearing housing			
11 July	Saloons with increased brake leverage	RQ-22055	226847	
16 July	Two-seater with increased brake leverage		226873	
	Tourer with increased brake leverage		227005	
	First A.A.L. tourer (low frame)		226017	
July	Clutch ring with Ferodo VM20, switchbox and cut-out, cable, colour scheme		230952	
9 September	Van, engine mounting stud		230960	
11 September	Barrel type piston ring			232501
20 September	Vans with increased brake leverage		232004	
28 October	Reverse gear wheel bush		234221	
November	Cast-iron fan spindle pulley, with wider flanges and single bush (Standard, Sports and Van)		235130	
	Cast-iron fan spindle pulley (Export)		235304	
27 November	Van with 2nd speed synchro	VJ-115	235580	
	Vans, E.L.P. tyres from body No. 501			
6 December	Positive earthing system		236210	
1936				
January	Speedometer dial	ARQ-30530	239165	
14 February	First Sports 65 with forced feed lubrication as for 75 m.p.h. model		240397	241541
21 February	Van silencer and longer tail pipe		241592	
11 March	Foot-operated dip-switch		241738	
13 March	1st and 2nd speed fork rod			
17 April	Pre-loaded pinion bearings	EB-729	244131	
16 April	Pre-loaded pinion bearings	VJ-1258	244241	

Year		Car No.	Chassis No.	Engine No.
1936				
20 April	Pre-loaded pinion bearings	RQ-34251	244397	
14 May	Cast-iron brake drum	RQ-35030	246176	
15 May	Cast-iron brake drum	VJ-1444	246325	
19 May	Cast-iron brake drum	EB-750	246006	
25 May	Steel brake shoes	RQ-35433	246835	
	Steel brake shoes	VJ-1486	246865	
5 June	Oilite for spindle bush	RQ-35652	247309	
16 June	Three-bearing crankshaft	RQ-35724	247765	249052
19 June	Three-bearing crankshaft for vans, also Borg and Beck clutch	AVJ-1625	248117	
22 June	Dynamo	AVJ-1597	248007	248149
	Distributor for 3 bearing crank, with greater advance		248850	
	Borg and Beck clutch	VJ-1625	248117	
	Borg and Beck clutch	RQ-36342	249066	
8 July	1st 1937 Saloon (R.R. 3) with Girling brakes, larger wheel centres, etc Chassis and car numbers combined from:		249701	
28 August	New type pistons			252915
5 October	Van Girling brakes and Silentbloc torque tube hanger		254226	
	Silentbloc torque tube hanger standardised on Low frame		254451	
24 October	Greaser for steering side tube		256148	
	Hourglass steering on Vans		256335	
27 October	Hourglass steering on Export models		256501	
	Hourglass steering on all Low frames		257866	
	Hourglass steering on Sports models		257211	
3 December	3-bearing cranks on Sports models		257842	
1937				
12 January	Clutch plate thickness		262654	264028
29 January	Riveted torque tube hanger bracket		264015	
1 February	Ditto, all Sports		263893	
15 February	Oil gauge with higher reading		264705	
	Steering box cover with bush		265295	
	Hourglass steering on Vans (L.H. steering)		266739	
13 March	Con. rod bearings on detachable metal backing		267634	268659
	Con. rod bearings on 1st Saloon		267906	
	Con. rod bearings on 1st Van		267746	
	Sports camshaft, with lower lift, and single valve springs			268770

Date	Description		
24 March	Oil jets on Saloon only ($\frac{3}{8}$ in.)		269660
9 May	Steering box with oiler in place of grease nipple	275488	
13 July	Van on Low frame	276126	
16 July	Shock-absorber front link lengthened	276213	
20 July	Brake shoe and spring anchorage	276596	
9 August	Oil seal for torque tube	276998	
28 August	Axle case and cover, electric horn	278543	
24 September	Van front and rear springs and bumpers	278708	
29 September	Vulcanised front spring packing. Van	278964	
	Vulcanised front spring packing. Standard	279753	
October	Front-brake rope swivel strengthened		279446
26 November	Oil seals in front and rear of gearbox	281472	
9 December	8 – 41 ratio		283618
	Split valve cotters	281955	
	3rd speed mainshaft gear and sleeve		
1938			
26 January	Newton-Bennett clutch plate	282122	
March	Shock-absorber, with flanged rubber bush	284581	
4 March	Steering wheel and switch plate combined	285305	
May	Prop. shaft needle bearing roller	286045	
June	Van silencer and tail pipe extended to off-side		288341
	Con. rod clamping nut	286413	
	Radiator and cowl to fit wider bonnet	286462	
	Full Girling brakes on rear	286571	
	Distance piece for pinion shaft bearing	286744	
July	Road wheels	287828	
	Road wheels Van from – 268733	288223	
	Van rear springs stiffer	286343	
	De Luxe with "On Top" metal roof	289118	
	Handbrake lever	289251	
31 October	Newton-Bennett clutch plate replaces Borg and Beck		
	Radiator filler cap		
1939			
January	Van – remainder with tail pipe on near side	290135	
17 January	Last Saloon (A.R.R.)	290570	
3 March	Last U.K. Van and last Seven H.P. (AVK)	291000	

Appendix 4
Austin Seven Servicing Data
Important extracts from Service Data Sheets issued by the Austin Motor Co Ltd between 1927 and 1940.

Removing
the Body

CERTAIN repair operations on the Austin "Seven" necessitate the removal of the body, and as the best procedure in doing this is not immediately obvious, the following instructions are given as a guide to repairers.

Disconnect the controls first. These are the air strangler (wire at clip on engine side of dashboard), accelerator at carburettor (split pin), throttle and magneto control rods, and the control levers must be removed from the bottom of the steering column. Disconnect also, the horn, dynamo, petrol pipe, and windscreen wiper connection.

Working inside the body, remove the floor mats, withdraw the control bracket with tubes and levers from the steering column, remove the steering wheel, and undo the clip holding the steering column to the dashboard.

Remove the brake and clutch pedal covers, and take off the pedal pads. Disconnect the speedometer drive at instrument end, the starter motor, and remove the latter with its housing, : it will have to be lifted vertically off its positioning dowels when the securing screws have been removed.

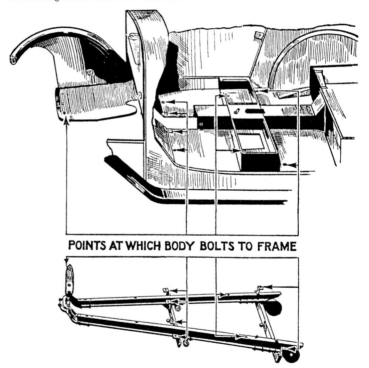

POINTS AT WHICH BODY BOLTS TO FRAME

The Fixing Bolts

There are eight body fixing bolts, their positions being as shown in the illustration, *i.e.*, four under the dash and two under each front seat. Additionally the three bolts on each side which hold the front of the body to the frame plates, the three bolts on each side of the radiator by which it is mounted, must be removed, also the bolt holding the bonnet strut to the radiator. The radiator assembly can be then left in position.

Lift the body up and towards the rear. One man should lift at the back, one at each side, and one in front should push the wings outwards to clear the engine as the body rises. While this is being done both clutch and foot brake levers should be held right down.

Refitting is a reversal of the above process. Care must be exercised in dropping the body over the brake, gear, and clutch levers, and steering column, and the magneto control lever (BF15). on the control spindle, should be lifted up clear of the steering box as the body is finally lowered. Ensure that the body is as far forward as possible, while it is being refitted, especially on the near side, otherwise the battery box will foul the cross member of the frame.

Replace the fixing bolts with locking washers under the nuts, and bend the washers up to lock the nuts when tight.

Although not essential, if the battery is removed, and any petrol in the tank is drained off, the body will be slightly easier to manipulate. The hood can be left up and the side curtains in position, but the windscreen should be closed to lessen the risk of breakage. Before refitting see that the felt strips along the top of the frame are in their correct places, also note that in refitting the radiator, the cowl fits inside the front end of the body, not outside.

AUSTIN SEVEN <small>Aug 1927</small>

The Saloon Model

Overloading.

IT has been found that, owing to the over-loading the public will impose on these cars, trouble has been experienced with the doors. In some cases, the panel has split, due to the excessive amount of strain imposed.

We are now fitting an extension to the frame—thereby supporting the back of the body, and reducing the strain on it in the event of overloading. We wish to point out, however, that this does not obviate the damage to the chassis resulting from overloading, but only relieves the body itself of damage.

The Frame Extension Member.

These extensions can and should be fitted by our Agents to all saloons made previous to those being supplied on new cars. Extensions required for the cars in your district can be obtained free of charge upon application to the Service Department, and fitting instructions are given below. When you have fitted these extensions to cars in your district, it will remove to a large extent the trouble caused by overloading.

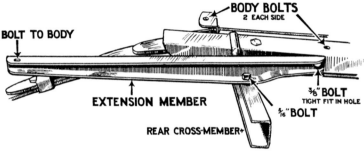

Instructions for Fitting.

The extension members are supplied drilled with ⁵⁄₁₆in. holes. It is not necessary to remove the body when fitting them. Slacken the body-bolts, particularly the two on each side at the rear, and wedge the body up from the rear ends of the chassis frame side members. Remove the one rivet on each side of the car holding the shock absorber brackets to the top of the rear cross member, and bolt the extension members to the

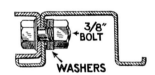

cross member at these points with ⁵⁄₁₆in. bolts. The extension members should then be flush with the top of the frame side members. Drill the frame through the hole in the end of each extension member, and ream out the holes to take ⅜in. bolts, the bolts being a tight fit, through each extension member and frame side member. This tight fit is important. The unthreaded portion of the bolt shank should be giving the fit in the holes, not the threaded portion, and washers should be placed under the nut to secure this condition. It is best to have the bolt head on the outside of the frame channel, and the nut and washers on the inside. The body can then be dropped into position on the frame, re-bolted, and drilled for the two ⁵⁄₁₆in. bolts to secure it to the end of the extension members, inserting a thin piece of felt or similar material between the body and each extension.

AUSTIN SEVEN
Relining the Clutch.

DETAILED below are the operations necessary for relining the clutch of the Austin "Seven." They are intended as a guide to repairers for when they have to effect this particular service.

Removing the Engine from the Chassis.

It is necessary to remove the power unit and the gearbox together from the chassis, before they are separated to give access to the clutch.

Work inside the car first ; remove the seat squabs and floor mats and the cover of the centre channel over the handbrake gear, so that the fixing of the brake ratchet (1 bolt) to the gearbox, can be removed. Access is also then afforded to the front fabric universal coupling, to disconnect it from the propellor shaft. The propellor shaft spider should be eased back off the universal joint bolts, to avoid pulling out the rear universal joint blocks.

Remove the gearbox top cover with the change speed lever and gate, and place a temporary cover over the studs to prevent the intrusion of dirt or small parts while the repair is in progress.

Undo the two nuts holding the accelerator control spindle bearings to the dash, disconnect the starter motor and battery, and remove the starter motor with its casing (lift it vertically off the positioning dowel). This leaves everything clear inside the car.

Working outside, disconnect the dynamo leads (at the dynamo—note the correct terminals for when re-assembling), ignition leads and control, carburetter controls, fuel pipe (from the float chamber union), oil pressure pipe (from its crankcase union), and the windscreen wiper tubing from the induction manifold.

The Radiator.

Turning to the cooling system, it is first necessary to remove the starting handle (retained by a set screw). Drain off the cooling water, disconnect the top hose

Set screw retaining the starting handle

7

connection at the radiator, and the bottom hose connection at the cylinder block. The radiator can be lifted clear when the three bolts holding it on each side to the front of the body and the screw holding the tie rod (except on models prior to 1927), have been removed.

This gives access for removal of the starting handle bracket and packing (if any) which bolts to the front member of the frame.

Remove the exhaust pipe-to-manifold-joint bolts, the induction manifold with carburetter, and the accelerator control spindle with the levers that it carries.

The Engine Bolts.

Next remove the four engine bolts. The front offside bolt is under the magneto coupling ; draw a line across the coupling, under the magneto strap, and take off the magneto to give access to the bolt.

Before the engine can be pulled clear of the frame, it is necessary to remove the clutch pedal lever from its spindle. This is the most difficult operation in removing the engine. The position of the pedal lever fixing is immediately behind the

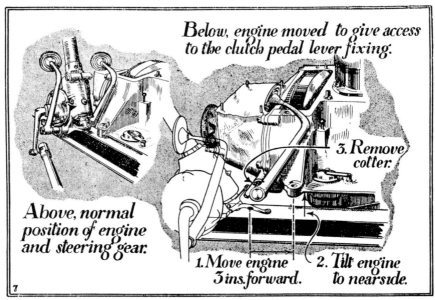

Below, engine moved to give access to the clutch pedal lever fixing.

3. Remove cotter.

Above, normal position of engine and steering gear.

1. Move engine 3 ins. forward.   *2. Tilt engine to nearside.*

steering gear (from the side of the car). The engine has, therefore, to be pulled forward about 3 inches, before the lever and spindle are clear of the steering box.

The lever is held on the spindle by a bicycle type cotter and the engine must be tilted over towards the near-side, to lift the cotter and nut above the frame. Then remove the nut, drive out the cotter, and prise the lever off the spindle, taking care not to lose the spring behind it.

Lift the front of the engine and pull the whole unit clear of the chassis, mount it on an engine stand and separate the gearbox from the engine.

The Clutch.

Removal of the six set screws in the flywheel cover, allows the cover with the declutching levers, the pressure plate, and the springs, to be removed, giving access to the flywheel. Lock the flywheel from turning by a bar inserted in one of the holes in the rim, remove the flywheel nut and pull the flywheel off its keyed taper with a flywheel puller (illustrated on page 16 of *The Austin Service Journal*, for May 1927). To dismantle the pressure plate from the flywheel cover, just pull them apart, guiding the declutching levers through the holes in the cover. Take care not to lose the springs.

Remove the old linings from the flywheel and the pressure plate and rivet on the new. The linings require careful riveting or they may be cracked, and the rivet heads on the back of the flywheel, should not stand up or they may foul the camshaft bearing. When re-lining the pressure plate the withdrawal pins should be in place, as the lining holds them in their sockets.

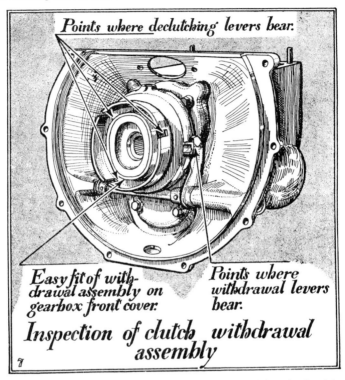

Points where declutching levers bear.

Easy fit of with-drawal assembly on gearbox front cover.

Points where withdrawal levers bear.

Inspection of clutch withdrawal assembly

Before Re-assembling It is as well, before reassembling, to examine the clutch withdrawal collar, left on the front cover of the gearbox, as clutch operation depends to a great degree on the condition of this collar. Examine the points shown in the illustration ; for wear where the declutching levers bear (uneven wear at these points will cause uneven clutch action—and if uneven wear is much apparent it is advisable to fit a new bearing pressure plate, BJ.19), also where the withdrawal levers engage (both should engage evenly), and for the movement of the withdrawal collar on the gearbox front cover, which should be easy, without any binding. Another point which should be examined for wear is the bearing in the withdrawal collar.

Reassembling is largely a reversal of the dismantling operations, but there are one or two points which deserve notice.

After reassembling the pressure plate and the flywheel cover together, with the springs between them, re-fix them to the flywheel, with the six set screws, the clutch plate being in the flywheel, in the same position as before removal, so that the timing marks coincide. Before tightening the set screws, centre the clutch plate (for particulars of the centring bar see page 16 of *The Austin Service Journal*, for May 1927), so that the gear box will fit up to it.

Adjusting the Declutching Levers.

When the six set screws have been tightened, and locked with the locking washers, test the distance of the end bearing faces of the declutching levers from the clutch plate face when they are about to act against the clutch springs. This distance

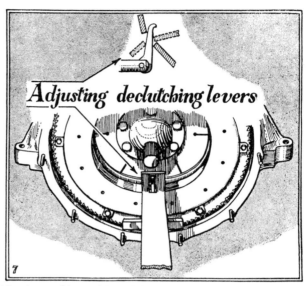

should be 1in. to 1$\frac{3}{16}$in., each lever being the same distance from the clutch plate face. If the levers require resetting adjust them by bending them with a slotted bar as shown in the illustration herewith.

After refitting the gearbox to the engine ensure that the clutch plate is free, when the clutch is out, by turning the flywheel by a bar in one of the holes in the rim, when the first motion shaft should remain still. If the first motion shaft (and therefore the clutch plate) moves, the clutch cannot be fully disengaged. Such a condition would be due to bad adjustment of the declutching levers, which should be readjusted so that the clutch can be freed entirely.

Replacing the Engine.

In replacing the engine in the chassis rest the accelerator control spindle with levers, just at the back of the cylinder block so that it will be in position for fitting to the dash.

Replace the clutch pedal lever on its spindle with the engine in the same position as for when it was removed. It is advisable to replace the spring on the spindle with its end in the small hole in the gearbox, before the engine is placed in the chassis.

When refitting the starting handle bracket, before tightening the bolts, line it up with the starting nut, by means of the starting handle.

In refitting the radiator, the cowl bolts inside the front end of the body ; not outside. On models which are not fitted with a radiator tie-rod, set the radiator in the right position, by fitting the bonnet, before tightening the three bolts on each side.

THE MAGNETO COUPLING
AND ITS USE.   Oct 1927

MANY a car is not giving its true performance owing to the ignition timing not being at its best position.

Description of the Coupling

We frequently find that the principal of the vernier coupling driving the magneto is not thoroughly understood, and we have endeavoured in this article to explain it in such a manner that our Agents' mechanics can readily attend to customers cars so that they can obtain the best from them.

When the magneto has been timed by No. 1 cylinder in the usual way, if on checking the contact breaker position, or if after the engine has been running the ignition timing seems either too advanced or too retarded, the fine adjustment provided by the vernier coupling can be used to set the timing as required.

The coupling has 20 teeth on the driving flange side and 19 on the magneto side, and the minimum amount of adjustment is the difference between the pitches of the two sets of teeth, namely 1/380th of a revolution. In terms of one revolution, the pitch of the magneto side of the coupling is 1/19th and that of the driving side 1/20th. Thus the difference is 1/19th less 1/20th.

$(1/19 = 20/380.$ $1/20 = 19/380.$ $20/380 - 19/380 = 1/380).$

To advance the ignition the flange on the magneto spindle must be moved relative to the driving flange *with* the direction of the magneto rotation, and to retard the ignition, the magneto flange must be moved *against* the direction of the magneto rotation.

How to use the Coupling

Suppose the ignition requires advancing. Before starting, draw a pencil mark across the two flanges and the rubber disc in case the original timing position is lost. Slacken off the magneto strap, and leaving the rubber disc engaged with the teeth of the driving flange, slide the magneto along its cradle until the teeth of the flange on the magneto spindle are well clear of the rubber disc, taking great care not to revolve the magneto spindle. The rubber disc is now withdrawn from mesh with the driving flange and turned one or more teeth *against* the direction of rotation of the magneto, being then put back into mesh with the driving flange. The magneto spindle not having been revolved, it will be found that the teeth on the magneto flange are not quite opposite their mating teeth on the disc. Now slide the magneto back into its place so that its flange teeth mesh with those on the disc. In so doing the magneto spindle will be caused to revolve very slightly in relation to the driving flange in the appropriate direction. The adjustment being so fine a movement of the disc of two or three teeth in relation to the driving flange will usually be found the smallest adjustment which makes any appreciable difference to the running of the engine as regards ignition timing. If further advance in the timing is considered necessary the rubber disc should again be turned more teeth.

To retard the ignition timing the operation is as for advancing except that the rubber disc is turned *with* the direction of rotation of the magneto.

(*On the next page are illustrations of the operations necessary for advancing the ignition as described above*).

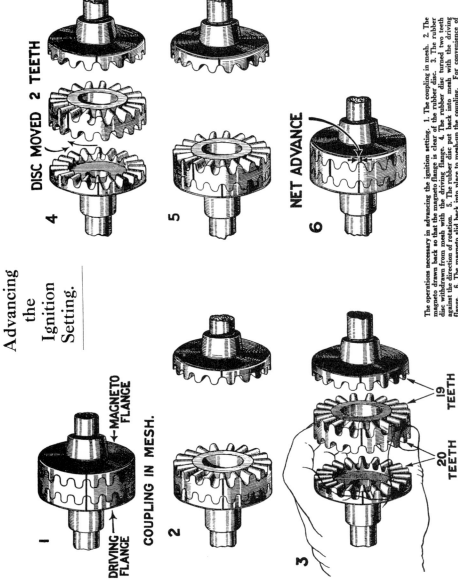

Advancing
the
Ignition
Setting.

DISC MOVED 2 TEETH

4

5

NET ADVANCE

6

MAGNETO FLANGE

DRIVING FLANGE

COUPLING IN MESH.

1

2

3

19 TEETH

20 TEETH

The operations necessary in advancing the ignition setting. 1. The coupling in mesh. 2. The magneto drawn back so that the magneto flange is clear of the rubber disc. 3. The rubber disc withdrawn from mesh with the driving flange. 4. The rubber disc turned two teeth against the direction of rotation. 5. The rubber disc put back into mesh with the driving flange. 6. The magneto slid back into place to mesh-up the coupling. For convenience of illustration the magneto flange is shown withdrawn further than is actually necessary.

Austin Seven Alterations in Design—*(Con.)*

from chassis 45016

Nov 1927

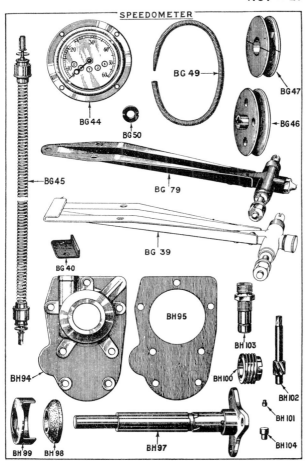

Illustration showing the new and superseded parts for the speedometer drive.

Parts for the belt type speedometer drive, illustrated above, and listed on page 29 of the "Austin Seven Spare Parts List" No. 353L, are, consequent on this change, not now used.

AUSTIN SEVEN Feb 1928

The Torque Tube and the Back Axle.

**Introduc-
tory.**

THE construction of the Austin "Seven" torque tube and back axle is straight-forward and simple as far as dismantling and reassembling are concerned. The time taken for this work, however, will be very considerably reduced if a knowledge is possessed of the best way in which it can be done. Moreover, there are several important requirements in dismantling and reassembling, which on no account must be overlooked.

The work is rather comprehensive, and covers several subsidiary repairs, which otherwise might well be complete in themselves. So for convenience of reference we will divide the following particulars under four main headings, viz. :—

> Removing the axle from the car, and refitting it.
> The Rear Hubs.
> The Torque Tube, and
> The Axle Centre.

Removing the Axle.

For simply removing the axle and torque tube assembly from the car, it is unnecessary to remove the wheels or hubs. But should the axle be overhauled, or require dismantling for a repair, the wheels and hubs will, of course, have to be removed, and in that event it is easiest to remove them while the axle is still in the chassis. Further, even though the axle may only be removed when not requiring further work on it, if the spring pins are particularly tight in the axle casing, it may be necessary to remove the wheels and hubs so that the spring pins can be driven clear from the hub side of the axle case end flanges. Here, however, we will describe the removal of the axle, without removing the wheels and hubs, for which latter operations refer to next page.

**The
Spring
Pin.**

The nut, on each side, securing the shock absorber arm link on the spring pin (BR58), being unscrewed, and the shock absorber link with its washers, sprung off the pin, each pin is free to be prised out of the axle case when the bicycle type cotter, securing the pin in the lug on the axle case, is removed. If, however, it has been necessary to remove the wheels and hubs to drive out the spring pins, the axle must be supported while this operation is in progress, otherwise it will fall, possibly get damaged, and badly strain the torque tube anchorage. The bolts are taken out of the brake rope ends, to disconnect the ropes from the brake cam levers, and then the axle is free except for the drive, and the torque tube anchorage.

**Torque
Tube
Anchor-
age.**

Reference to the illustration on page 112, will show the operations necessary at these points. The drive is disconnected at the propeller shaft flange that fits up to the universal joint socket (BP10), by the four nuts being removed, and the socket being pushed back to bring the studs clear of the flange. The torque tube anchorage is freed by bending up the tangs of the locking washer, slackening the lock-nut, and unscrewing the seating nut and lock-nut. The lower seating (BP68) is then removed and the torque tube socket (BP66) is lifted off the ball flange on the frame. The top seating (BP67), may drop out ; it must not be lost.

The socket is twisted round slightly to clear the frame cross-member and the floor of the body, and the entire axle is drawn back. The axle is thus free to be taken from the car.

Refitting the Axle to the Car.

In refitting the axle and the torque tube assembly, the spring pins should be inserted in the axle and through the spring eye, up to the collar on the outer end, and in the right position for the bicycle type cotter to be inserted to secure the pin in the axle. The cotter is driven home while the nut on it is tightened. The shock absorber arm links, with their washers, are then resecured on the spring pins and the brake ropes are connected up to the brake cam levers.

The ball seatings anchoring the torque tube are secured round the ball flange on the frame (the top seating located by the slot in the top being up round the ball adjustment locking bolt), so that there is no play, and they are given sufficient lubricant.

Finally the drive is connected at the propeller shaft flange, the nuts on the four set screws being secured with locking washers.

The Rear Hubs.

Jacking up the Car

For removing the hubs, first the rear wheel nuts are slackened. The car is jacked-up and supported from the rear cross-member of the frame. Each rear wheel can be then taken off its studs when the wheel nuts have been unscrewed. The brake drums usually come away with the wheels, but in any event they are removed. Access to the hubs is now afforded. The axle nut, secured by a split pin, is removed, the hub being prevented from turning while this is done, by a bar placed between one of the wheel studs and the hub shell. Next, the three screwdriver screws, holding the two portions of the hub together (BO45 to BO87), are taken out, and the hub puller (illustrated on page 100, of the *Austin Service Journal* for January), is screwed on the hub well up to the shoulder. On the centre screw of the puller being tightened up home to the axle shaft end, it is given a sharp blow, and then turned, to pull the hub off its keyed taper. The hub being off, the key is removed from the shaft. Take care of the paper joint washer that will be found between the two portions of the hub.

At this point end play to the extent of about $\frac{1}{4}$in. to $\frac{3}{8}$in. will be evident in the axle shaft. This must not be taken as a sign of wear or failure. The differential gear being of the straight tooth pinion type, there will always be this end play when the axle shaft is free at the hub end.

The Bearing Nut.

The journal bearing nut (BO52) is next removed, the tang of the locking washer being bent back. The locking washer is withdrawn (one of its tangs projects into the axle casing), and the inner portion of the hub is then free to be prised off the end of the axle casing. Sometimes, however, it is too stiff to be removed in this way. So the outer portion (BO45) is refitted up to it, by screwing up the wheel nuts on their studs. The puller is then used, as before, but to extract both portions of the hub together. The brake springs are then unhooked from the shoes, and the shoes lifted clear.

The ball journal can be now prised from the inner portion of the hub with screwdrivers or bars inserted from the back. Then the washer plate and oil retaining washer can be removed, but this is necessary only if oil leakage to the brakes is suspected, or if the washer has been disturbed while prising out the bearing. The ball journal is examined for wear so that on re-assembling it can be replaced by a new one if necessary.

The effect of all these operations is to be seen clearly from the illustration below.

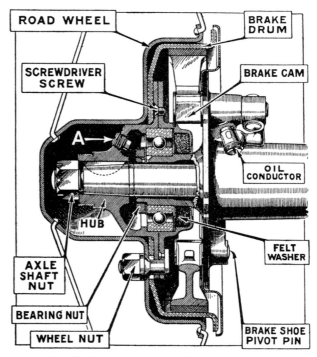

ROAD WHEEL   **BRAKE DRUM**

SCREWDRIVER SCREW   **BRAKE CAM**

A→

OIL CONDUCTOR

HUB

FELT WASHER

AXLE SHAFT NUT

BEARING NUT

WHEEL NUT   **BRAKE SHOE PIVOT PIN**

Reassembling.

When re-assembling, the brake shoes are refitted, with their springs, on the cam and pivot pins. The inner portion of the hub, if the ball journal and felt washer have been removed from it, has a new felt washer fitted, the washer being soaked in melted tallow and fitted while warm. The washer plate, dished side outward, is next inserted into the half hub, and then the ball journal, and the paper washer, or a new one, lightly greased both sides, is fitted over the wheel studs on to the joint face. The bearing nut being screwed home and locked by its locking washer, the key is fitted in the axle shaft, and the outer portion of the hub is drawn up to the inner portion by the wheel nuts.

The axle nut can be screwed home and locked with a split pin and the three screwdriver screws can be then inserted and tightened.

The Torque Tube.

Removal from the Car.

The torque tube assembly if desired, can be removed from the car without removing the back axle. The drive and anchorage are disconnected as previously described (see page 109).

The nuts securing the torque tube on the six studs in the centre case of the axle are removed, and the torque tube is pushed upward and withdrawn from the axle forward, bringing with it the propeller shaft, and bevel pinion. Care is exercised not to lose the packing shims (BP52). Between the torque tube flange and the axle facing, for the same number must be fitted when re-assembling to ensure the correct meshing of the bevel pinion with the crown wheel, unless of course, these parts have to be replaced by new ones.

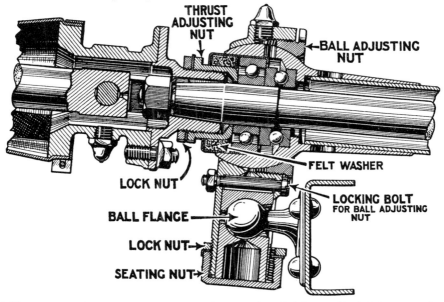

THRUST ADJUSTING NUT

←BALL ADJUSTING NUT

FELT WASHER

LOCK NUT

BALL FLANGE—

LOCKING BOLT
FOR BALL ADJUSTING NUT

LOCK NUT→

SEATING NUT→

Dismant-ling.

To dismantle the torque tube, the nut on the end of the propeller shaft is unscrewed, the locking washer being bent back, and the propeller shaft flange is extracted off its keyed taper, bringing with it the thrust adjusting nut and lock-nut. The shaft, when the key has been removed can be driven out of the tube leaving the ball journal and thrust in the front end of the tube, and bringing with it the ball thrust and inner race (with rollers) from the rear end. The outer race for the roller bearing can be prised out of the torque tube end, but this is necessary only if it is pitted and worn, so that a new bearing is required.

The torque tube felt housing holding the felt and ball journal, remains to be taken from the tube, being driven out from the rear end by a rod inserted through the tube ; then the ball thrust will fall clear. Turning to the torque tube socket, the bolt locking the adjusting nut is removed, so that the nut can be unscrewed, and the socket taken from the tube.

The felt housing, containing the felt and ball journal only need be dismantled if a new felt, or a new bearing is necessary. As the housing will have to be scrapped, in any event if dismantling is necessary, the easiest way to remove the felt and bearing is to saw through the housing.

The inner roller race and rollers on the bevel pinion end of the propeller shaft are driven off by a taper punch rested between the bevel pinion teeth at different positions round the race to drive them off evenly. This operation requires care, or otherwise the race will be damaged.

Testing the Propeller Shaft.

With this done, it is possible to test the shaft for truth. The finished ends on which the bearings fit are rested on vee blocks, and the shaft is tested with a dial indicator in the usual way, and straightened as necessary.

Next, the torque tube is tested for truth. The roller race and rollers are refitted on the propeller shaft, and the outer race for the rollers, if previously removed, is refitted in the rear-end of the torque tube. The propeller shaft is replaced in the tube, with the ball thrust in the rear end as packing, and the felt housing with bearing in the front end. The tube with shaft is then spun between centres and tested for truth at the faces at each end (*i.e.*, the ball end, and the end fitting in the axle casing). On the propeller shaft and bearings being removed from the tube, it can be corrected as necessary.

Reassembling.

When the torque tube is being re-assembled, the ball thrusts and their seating faces in the tube, are cleaned carefully so that they bed properly ; and all bearing parts are given sufficient grease.

The torque tube socket is fitted before the propeller shaft ; it cannot be fitted after the propeller shaft flange is in place. The socket is placed on the ball-end and the adjusting nut is screwed up to make the movement of the socket moderately stiff. The ball adjusting nut is then locked by the bolt being inserted and secured below the socket.

The propeller shaft with the ball thrust, rollers, and inner roller race is fitted in the tube first ; then the front end ball thrust is fitted.

The Felt Washer and Housing.

If previously removed, the ball journal or its replacement part is refitted in a new felt housing ; the inner washer plate is fitted next to it, with its dished side towards the bearing. The felt washer is dipped in oil and fitted, and the outer plate is placed over it. The thrust adjusting nut is unscrewed from the propeller shaft flange, and is inserted into the felt and pushed up to the bearing ; then the felt housing tangs are turned down to secure the felt. By inserting the thrust adjusting nut, the felt is prevented from spreading, which would make the seal inefficient when the unit is finally re-assembled. The nut is removed from the felt washer and screwed well up on the propeller shaft flange with the lock-nut and locking washer above it. The felt housing is then inserted in the torque tube end over the propeller shaft, and pushed up home to the ball thrust. The key is replaced in the end of the shaft and the flange is tapped up over it on to its taper ; when the nut, with locking washer under it, can be tightened home on the end of the shaft.

Any end play of the propeller shaft can now be taken out. The thrust adjusting nut is turned up tight ; and then it is slackened back about half a turn at which position it is locked by the lock nut and locking washer.

Fitting new ball thrusts in the torque tube does not affect the mesh of the bevel pinion with the crown wheel to any vital extent, so when it comes to re-assembling, if new thrusts have been fitted, it is not necessary to alter the number of packing shims between the torque tube flange and the face on the axle case to which it fits. If, however, a new bevel pinion end propeller shaft is fitted (and a new crown wheel in the axle), this adjustment will have to be checked, and modified if necessary, to give correct meshing. Of this we give particulars later. Connecting up the drive and anchoring the torque tube socket, is described in the section dealing with the removal of the axle.

The Axle Centre.

Marking the Casing.

A necessary preliminary to dismantling the back axle is to remove the drain plug and allow time sufficient for the lubricant to drain away.

The back axle itself, before being dismantled, must be marked for the correct reassembling of the side cases to the centre case. A mark is made on the centre case near each of two of its studs, an opposite sides, but in line. The side cases are marked to correspond with these studs.

The side cases are removed from the centre case, on the six nuts on each side being unscrewed. (Care is exercised not to break the paper joint washers).

The axle shaft, crown wheel, and differential assembly is then clear. The ball journals supporting the differential case, will come away with this assembly, and the ball thrusts will be free. Behind the thrust race in each side case is a washer plate, and an oil retaining felt washer in a housing.

On lifting the felt housing out of the side case some packing shims will be revealed. A certain number of these shims are fitted between the felt housing and the side case on each side, and they determine the mesh of the crown wheel with the bevel pinion. It is important to count these shims, or to keep those for each side separate, so that the drive can be properly meshed without any setting on re-assembling, unless, of course, a new drive or new ball thrusts have been fitted. When the axle shaft, differential and crown wheel assembly is removed, with the ball journals on the differential case, it is supported at the journals on vee blocks, and the crown wheel is tested for lateral truth with a dial indicator. If it is more than .003in. out at the extreme diameter, it will have to be corrected when being re-assembled.

The Differential.

The differential case cover is secured by three bolts and three studs. The bolts are removed, and the nuts are taken off the studs. The cover will then come away and leave the crown wheel and the differential pinions free to be removed. The axle shafts then can be withdrawn from the casing and the cover, respectively.

We may mention here that it is advisable not to confuse the parts, so that the axle shafts, ball journals, and ball thrusts are re-assembled on the same side of the axle as they were before removal, as with the shims.

So far as the crown wheel is concerned, it is advisable to mark it, so that it can be refitted in the same position on the differential case.

The bearings and differential pinions are cleaned and examined for wear and replaced by new ones if necessary. The pinion spindles, which are secured in the differential case and the cover, three in each, by taper pins, are also examined for wear, and renewed if necessary ; the same applies to the bushes in the case or cover for the axle shafts.   Each axle shaft is tested for truth while mounted on vee blocks, with a dial indicator, and corrected if necessary.

Before re-assembling the crown wheel flange is carefully cleaned on each side, also the faces on the differential casing and cover, which bed up to it.

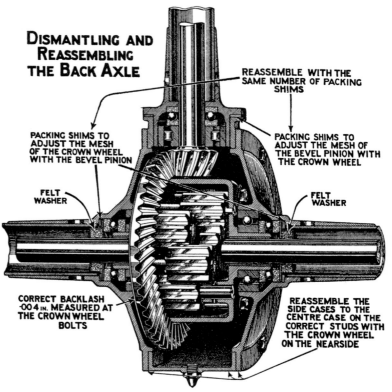

DISMANTLING AND REASSEMBLING THE BACK AXLE

REASSEMBLE WITH THE SAME NUMBER OF PACKING SHIMS

PACKING SHIMS TO ADJUST THE MESH OF THE CROWN WHEEL WITH THE BEVEL PINION

PACKING SHIMS TO ADJUST THE MESH OF THE BEVEL PINION WITH THE CROWN WHEEL

FELT WASHER

FELT WASHER

CORRECT BACKLASH ·004 IN. MEASURED AT THE CROWN WHEEL BOLTS

REASSEMBLE THE SIDE CASES TO THE CENTRE CASE ON THE CORRECT STUDS WITH THE CROWN WHEEL ON THE NEARSIDE

Reassem-
bling.
The axle shafts are replaced in the differential case and cover respectively.   Three of the differential pinions are placed over the spindles in the differential case, and the other three are rested between them.   The crown wheel is then fitted over the studs in the same position as before, according to the marking made when dismantling.

The end cover (with the axle shaft in it) is fitted outside the crown wheel on to the three studs, with its three spindles passing through the three differential pinions (resting in the case), into the case.   The end cover, and the case are numbered and these numbers must be opposite when the cover is fitted.   The nuts are screwed home on the studs with locking washers under them.   The three bolts are then inserted, and their nuts also having locking washers under them, are tightened home.

The assembly, including the ball journals on the differential case, is mounted on vee blocks, as it was before being dismantled and a similar test is taken.

If it is more than .003 out at the extreme diameter the assembly is dismantled, and then re-assembled with the crown wheel in one other of the three positions in which it can be mounted. The differential case is also tested for truth, as if this is out, the crown wheel most likely will be out also. If all three positions for the crown wheel are tried, and still there is too much error indicated, it can be rectified by correcting the differential case (if that is out), or by scraping the surface of the differential case which mounts up to the crown wheel flange.

The important point in re-assembling the differential case, cover, and crown wheel, is to have all the surfaces that mount together, absolutely clean, so that the crown wheel is mounted correctly.

Reassembling in the Axle Case.

Re-assembling is only a matter of placing the ball thrusts (with cleaned surfaces) on the axle shafts, and the felt plates with the felts (soaked in oil) in their housings, and the correct number of packing shims on each side, to give the right mesh. The paper joint washers are greased and fitted over the studs on each side of the centre case. The offside side-case is refitted to the centre case in the same position as marked, as it was before dismantling. The axle shaft, crown wheel, and differential assembly, is replaced in the side-case and centre case, and the nearside side-case is refitted on its correct studs. The only reason for re-assembling the side cases in this order, is that the crown wheel must be on the near side of the bevel pinion, and this ensures that it is. The torque tube assembly is refitted up to the centre case, with the same number of packing shims interposed, and the securing nuts are locked with locking washers.

If a new crown wheel and pinion have been fitted, before going thus far with the re-assembling, it will be necessary to adjust the mesh.

Final Drive Adjustment.

The crown wheel and pinion are marked with a certain number, such as 36 or 38, which indicates thousandths of an inch. The correct mesh of the pinion with the crown wheel is given, when, with the torque tube bolted up to the axle centre case, the end face of the pinion is 5.918ins. plus the number of thousandths of an inch marked on it (according to our example above, .036 or .038), from the machined internal diameter of the side flange of the centre case. This measurement, at the works, is determined by a gauge.

When meshing the gears together, both or either of the side cases, as may be necessary are mounted up to the centre case, with the paper joint washers (BO2) fitted. The crown wheel, as we have mentioned is meshed up to the pinion by the packing shims. First, the centre case has the torque tube fitted to it, with the pinion at its correct position ; also the off-side side-case is fitted. The felt housing without the felt is placed in the offside side-case, with several packing shims under it. The ball thrust is then fitted, and then the differential and axle shaft assembly, with the crown wheel meshing with the pinion. Being pressed home fairly tightly, as it would be if the nearside side-case were fitted, the back-lash between the crown wheel and the pinion should be about .004in. measured at the centres of the crown wheel fixing bolts.

Shims are added, or removed from, behind the felt housing, until this degree of backlash is attained. The shims already fitted will show a slight pressure marking if the correct pressure is being applied to keep the assembly in the axle case while the test is being made. This marking is caused by the shims spreading outward round their inner diameters as they only bear against the axle casing at the outside.

If new shims are fitted, it is ensured that their edges are clean, not burred or the adjustment will not be satisfactory. All shims should of course, be clean. Also, it may have been noticed that we advised refitting the felt housing, without the washer while meshing the gears. This is desirable because the washer, acting as a brake on the movement of the crown wheel, will make the backlash measurement more difficult to take.

For ascertaining the correct number of packing shims to be fitted in the nearside side-casing, the same procedure is followed. This careful meshing will ensure the axle being silent, and will obviate wear in the drive.

An Alter-native Method.

A method of meshing alternative to the above, is to mark the crown wheel teeth with lamp black and oil, blue, or any of the marking mediums. The axle is then assembled with a certain number of shims on each side of the crown wheel, and between the torque tube and the axle centre case. These shims are varied until the correct meshing is attained.

The marking, if the crown wheel is rotated several times in both directions while in mesh with the pinion, will show the contact of the teeth. This should be along the side of the tooth, almost for its full length, neither engaging right to the top of the tooth, nor to the bottom, but over the maximum area within these limits.

If contact occurs along the top edge of the tooth, the pinion is not far enough in mesh with the crown wheel, and a packing shim (or shims), is taken from between the torque tube and the centre case. If the tooth contact is too near the bottom of the tooth, a shim or shims, must be added.

Similarly, if contact is being made more on the toe of the crown wheel tooth (*i.e.,* at the inner end), the crown wheel is too close to the pinion ; and if the contact occurs more on the heel of the crown wheel tooth (*i.e.,* towards the outside diameter), the crown wheel is too far from the pinion.

The adjustment in either instance is made by altering the number of packing shims in each side-case.

When the correct mesh is obtained there should be the .004in. back-lash as already described, and the packing should show the slight pressure marking as detailed previously. With the mesh adjusted correctly the axle can be finally assembled, and fixed to the car, as already described.

Finally the axle is lubricated. It requires about 3lbs. of grease and oil of equal parts, well mixed. The total capacity is about 4lbs. of the mixture, but with the grease used in re-assembling, 3lbs. should give a sufficient charge.

AUSTIN SEVEN - 1929

Rear Axle and Torque Tube Assembly.

WHEN assembling a rear axle and torque tube to a 7 h.p. chassis, it is usually necessary to turn the torque tube socket assembly round, until it is pointing vertically downwards. In the event of this socket being adjusted to a fairly tight fit on the torque tube ball, it is quite possible that, unless the torque tube clamping bolt has been tightened up securely, the torque tube will turn with the socket, and thus upset the setting of the mesh of the pinion with the crown wheel.

The torque tube clamping bolt should be tightened up immediately after the pinion adjustment has been made, and even so, every precaution should be taken to see that the torque tube does not move, as the leverage created when the socket assembly is turned (should it be adjusted too tightly) is sometimes sufficient to turn the torque tube with the clamping bolt tight.

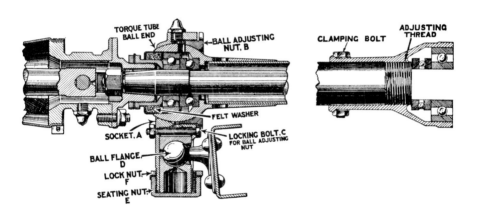

AUSTIN SEVEN

Overhauling the Steering.

Removing the Column from the Car.

WHEN removing the steering column from the car, the first thing to be done, is to remove the small control levers at the base of the steering box. This done, the horn wire is disconnected from the horn. The controls, and friction disc, at the top of the column, are now removed, by slackening the clamping pin, which holds the friction disc on to the control bracket tube, and then drawing the disc, controls, and the control tubes, out of the column.

The steering side tube is disconnected from the steering lever, and the steering wheel turned, until the steering arm is in a vertical position.

The foot brake adjustment is next released, in order to remove the brake pedal fulcrum pin, which passes through part of the steering box casting. The thin nut, on the outside of the fulcrum pin is removed, and the brake pedal is driven off the pin. The fulcrum pin is removed, after undoing the nut, on the inside of the frame channel. The steering wheel, and the steering column bracket, which is under the dash, are now taken off. (On the latest types of Seven, the steering wheel fits on to a splined section, at the top of the inner steering column, and is held in position by means of a large nut. On older types, it is fastened to the top of the inner column by means of a clamping bolt). When these have been removed, the complete steering column may be withdrawn from the front of the car.

Dismantling the Column.

When the column has been removed from the car, it is held in a vice, by means of the outer column. The steering box locking washers are knocked back, and the holding down bolts are removed. The steering box cover is next taken off, complete with the worm wheel, and steering lever. The steering box clamping pin is removed, and the set screws taken out. The box is now free to be unscrewed from the base of the column, bringing with it the control bracket tube. When these two components are removed, the steering inner column, with the steering worm and thrust washer, is removed from the outer column. All the components are now thoroughly cleaned, and dried.

The worm and worm wheel are now examined for wear. If the worm is badly worn, a new inner column will have to be fitted complete.

Removing the Worm Wheel.

To remove the worm wheel from the steering lever spindle, the lockwasher is knocked back and the nut which holds the worm wheel on to the taper, is unscrewed. The wheel is now removed from the spindle by means of a mandrel press or similar hand press. On no occount should any attempt be made to drive out the spindle with a hammer, as if this is done one is liable to damage both the cover and the spindle.

A special note should be made at this point, of the keyway which was in use before the worm wheel was removed.

The spindle is now examined for wear in the bush. If any excess wear is found, the key is removed from the spindle, and the spindle itself pulled out. The felt washer housing, which fits on the outside of the cover is removed, bringing the felt washer with it. The worn bush is pressed out and a new one fitted. This is

Austin Seven.   Overhauling the Steering.—*Contd.*

reamered out to fit the spindle and the felt housing and felt washer, or a new one if necessary, refitted.   It sometimes happens that the housing is damaged in getting it off.   In this case, a new one is fitted, and is centre punched in two or three places around its base to hold it in position.   The spindle is now refitted and the key replaced in its keyway.

Re-fitting the Worm Wheel.

The full travel of the steering arm in service is only 120 degrees, so that only one-third of the teeth on the worm wheel will be worn. It is for this reason that three keyways are cut in the wheel so that it may be refitted to the steering lever spindle using another keyway—thus bringing another set of teeth into mesh with the worm.

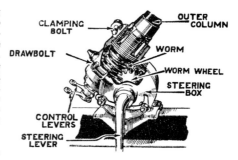

Before refitting the worm wheel to the spindle the taper on the spindle and the taper in the wheel are wiped thoroughly clean.

The dropped portion of the steering lever is now held in a vice with the spindle pointing vertically upward.   The wheel is fitted on to the taper using another keyway.   The lockwasher or a new one if necessary, is fitted, with the three tangs fitting into the three keyways in the wheel.   The nut is now put on, and tightened down until the worm wheel is pushed home on to the taper.   The lock washer is then knocked up.

Re-assem-bling.

The column is held in a vice and the inner steering column fitted, care being taken not to forget the thrust washer which fits between the worm and the base of the outer column.   The control bracket tube and the steering box are now offered up, and the box screwed on to the base of the outer column—sufficiently far to take up all end play in the inner column, but not so far as to cause undue tightness.   When this condition has been attained, the set screw is re-engaged with one of the serrations on the base of the column and the clamping bolt tightened.

A new paper washer is now fitted on to the joint face of the steering box and the cover, with the worm wheel and spindle, is replaced.   New lockwashers are fitted, and the nuts screwed down until they are finger-tight.   The mesh of the worm wheel and worm is now adjusted by means of the drawbolt and nuts provided for that purpose.   The adjustment is carried on until there is only the slightest amount of backlash in the steering lever.   The nuts are then tightened down but the locking washers are not knocked over.

If there is any end play in the worm wheel spindle when this is assembled and bolted into position, the cover should be removed and the thrust button at the bottom of the box driven out and fitted with packing shims underneath until all end play is taken up.

Austin Seven.   Overhauling the Steering.—*Contd.*

The worm and worm wheel are now smeared with a small quantity of grinding compound, of a tacky nature, and the cover is bolted down again.   Great care must be taken to see that no compound gets into the bushes.   The high spots on the gears may now be ground off, by refitting the steering wheel to the column and moving it backwards and forwards so that the steering lever moves through the same arc, that it will move through in service.   That is, roughly, from end to end of the machined portion of the box which fits down on to the chassis.

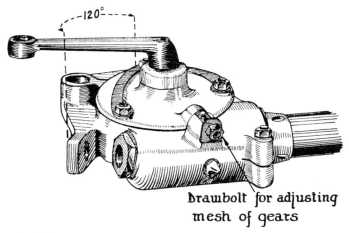

**drawbolt for adjusting
mesh of gears**

As the grinding is continued the mesh of the gear should be continually adjusted for backlash until a state of affairs is reached where the movement of the arm is smooth throughout the length of the necessary travel, and there is only the requisite amount of backlash.

The whole of the steering column is now dismantled once more and washed thoroughly, first in paraffin and then in petrol to ensure that all parts dry quickly and clean.   It is then rebuilt once more, the steering box filled with graphite grease, and all the locking washers knocked up.

AUSTIN SEVEN
Torque Tube Ball End

IN the last issue of the *Service Journal*, for the purpose of illustration, a drawing of the old type torque tube ball end was used in connection with the article on Rear Axle and Torque Tube assembly. In order to prevent any misunderstanding we reproduce herewith, a drawing of the latest type of ball end. The list of alterations dealing with this particular part, were given in the May-June 1929 issue of the *Service Journal*.

It will be seen by comparing the two drawings, that the thrust race has been done away with in the later type. Its place has been taken by a double purpose bearing, which, as its name implies, does the job both of the thrust race and the journal bearing.

Another alteration which is shown in the drawing, is the substitution of an oil retaining washer, for the felt washer used in the older type of ball end. This washer also serves to hold the bearing in place.

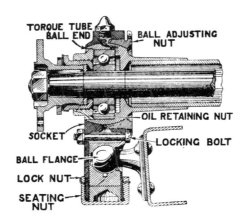

Index